ART OF MITRING

(or How to Join Mouldings or,
The Arts of Mitring and Coping)

by Owen B. Maginnis

CARPENTRY AND JOINERY FOR AMATEURS

by James Lukin

Art of Mitring / Carpentry and Joinery for Amateurs
Printed and bound in the United States of America by
Popular Woodworking Books, an imprint of F+W Media,
Inc., 10151 Carver Rd. Blue Ash, Ohio, 45242.

Distributed in Canada by Fraser Direct
100 Armstrong Avenue
Georgetown, Ontario L7G 5S4
Canada

Distributed in the U.K. and Europe by
F+W Media International, LTD
Brunel House, Ford Close
Newton Abbot
Devon TQ12 4PU, UK
Tel: (+44) 1626 323200
Fax: (+44) 1626 323319

Distributed in Australia by Capricorn Link
P.O. Box 704
Windsor, NSW 2756
Australia

Visit our website at **PopularWoodworking.com** or our
consumer website at **ShopWoodworking.com** for more
woodworking information.

Other fine Popular Woodworking Books are available
from your local bookstore or direct from the publisher.

ISBN-13: 978-1-4403-4534-0

19   18   17   16   15   5   4   3   2   1

PLAN OF A GEOMETRICAL WOODEN CEILING.

Owen B. Maginnis, Designer.

HOW TO JOIN MOULDINGS;

OR,

The Arts of Mitring and Coping.

A complete treatise on the proper modern methods to apply practically in joining mouldings. A book for working carpenters, joiners, cabinet-makers, picture frame
makers and wood-workers. Clearly
and simply explained by over
40 engravings, with
full directive
text.

By OWEN B. MAGINNIS,

AUTHOR OF " PRACTICAL CENTRING," " THE CARPENTER'S HANDOOK "
(LONDON), ETC.

NEW YORK:
WILLIAM T. COMSTOCK,
23 WARREN ST.
1892.

INTRODUCTION.

THERE is no carpenter, cabinet-maker, or other artisan, who will not find it a benefit to be thoroughly familiar with the proper methods to follow in joining mouldings together, or, as it is technically termed, "mitring" them, etc. As there has never been any book printed treating at length on this important art, I have carefully prepared this little work, and feel confident that it will be found of great service in and out of the shop, both by practical men and amateurs. The contents are all gathered from practical experience, and can therefore be followed in actual work without any doubt as to their accuracy.

I beg to acknowledge the kindness of the publisher of the *Manufacturer and Builder*, who has permitted me to reproduce the "Art of Coping."

THE AUTHOR.

CONTENTS.

CHAPTER I.

The Definition of a Mitre—Mitre Boxes: How to Make and Lay Them Out.............................. 9–15

CHAPTER II.

Sawing the Mitre Box—Mitring Simple Mouldings and Proving the Cuts in the Mitre Box................. 16–24

CHAPTER III.

Mitring Panel and Raised Mouldings................... 25–30

CHAPTER IV.

To Mitre on Octagon and Polygonal Figures—The Mitres Formed by Straight Mouldings Intersecting with Circular Mouldings; also Mitres of Circular Mouldings Intersecting.................................... 31–40

CHAPTER V.

Mitring Crown or Sprung Mouldings—Base and Wall Mouldings, or Door Trim........................ 41–48

CHAPTER VI.

Mitring Chair Rail, Picture Moulding, Column Bases, and the Use of the Mitre Templet.................... 49–54

CHAPTER VII.

Varying Mitres in Both Straight and Circular Mouldings.. 55–62

CHAPTER VIII.

A Description of a Combination of Many and Various Mitre Joints, Illustrated by the Frontispiece—A Geometrical Ceiling Design......................... 63–65

CHAPTER IX.

The Art of Coping Mouldings........................ 66–73

CHAPTER I.

THE DEFINITION OF A MITRE.—MITRE BOXES:
HOW TO MAKE AND LAY THEM OUT.

"MITRE" is defined architecturally by
Webster as the "joint formed by two
pieces of moulding each cut at an angle
and matching together; to meet and match
together on a line bisecting the angle of
junction, especially when at a right angle;
to cut the ends of two pieces obliquely and
join them at an angle."

The above definition of the great lexico-
grapher is really in substance the full definition of the term and the way it is employed, so we will at once proceed to describe the different forms of mitres, from
the simplest to the most difficult, giving
each in detail and illustrating all methods
in full, with the appliances necessary for
accurate cutting, etc.

THE MITRE BOX.—This indispensable
adjunct for the purpose of cutting mouldings on an angle is well known, yet so important is it that it must be perfectly and

accurately constructed so as to insure the
perfection of the mitre. Fig. 1 represents
a mitre box as it ought to be made by carpenters in the shops or building, and, as
will be seen, consists simply of three pieces
of wood joined together, the size of the
pieces being as near the following dimensions as possible for ordinary mouldings
up to 3½ inches wide and using a 20 or 22-
inch panel saw. The length of the box

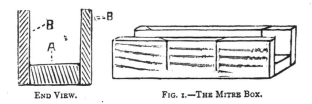

END VIEW.   FIG. 1.—THE MITRE BOX.

should not be less than 18 inches nor more
than 2 feet six inches long. The bottom
should be 2 inches thick by 4 inches wide
inside so as to insure the sides being firmly
and strongly fastened to its edges; sides,
1¼-inch stuff by 6 inches wide. Either
pine, oak or soft ash may be used for the
material. I cannot by any means recommend any of the other woods for this purpose, as they are entirely too subject to at-

mospheric changes. Experience has proven
that pine is preferable to any other wood,
even though the cuts may wear out sooner
through the friction of the saw sideways.
If the box be made long enough new cuts
can be put in in a few minutes, while the
oak box is heavy and unwieldy, though it
has the virtues of wearing well.

To construct a mitre box properly the
bottom piece, A (see section), must be
placed upon the bench and taken out of
wind with the fore plane by using straight
edges or winding sticks and placing one
across each end of the surface to sight
across them until they show parallel. If
one corner should be higher than the other
it must be planed down perfectly level;
this being done one edge is straightened
with the try-square, after which it is
gauged to a parallel width, and the other
edge squared. The sides, B B, must also
be taken out of wind and one edge
straightened. For very good work the
sides should also be gauged and planed to
a thickness of say $1\frac{1}{8}$ inch when $1\frac{1}{4}$-inch
stuff. This planing and gauging must be
very well done to gain a perfect box. Be-

fore fastening the sides on the bottom they must be carefully gauged with a line 4 inches down on the face side, or on the side which was taken out of wind, which must be done on both sides of the box. A small wire nail can now be driven close to each end exactly on this line and the side can be placed on the edge of the bottom, keeping the wire nails close down on the face of the bottom, or rather the gauged line fair with the face of the bottom, and the side can be nailed fast to the edges of the bottom, keeping the fastening nails about the centre of the edge. Should the above work be properly done the inside of the box will measure 4 inches deep, 4 inches wide and be perfectly parallel from end to end, top and bottom at 4 inches, and the sides will stand square to the bottom. On looking across the top edges of the sides they will be out of wind and show as one. If a box be made in this way it will cut a mitre exactly to a square mitre.

There are two or more ways by which the box can be marked for sawing, but only two which will be accurate. The first consists in taking a drawing board or clean piece of stuff with a straight edge, as Fig. 2, and laying off on it a square whose side is equal to 8 inches, and drawing two diagonals from corner to corner, as shown, then setting a long bevel to one of the diagonals and screwing the blade

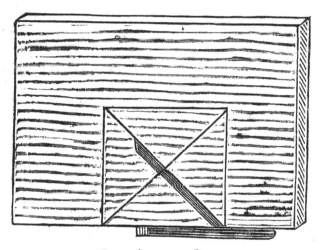

FIG. 2.—SETTING THE BEVEL.

fast in the stock; now take the bevel and lay it across the edges of the sides of the box, and, applying it from the outside of the box, holding the blade firmly down with the left hand, mark the cut with a sharp pen-knife on the edge with the right

hand.   Next, reverse the bevel for the left
hand cut, as Fig. 3, and mark it similarly,
which, being done, take the try-square and
square down from the edges on the outside
of the sides to the level of the bottom,
also with a knife, watching that the square
does not move and that the line is perfectly straight.   This is one way to lay out
the cuts.

Another method by which it can be

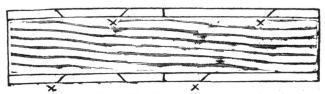

FIG. 3.—TOP VIEW OF MITRE BOX.

done is to take the width of the box inside,
4 inches, and lay it off on the inside arrises of the sides, square, and with the
straight edge and knife, to mark the direction of the angle of 45°, which is now being treated, and square down as before.
I would scarcely recommend that the box
be marked by taking two equal numbers
from the heel of the steel square, because
it is difficult to hold it firmly in position

and there is always the likelihood of the squares being out of true or worn, which will, of course, affect the direction of the cut, though it can be done when the bevel is not available. The reverse cut can either be marked across the right or at the opposite end, but the first has the advantage of leaving the remainder of the box sound for making new cuts when the first ones are worn too wide to be accurate in sawing the moulding.

CHAPTER II.

WHEN the box has been properly marked
the next thing to be done is to saw it, or
rather to saw into the sides exactly to the
knife mark. The saw should not be run
down the centre of the mark, but to one
side of it, so that the operator may see that
it moves down in sawing just to the line.
It is therefore best to keep the thickness of
the saw blade to the right of the line both
across the top edges and on the sides,
kerfing both edges simultaneously and reversing the box at intervals to make sure
that the saw is not running from the mark,
which would throw the cut out of square
and spoil the box for good mitring. It is,
of course, necessary that the teeth of the
saw be sharp and well set and not coarse,
so that the cut on the mouldings may be
clean enough to obviate planning. An-

other point I would also strongly recommend is that the saw with which the box is cut, be used in cutting the mitres, because, as it fits best into the kerfs, it will run steadier and more accurately than one which is thinner and has less set. Again, by using a saw with more set the kerfs in the sides are liable to be thrown out of true when placing it in the box. I would decidedly prefer a long saw in preference to a tenon or panel saw, still a 22-inch panel saw is very handy for the box described, as the longer the stroke the better for accurate cutting. Some carpenters prefer to insert a square cut in the box to make butt joints, especially when fixing mouldings in buildings, and it is a judicious and economical practice, when necessary, though, as we are now dealing with the elements of the science, we will proceed with the methods of obtaining ordinary mitres.

Supposing Fig. 4 to be a fillet of wood of any length and it is desired to saw it into such a shape that two or more pieces will be joined at right angles, or square, so as to show a continuous grain and be a close joint, how is it to be done? With

the aid of the box just described, very simply. Make the piece long enough to be
handily placed in the mitre box, which we
will presume is placed upon a bench or
table, or even a saw bench, and there fastened by a nail driven diagonally through
the ends of the bottom into the bench to

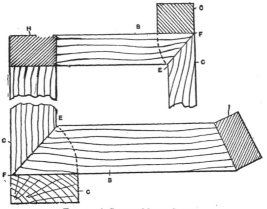

FIG. 4.—A SIMPLE MITRE JOINT.

hold it firmly in one position, then place
one piece in the box in the bottom corner
against the farthest side, as at A, Fig. 5,
and hold it fast there with the thumb of
the left hand, the fingers spanning the top
edge of the side. Now lift the saw with
the right hand, and, inserting it in the kerfs

of the box, move it back and forth lightly
until it touches the bottom and the end of
the mitred piece drops off. We are now
presumably making the right hand cut, as
B, Fig. 4. Care must be taken to hold the
piece immovable in one place until the saw
has gone entirely through, as the slightest
movement will destroy the shape of the
cut and render it inaccurate. The saw
will point from left to right in making this

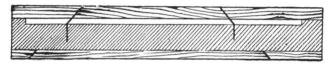

FIG. 5.—TOP VIEW OF BOX WITH SADDLE.

cut, and be placed in the left hand kerfs
of the box. To make the left piece that
will fit against this, as C, Fig. 4, it will only
be necessary to place and hold it in the
box as before and saw in the right hand
cuts from right to left. When the two are
placed together on a level board or surface
they will be as represented in Fig. 4, and
the mitre joint will be as E F. The inside
and outside angles will be 90° and the
pieces will be square to each other, giving

a continuous grain on all sides and a perfect, if not invisible, joint on the mitre.
G, Fig. 4, is the section of the mitred ends
which will, of course, be longer than the
cross section of the fillet, H. The accuracy of the cuts in the box can now be
practically proven by placing the mitred
pieces together and holding them with one
hand or a hand screw while inserting a
true try-square in the angle. If the stock
and blade of the square touch every part,
then the box is correct; if not, then the
box is out of true and there is no remedy
but making new exact cuts or kerfs in the
sides, using more care in doing so. T is
the section of the fillet when sawn at an
octagon, or on the angle of $22\frac{1}{4}$ degrees,
below which is seen the fillet mitred on
the edge and the section of the mitre cut.

The process of mitring, just described,
is applicable to all fillets and simple mouldings. For exam-
ple, the quarter-
round, Fig. 6,
the half-rounds
or beads, Figs.
7 and 8, the round or torus, Figs. 9 and 10,

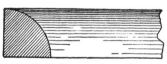

FIG. 6.—A QUARTER-ROUND MITRED.

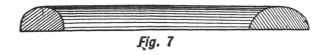

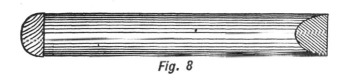

Fig. 7

Fig. 8

Fig. 9

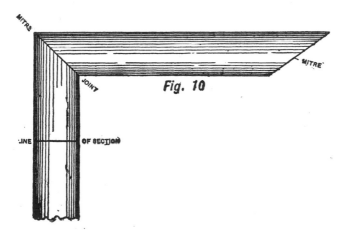

Fig. 10

are all similarly mitred, as are also the "scotias" or "cavettæ," Figs. 11 and 12, which are shown mitred and in projection.

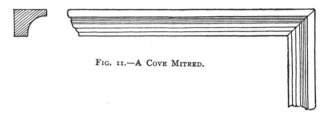

FIG. 11.—A COVE MITRED.

When a fillet or moulding is to be mitred to a fixed length a regular method must be followed to insure its being, when mitred, the exact length required. It is usual to mitre the left hand corner and end first, and then having marked the measurement on the top arris of the piece, as E, to place it in the box, keeping the mark to the side of the saw kerf in the box,

FIG. 12.—BACK VIEW OF COVE.

because, when it is sawn, the mark must just be on and nothing more. It would leave the piece short by the thickness of the saw blade were this precaution not taken and the mark placed carelessly at the kerf.

It will be seen from the above that extreme care is always requisite for proper mitring, in order that the beveled ends formed by sawing in the box may fit to form the angle required *without planing*, which is rarely done neatly enough to make a close joint and causes much waste of time.

A good mechanic will never plane his mitres, but saw them so accurately that they will fit to a hair when placed together.

FIG 13.

Fig. 13 shows the right hand mitre of a compound raised moulding mitred in the box, A being its cross section and B its mitred section.   In order to acquire practice I would advise a beginner to mitre four pieces of wood, fillets, or mouldings, like Fig. 4, together, forming a picture frame, as it were.   This can be done by first mitring them, say, two 8″ and two 12″ long, and tacking each one as it is mitred round on a flat board till they

form a border or frame and the joints
come close. There are many who claim
that it is impossible to cut four pieces or
eight mitres so precisely as to fit all round.
This is a fallacy, and after doing it several
times the beginner will see that if his mitre
box be true they will all fit and the frame

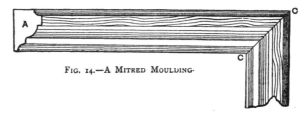

FIG. 14.—A MITRED MOULDING.

will be square. The latter he can determine either by placing a rod across from
corner to corner inside till the diagonals
are equal, or by the method before described with the try-square. Fig. 14 is a
panel mould mitred for a picture frame,
A being the cross section and C C the
joint of the mitre.

CHAPTER III.

MITRING PANEL AND RAISED MOULDINGS.

HAVING considered the simplest form of the science, I will now describe how a raised or rebated moulding can be inserted in a

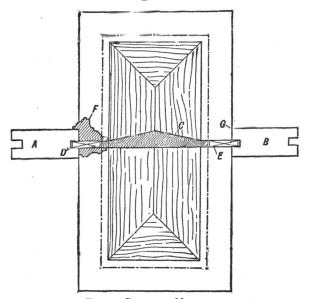

FIG. 15.—PANEL AND MOULDINGS.

panel. Supposing the panel at Fig. 15 to be a panel in a door of any kind, either for a

room or wardrobe, A B being the section
showing the two stiles of the frame A and
B, C the panel, D E the fillets and F the
panel moulding, which has to be mitred
round the inside edges of the frame and
to cover the joint at the arrises, as G, by
the rebate or lips on the moulding F.

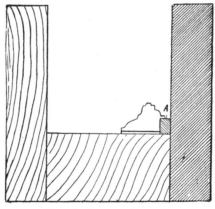

FIG. 16.—BOX WITH SADDLE.

Should the frame be so carefully made and
planed off that the sinkage of the panel
be equal all around, then all that is necessary is to make a saddle as A, Fig. 16,
equal in width to the depth of the sinkage,
which is here $\frac{1}{2}''$, about $\frac{1}{4}$ or $\frac{3}{8}''$ thick, and
place it in the mitre box in the position

shown in the drawing, so that the lips of
the moulding may rest upon it. Fig. 5,
being a plan of the box, illustrates this
more clearly, also how the marks for determining the length are scratched with a
knife on the bottom by squaring out from
the mitre point where the saw intersects it.
Should there be any difference in the sinkage between each corner or angle, then a
saddle, the width of which is equal to the
neat depth, must be used when cutting
the mitres at each individual corner. This
must be strictly adhered to when there is
a marked difference in order to make the
mitres fit closely, the rebate to come closely
down to a joint on the frame and the inside edge of the moulding close down on
the panel, thereby making a good job.
When the latter is being done the best
method to follow is to place the pieces
round in the panel, just feeling, making
the profiles of the moulding intersect
equally, commencing at the left and working round, and when the four are in to tap
them gently down, using a block, so as
not to bruise the moulding, and a hammer,

making sure that they all fit snugly in their places.

The usual way to mark the length of this description of rebated moulding is to place it in the sinkage of the frame, keeping the left hand mitred end closely into the corner, and then marking it with a pocket knife. This mark is placed to the square line at Fig. 5 in the mitre box and when it is sawn it will be just the exact length required.

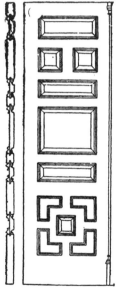

FIG. 17.—DOOR WITH RAISED MOULDINGS.

The front door illustrated in Fig. 17 has both flush and raised panels, but a raised inch moulding on one, the face side, and a common o-gee chamfer moulding on the other. The full size section, Fig. 18, gives the full profile of each. This door is a very good example of mouldings cut in the way I have just described, with the addition of having a central panel with L panels grouped around,

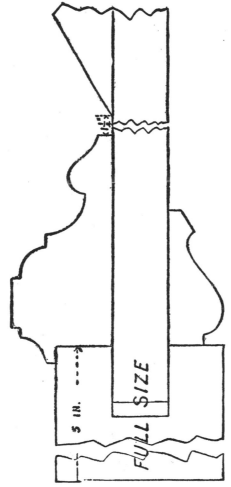

FIG. 18.—SECTION OF FIG. 17.

which gives four outside mitres. Here the difference between outside and inside mitres must be explained. An inside mitre is one in which the profile of the moulding is contained, or the outside line and highest part is contained within the angle, and an outside mitre is one which is directly its opposite, or the whole of the moulding is cut round outside the angle. The mitres are similarly sawn in the box, with the exception that the direction of the cut is changed, and instead of being an inside angle the profiles of the moulding intersect on an outside, as shown on the door. As it often happens from faulty construction that the rails and stiles of a door are slightly out of square, it is advisable to place a try or set square over or in the angles, to make sure that they are correct, or the mitres will show an open joint according as they vary. When this is the case the best way is to place a thin shaving or strip of cardboard, when mitring, behind one end of the moulding to make it vary likewise to suit the framing.

CHAPTER IV.

TO MITRE ON OCTAGON AND POLYGONAL
FIGURES.—THE MITRES FORMED BY
STRAIGHT MOULDINGS INTERSECTING
WITH CIRCULAR MOULDINGS, ALSO
MITRES OF CIRCULAR
MOULDINGS INTER-
SECTING.

THE moulding should also be carefully
examined to see that it is stuck the full
thickness, that the rebate is square and
fully fit for the purpose for which it is intended, and it is best to plane the back off
a little on a bevel so that it will fit easily
into its place and tighten as it goes down.
When the moulding is too thick for the
sinkage then it must be backed off until
the distance from the lips to the bottom is
slightly less than the depth from the face
of the frame to the fillet or panel. Ma-
chine-made mouldings often vary in their
outline and thickness, and the operator
will find that when the pieces are driven

into their places one piece may rise over its fellow and require trimming off to make the joint exact and the profiles of the members continuous. As just stated, when the character of the work is high, as in cabinet work or the construction of hardwood finish for or in buildings, it is best to take precautions to prevent the occurrence of faults which will necessitate remedies likely to mar the finished appearance of the workmanship.

Concerning the subject of mitring on all other angles besides that of 45°, it is to be said that for this purpose the mitre box is also requisite, the method of kerfing for the octagon cut being similar excepting that the direction of the cut across the box is only 22½° instead of 45°. All octagons on different designs are of different sizes, and a fixed method should be followed for this and all other sided figures to determine the direction of the line which will exactly bisect the angle formed by the junction of the sides, or, technically speaking, the mitre. In Fig. 19 the methods of finding this line will be seen,

embracing the pentagon or five-sided

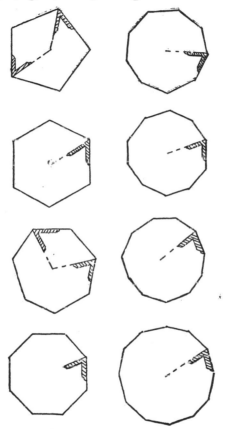

FIG 19.—POLYGONAL FIGURES.

figure, the hexagon or six-sided, the hep-
tagon or seven-sided, the octagon or eight-

sided, the enneagon or nine-sided, the
decagon or ten-sided, the undecagon or
eleven-sided and the dodecagon or twelve-
sided. Therefore, all that is required to
find the angles by which the box must be
marked for the mitre is to set a bevel to
the lines laid down as here shown and to
the size desired and to line across the box
for the kerfs.

Fig. 20 shows a moulding mitred together on the outside and inside cuts of an
octagon, also the mitre of a straight piece
with a piece on the octagonal cut of $22\frac{1}{2}°$,
which often occurs in practical joinery
and demands care in making. In connection with this it might be mentioned
that a very simple method to find the bi-
section or mitre of any angle is shown at
Fig. 20a, which consists of taking any two
points equi-distant from the apex of the
angle, as A and B, and with a pair of
compasses, set to any radius, to strike two
intersecting arcs. By joining the points
of intersection with the apex by a line,
this line will be the exact mitre. This
method can be applied here with perfect

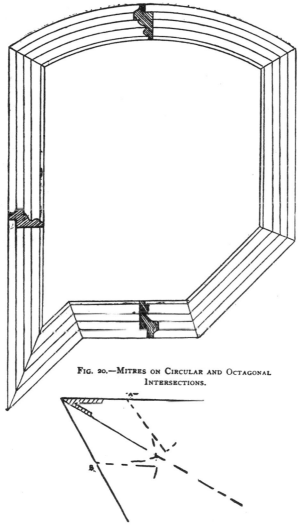

FIG. 20.—MITRES ON CIRCULAR AND OCTAGONAL
INTERSECTIONS.

FIG 20a.—TO FIND ANY MITRE.

success. At the opposite end of Fig. 20 is illustrated the mitring of a straight piece of moulding with a curved or circular piece. As the moulding embraces a part or arc of a circle, it follows that, being cut by the circle inside the circumference, the mitre will be a straight cut.

The feature noticed is amply illustrated in Fig. 21, which is the junction of a circular and straight moulding, the straight piece being tangent to the circular and each having similar members they mitre perfectly and show good workmanship. This sketch also shows the joint of a circular moulding with a straight one when the sweep is a semi-circle, and the sections, as drawn, will give the reader a clearer explanation of the manner in which the various members lapse into each other in passing. The writer considers this subject of circles in mitre of so much importance in the construction of decorative joinery that he would strongly recommend all those interested to closely examine and study all existing examples of work already executed. It is capable of

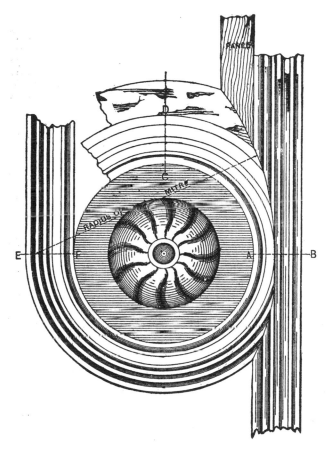

Fig. 21.—Circular and Straight Mouldings.

much variation, involving very careful study in working out in practice.

Fig. 21a is the mitre formed by tangent circles, which is also a curve. In connection with this subject it must always be remembered that all curved mouldings should be turned to a like profile to intersect properly. This I show at the section on the line of the mitre.

The drawing, Fig. 22, gives the reader

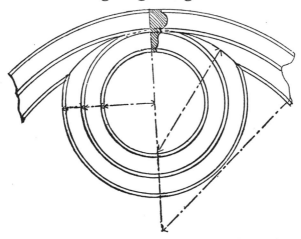

FIG. 21a.—MITRE FORMED BY CONCENTRIC MOULDINGS.

a description of how two circular contiguous mouldings of the same radius and profiles must necessarily form a mitre whose direction will be a straight line, but if two circles intersect which are contiguous and radii of different lengths, then the mitre joint will be a curve.

By referring to the geometrical design for a ceiling, Fig. 23, the student will see

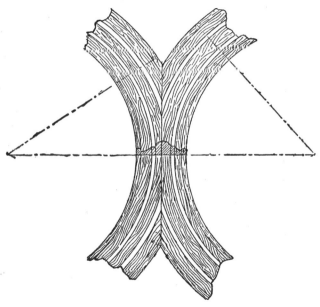

FIG. 22.—MITRE OF TWO ECCENTRIC MOULDINGS.

another and more advanced feature, namely, in the mitring of a straight moulding into one whose peripheral is a

circle, the direction of the straight one being through the diameter, which makes a
straight joint when mitring, also another

FIG. 23.—A MITRED CEILING.

circle cut toward the centre by another
which does not pass to it at right angles
but on an acute angle.

CHAPTER V.

CONCERNING the subject of mitring crown mouldings I would state that there is only one way to mitre a sprung moulding properly, whether it be a crown mould or any kind, and that is to place it in the mitre box against the further side with the side that is to stand perpendicular as on the side of the wall. The two most common kinds of mitre cuts usually made on crown moulds are those on the inside and outside mitres, as A and B, Fig. 24, where the mitred pieces are shown as they will appear from above. When a piece has to be cut on an outside mitre, as on the corner of a building, it is mitred from the corner, or as B, Fig. 24; that is, the direction of the cut will be outside the right angle made by the building; but if it be an inside mitre the mitre joint will be con-

tained within the angle of the building
and it will bisect it.   It is to be said, how-

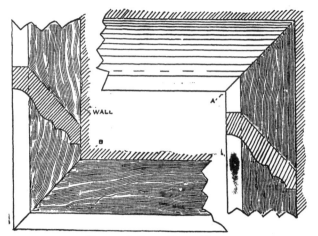

FIG. 24.—A CROWN MOULD MITRED.

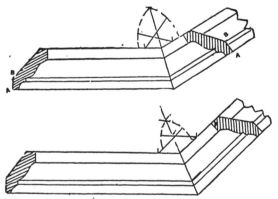

FIG. 25.—HOW TO FIND THE INTERSECTION.

ever, that inside angles, like A, are usually
coped, and the method of doing this will
be explained hereafter. Fig. 25 illustrates
the manner of mitring a level moulding
with one on the pitch on the same surface.
Some carpenters maintain that the same
conditions prevail here as in the case of a
moulding on a pediment mitring and
with one on a level, namely, that they
won't intersect. This is an error, as the
sketch clearly proves, because each moulding has the same profile, and the only
thing essential to insure a perfect intersection is to determine the exact line of the
mitre. It can be done as shown by taking
any two points and striking arcs cutting
each other, and the point of section being
joined with the apex of the angle will give
the direction of the mitre joint. As it
often happens that there may be only one
gable or pediment on a building, or two
of a different pitch, it would scarcely be
necessary to make a box for the four or
eight cuts, and a very rapid and simple
way which I have found to work well is
to lay out the direction of the cut on the

plumb side which nails against the wall or fascia and square across the bottom edge.

A carpenter with a well filed saw and steady hand can cut this joint clean and straight from the back. Another way which some prefer is to lay the running directions of the moulding out on a board and set each piece up on the laid out lines, then to place the moulding to the lines and square up with a try-square from the line of the mitre as laid out. This method saves more time than by making a box.

To prove that the angle does not regulate and alter the intersection I illustrate at Fig. 26 a large 5-inch crown moulding of ten members which will intersect and be continuous, each to each, provided the profiles run on each piece in the sticker and be entirely alike. I find from experience that by reason of the peculiarity of some stickers there is a variance of some mouldings, and it is therefore wise in the carpenter to measure each piece carefully to insure their intersection and save time in trimming them off to a like profile.

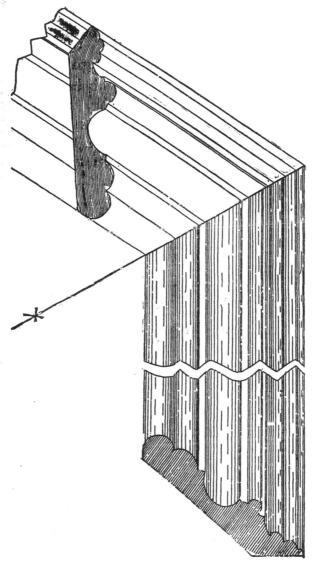

FIG. 26.—LEVEL AND PITCHED MOULDING.

This is rarely done neatly enough to make a clean job because it is necessary to trim as far back as 8 or 9 inches from the mitre to prevent each member appearing round.

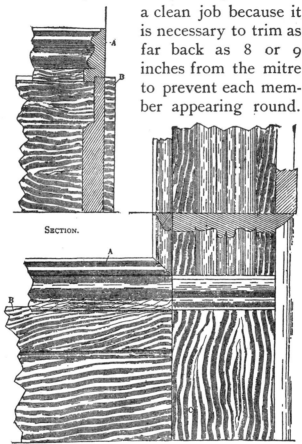

SECTION.

FIG. 27.—A BASE MOULDING AND CASING.

Regarding the mitring of sprung mouldings on a curve much the same conditions prevail as with those stuck flat, but should the reader desire to become thoroughly acquainted with this subject I would refer him to some of the very excellent works written by various authors treating on it. There is very little occasion for this class of work at present, and, even were it so, I should still refrain from taking and accrediting to myself those ideas which have been so clearly explained and illustrated before.

Fig. 27 will explain how the mitring on door trimming is usually done. A is the base moulding or top member of the base. As will be noticed it has three principal members, comprising the square or flat surface on the bottom, the main o-gee and the upper compound moulding. When the base mould, A, is fitted against the trim and base block, C, the two bottom members are cut square in the mitre box, and the top member is mitred to permit the wall moulding (which is really the top member, to run in separate lengths) to mitre. It is used for the pur-

pose of covering the joint likely to open
between the back side of the door casing
and the wall plaster

CHAPTER VI.

MITRING CHAIR RAIL, PICTURE MOULDING. COLUMN BASES AND THE USE OF THE MITRE TEMPLET.

FIGURE 28 shows the reader an elevation and section of a piece of chair rail mitred

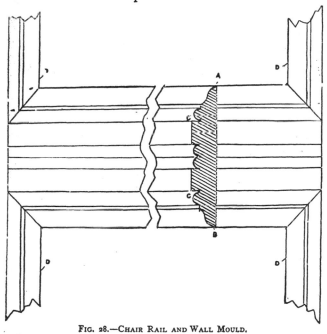

FIG. 28.—CHAIR RAIL AND WALL MOULD.

into the wall mould of a door or window trim.   A B is the section of the mouldings, and it will be noticed that the two upper members, C A and C B, though they are 'stuck solid on and form part of the chair rail, are of the same profile and mitre with facility with the wall moulding, L.   In many sections of the country this style of finish is not used, but in some of the East-

FIG. 29.—PICTURE MOULD.

ern States and in New York City it is the usual method, and has, I think, many good qualities which would recommend its adoption.

The picture mould shown in the drawing, Fig. 29, where it is represented as being nailed on a wall on which the wall paper has been pasted, conveys to the reader the way in which this moulding is placed beneath the frieze. This moulding usually is cut on square inside and outside angles. There is very little to be said explanatory of how it should be mitred, excepting that when gilt moulding is being mitred a very fine tooth saw should be employed in order to avoid breaking the plaster of Paris composition which covers the profiles of the members. Another thing is that the inside angle should never be coped but should invariably be mitred, for the reason that it is almost impossible to cope it with the pen-knife without injuring the gilding.

Fig. 30 represents the mitring of a base moulding round a column whose plan or section is a hexagon. It will be noticed that the base is composed of nothing more than a large moulding stuck in the machine to the design shown in the sketch. Readers will understand for the accurate mitring of such a moulding as this it would be best to construct a special mitre-box, and, after setting a bevel to the angle desired, so mark the box from it and

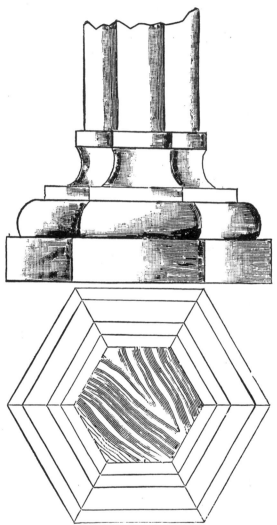

FIG. 30.—A COLUMN BASE MITRED ROUND.

thus insure the accuracy of the length of each piece. Nail or glue on each side of the hexagonal piece. I would here like to impress one thing on all readers, and that is the necessity of making sure that wide mouldings are straight or even a little hollow on the back side. This is necessary when the pieces are affixed to surfaces, and

FIG. 31.—A MITRE TEMPLET.

a good plan to follow is to place the edge of a blade of a try-square across the back, and, if it be rounding, to plane it to a slightly hollow surface with a smoothing plane.

Fig. 31 represents what is commonly called by carpenters a mitre templet, and it is used for the purpose of marking all small mouldings, as beads, quarter-round, etc.

Fig. 32 shows its application to a quarter-round. The introduction of mitre squares, bevel squares and other modern tools have rendered the use of this instrument more

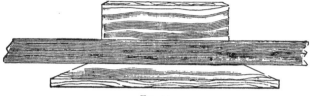

FIG. 32.

or less obsolete, but the older mechanics regard it as essential in their tool chest and use it largely in putting together beaded framing or other work where small mouldings are to be mitred.

CHAPTER VII.

VARYING MITRES IN BOTH STRAIGHT AND CIRCULAR MOULDINGS.

IN THE ordinary routine of work pertaining to each of the different wood-working crafts, there are certain forms of joints, cuts or important details of construction and decoration which are well known and occur almost daily, and other forms of the same which are varying. As those which are most in use are more easily worked and familiar to the operator, so it must of necessity follow that unusual forms will call forth more labor of brain and manual skill to effect their successful completion. This is particularly applicable in the case of the mitre joint, which every wood-worker is in daily contact with. It is being continually employed in different parts of joinery, in all places where a continuous grain or moulding is required, but the most difficult of all its employments to execute is the mitring of mouldings, both flushed and raised, in framing. Here the intersection of the profile, especially those with many members, necessitates great care in marking the mitre box and sawing it, marking and sawing the moulding, and insuring its perfect intersection before driving the pieces to their permanent place in the panel. Concerning a simple square mitre of the angle of 45°, as it is too well known to require special comment here, we will avoid its consideration, except to recommend readers to take careful heed of three important points, essential to perfect mitring :

First—To mark the mitre box by a bevel set to the diagonal of a square about four inches wide, laid down with a knife on a clean board.

Second.—To mark the box also with the knife and saw, carefully, keeping the saw kerf to one side of the knife mark.

Third.—Saw moulding exactly to the mark made on the panel, and out of one continuous piece for each panel, round the sides, and intersect perfectly before driving down.

Care and exactness will help to perfection and save trimming off afterward.

Fig. 33 represents a piece of ash paneling designed to stand under a stair string.

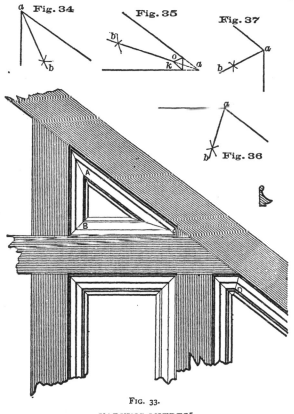

FIG. 33.

VARYING MITRES.

To find the mitre at A, strike out the angle inside the framing at A, like Fig. 34. Take any two points equi-distant from A, the apex of the angle. With the compasses strike the crossed lines shown and draw a line joining their crossing with the apex of the angle. This line will be the exact mitre, and if a level be set to it and marked on a good box, the cut can be got direct from the saw. Fig. 35 shows the compound mitre at C. It is rendered compound by the insertion of a small piece necessary to continue up the mullion below the rail show, and the mitres are found thus : The angle at the corner of the rail and raked piece, being even less than at A, B, will be longer, and this line is gained by the method used above. B being a right angle, the mitre for it is cut in an ordinary 45° box, but C must be cut differently, as its length renders it unhandy for a box. It is recommended that the moulding be marked on the bottom side and the mitre cut square to the bottom to insure a close joint above. This method will always be found suitable for very long cuts. The fifth mitre, shown in Fig. 33 at D, is obtained by the same process as before, and, being short, can be marked on Fig. 36 and cut in the mitre box. Experience has taught that the only way to obtain a perfect mitre is from the saw alone, as it is invariably the case, no matter how carefully the block plane is used, the joint can never be evenly surfaced or satisfaction gained.

Fig. 38 is a diagram of an opening for a panel in a partition or door, etc., showing two methods of ornamenting the angles. The cross sections of the mouldings X^4 are similar, but the shape of the opening would vary according to the arc used, whether internal or external. The circular mouldings B B C are similar, and are of the same section as the straight portions, but A is expanded to conform to the conditions laid down in the plan—*i.e.*, that all the intersections shall be at a true mitre ($45°$). B B joins the straight parts with a butt joint, C is the same section, and would intersect in the same manner as B if it were in that position ; but, following the

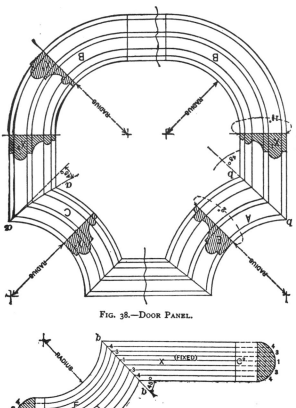

FIG. 38.—DOOR PANEL.

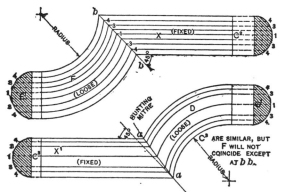

FIG. 39.—VARIED INTERSECTIONS.

plan, it will be seen that it intersects not a true mitre. But the joint is not a right line, and it is impossible to make the joint in the ordinary manner—*i.e.*, with the saw and plane (for woodwork). This joint is sometimes called a "hunting mitre," and it must be carved to its true shape. It will be noticed that it is formed of a pair of curves. This will perhaps be clearer from an inspection of Fig 39, and to those interested in the subject (and it is a practical one) if they construct a model from that plan a curious result will be seen.

X, X' are straight lengths of mouldings (any section—in this case semi-circular for simplicity); but the principle can be seen better if a good half-round moulding be selected.

D is a quadrant of a circle, section as X, X', joined so that the marginal lines intersect. The form of the curved joint *a a* is found by a series of straight and curved auxiliary planes parallel to the axes of D and X'.

F is an arc similar to D internally which intersects X at *b b* at an angle of 45°. The result is that the point where the angular line cuts the horizontal line is the position where the arc must join the straight line, therefore F is expanded; its true section is shown at E'.

This explains why many workers cannot get a turned moulding and a straight one to intersect at a true mitre, when both are similar in cross section. When the model is made, alternate the positions of D and F with X and X'.

CHAPTER VIII.

A DESCRIPTION OF A COMBINATION OF MANY
AND VARIOUS MITRE JOINTS ILLUS-
TRATED BY THE FRONTISPIECE—
A GEOMETRICAL CEILING
DESIGN.

THE ceiling decorated in this manner
would be of the kind technically termed
"planted," or the design of hardwood
planted or nailed on a wooden ground or
smooth ceiling· surface, which would be
covered with a prepared cloth capable of
taking paint. The panels are, therefore,
the paneled surface, and the ·outline of
the design or woodwork.

We will suppose then that the whole
area has the canvas or cloth tacked on and
that it has been given a coat of size to
render it capable of receiving the paint.
It is desired to work out the design in
wood ; how shall it be done ?

First, the design must be detailed ; that

is to say, the main features of the construction will require to be drawn to a
large scale or the actual constructed
size, so that each part may be distinctly
comprehended by the wood-worker and
carpenter.

A very simple detail will be necessary
here, and merely a section will be needed.

All mitres are simply intersections, and
the mitre joint proper is the line of direction which the several and separate members form in blending into each other,
each to each, in maintaining their contin-
uity. It will then be clearly seen that if
the operator place the pieces, be they
either one straight or one curved piece,
two curved pieces crossing or intersecting
either in a tangential or eccentrical direction, or two straight pieces placed at any
angle, the direction of the mitre-line or
"joint" will be easily found by laying
down the lines which indicate the several
members.

Thus it will be readily comprehended
that the main lines which form the whole
geometrical part of the ceiling are the

lines which indicate the members of the mouldings, and all that it will be necessary to do to determine the line of direction of the mitre joint will be to place each moulding where it belongs and mark the intersections.   There are fifteen different mitres illustrated in this design, and I think I would be justified in saying that if any practical readers will go to the trouble of making a scale model, they will receive a practical lesson in the art of mitring which will give them the power to obtain any possible mitre on flat surfaces.

CHAPTER IX.

THE ART OF COPING MOULDINGS.

ONE of the means employed by cabinet-makers and carpenters in making joints in r'entrant angles is the art of coping.

The verb "to cope" is used in contradistinction to "to mitre," a method entirely used for joining pieces of joinery of a continuous grain on exterior angles. Webster gives the word as, to cover; to match against; a covering. So it is admirably adapted, and very appropriate, as when an operator copes, he really covers and matches against.

Coping is principally used for mouldings, square and flat surfaces being fitted together, one piece abutting against the other; but curved or moulded surfaces can only be coped to a successful inside joint.

Mitring interior angles is very faulty, and is rarely done by mechanics of ability, on account of the liability of one or the

other joint slipping past its fellow, breaking the intersection, and showing end
wood, added to the difference of the profiles of mill-run mouldings. Against
plaster the inside mitre is useless, as one
piece is almost certain to draw and open
the joint when nailing into the studding.
The best way, then, to make this joint is
to cope it.

Fig. 40 represents
a very simple cope,
being a common
shelf cleat, coped
at right angles
against another.
As will be seen, it
is the end cut to
the profile of the
moulding, or bevel,
of the cleat, so that

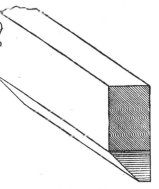

FIG. 40.—A COPED CLEAT.

it will fit tight against it and look as if
mitred.

In order to gain this joint, the piece is
first placed in a mitre box and cut on the
mitre on the side to which the joint fits;
in this case, the right hand. The dotted

line denotes the line of the cut. When
this is done, the piece is cut through at an
angle, slightly under, so that the joint may
touch in every point on the face. When
placed in position, if the piece be cut
slightly long, the joint will come perfectly
close and fit well; but the piece coped to
must always be nailed well back and solid
before marking the piece to be coped, as it

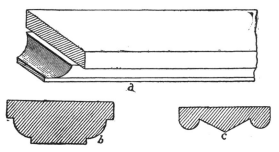

FIG. 42.—MOULDED STRIP COPED.

is certain to yield to the concussion of the
hammer. This is a vertical, or plumb,
cope.

A horizontal cope is drawn at Fig. 42
and shows a ceiling strip or piece of astra-
gal coped to an ovolo, or rule-jointed
edge; *a* is the coped end, done by placing

the entire moulding on its back in the
mitre-box and mitring each moulding on
each side square across the piece, and
afterward sawing or chiseling the end out
to the profiles made by the saw in mitring,
until it appears as in the sketch *a*, and will
fit closely against the section at *b*. This
cope ought to be slightly hollow, so as to
press against the surface of the moulding
on the arms of the cope.

The moulding shown at Fig. 42, *c*, cannot be coped, as some of its members are
incapable of being so, or sink below
others. This will be seen at a glance and
the moulding mitred.

It is only in mouldings of this kind
where the art cannot be profitably applied;
but interior mitres (if they must be used)
should be nailed and glued together before
setting in position.

When it is found necessary to cope an
architrave moulding, like Fig. 43 (a series
of compound curves and squares), the
mitre box is again brought into requisition
and the end brought to the mitred line,

always beveling it slightly under, to bring
the cope close on the line of A B.

A sharp penknife is essential for good
coping, to cut away the wood on the
curves exactly to the mitred line, something which can scarcely be done correctly
with the compass saw, gouge or chisel, as
in soft wood the arris is very liable to
break under the pressure of the hand, even

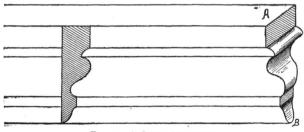

FIG. 43.—A COPED ARCHITRAVE.

though the edge be keen, whereas the
small blade of a good pocket-knife, if
reasonably sharp, can be very handily
swept around the quick curves, and will
also cut obliquely against the grain without injuring the edge of the end wood,
the grain of which is often short and
fragile.

A difficult cope is drawn at Fig. 44, being a section of rebated wainscot capping, with its wall moulding and another piece coped to it in a r'entrant corner, at right angles, left hand. The capping is mitred in the left hand cut in the box, and then sawn out close to the mitred line with a compass saw, and afterward being neatly

FIG. 44.—COPED WAINSCOT CAPPING.

pared exactly to the line, in order that the joint may show one line. The wall moulding is similarly treated ; but for all mouldings when coping, pieces of the same thickness and profile ought to be selected.

Obtuse angles might also be coped, taking care that the end is beveled well enough to clear the piece running behind it, otherwise the joint will be *hard* on the back and open; acute angles will cope easily.

Coping obtuse angles gives a splendid chance to bring the joint close by nailing through the cope into the piece behind, something which can never be done with an inside mitre.

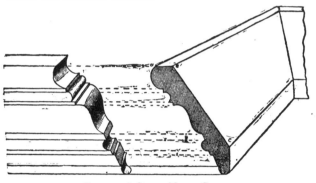

FIG. 45.—A CROWN MOULD COPED.

The crown mould is also fitted by this method when it is returned on inside corners, as on wardrobes, cases, an angle in a house cornice, etc., mitring as before, by placing the length of mould in the box upside down, the part that stands plumb, as *e c* in Fig. 45, against the side of the box, the level part, or cope *d e*, resting flat on the bottom. When cut to an inside mitre, the end is *coped*, or cut out, to cover over the profile *d b*, the coping being all level, or parallel, to *d e*, in the manner represented in the perspective sketch.

Coping on the angle, as on a gable with an eave moulding, can also be done, but the pieces must be wrought so that they will intersect, and continue true—member with member.

In conclusion, it may be said that the system is universal in its use in modern joinery for chair rail, picture mould, crown mould, base necking, wall members, etc., and is very popular among wood-workers, as they cannot, like plasterers, mitre their pieces and then close the joint with putty. It is a rapid, certain and accurate system, and when properly done, especially in the hard woods, produces a good mechanical job.

Carpentry and Joinery
for Amateurs.

CONTAINS

FULL DESCRIPTIONS OF THE VARIOUS TOOLS REQUIRED
IN THE ABOVE ARTS, TOGETHER WITH PRACTICAL
INSTRUCTIONS FOR THEIR USE.

By the Author of

"TURNING FOR AMATEURS," "WORKING IN SHEET METAL," &C.

LONDON:

"THE BAZAAR" OFFICE, 170, STRAND, W.C.

LONDON:
PRINTED BY ALFRED BRADLEY, 170, STRAND, W.C.

Carpentry and Joinery for Amateurs.

INTRODUCTION.

Of all the arts which conduce to the comfort and well-being of the human race there are two which claim precedence for their antiquity: namely, masonry and carpentry; and in this respect the latter probably bears the palm, for the wooden hut generally precedes the stone building. The earliest mention we have of either or both of these arts occurs in the 4th chapter of Genesis, where we are told that Enoch, Cain's son, built a city in the land of Nod, and called it after his own name.

Almost at the same period we read of the early manufacture of brass and iron, which were probably formed into rude tools, to be used upon wood and stone, succeeding perhaps the flint implements of earlier generations, if such existed upon the earth. It is quite possible that what is here styled a city was little else than a collection of log huts, or cabins of mud and stone, but at the same time it need not be absolutely taken for granted that such was the case; for the archæologist is frequently brought into contact with imperishable proofs of skill in the construction of buildings, which suggest a far higher development of mechanical and engineering knowledge in the earlier epochs, than we should have been prepared to expect. Looking back, indeed, upon ancient records, we are fairly staggered at the accounts of buildings we there meet with, corroborated as they undoubtedly are by recent discoveries in Nineveh and elsewhere. It seems as if generations of old were even better versed than ourselves in arts of construction, but that from unexplained causes, this knowledge had died out in the course of time, to be again taken up and studied in later ages. No doubt the masonic craft will claim that these monuments of antiquity prove rather the earlier development of their own art than that of the carpenter; but it must be remembered that timber decays where stone remains intact, and that therefore we should expect to find the merest traces of woodwork where the more durable material might remain uninjured from generation to generation. It is most probable that the two arts were developed side by side, the one as the handmaid of the other, and if the city of Enoch were built of stone or similar material, the ark of Noah stands forth a standing proof that the science of timber framing and substantial carpentry was known and practised at an almost equally early period. It is not only, however, the materials of these early buildings that interests us, but the tools used in their construction; and it is a matter of regret that the early records of man's doings supply but a meagre account of ways and means. We can scarcely imagine that capacious ark, with its several rooms and fittings, to have been constructed without the use of two tools at least—the axe and saw; and the moment we allow these a place, we recognise the necessity of other appliances for their formation, as for instance, a file, or its substitute, for sharpening the teeth of the latter. As to the real or approximate date of the introduction of such tools we must, however, rest contented with our profound ignorance; but we may perhaps not unreasonably hazard the conjecture that the same Providence which in just judgment laid on man the necessity of providing himself shelter from the inclemency of the weather, instructed him also in the ways and means of accomplishing his desires. It is scarcely probable that mere accident should have taught him to smelt and manufacture, for example, iron and brass, unless the so-called accident were purposely ordered by a higher power—a power which no sooner lays on man the need of suffering or of toil than he points to means of alleviating the one and lightening and sweetening the other.

CHAPTER I.

TOOLS AND THEIR APPLICATION.

CLASSIFICATION—THE AXE—THE ADZE—THE HAMMER AND MALLET—THE CHISEL—THE DRAW KNIFE—THE SPOKESHAVE —THE GOUGE—THE SAW—THE PLANE—BORING TOOLS— APPLIANCES FOR SHARPENING TOOLS — THE BENCH — THE HOLDFAST—THE MITRING BOX—THE SHOOTING BOARD.

WE must now take "a big leap" from the past to the present, and commence our proposed instructions in the art of modern carpentry. In this book we shall, as far as possible, follow the plan of our little work on "Turning for Amateurs," to which this is intended to become the companion volume. As we commenced with the lathe and tools of the turner, we shall now first describe the tools used by the carpenter and joiner, pointing out at the same time what are absolutely necessary and what may be omitted in the tool chest of the amateur.

These tools are capable of a certain systematic arrangement, and may be divided into the following groups :

1. Those which act by percussion—namely, the axe, adze, hammer, and mallet, and as the latter is used invariably in conjunction with the mortise chisel, in order to give it due effect, this chisel may also be fairly classed under the same head.

2. Tools which act by cutting but without any percussive action, and which have no attachment of any kind to guide the direction of their cutting edges. Such are the paring chisel, firmer chisel, draw knife, or double-handled shave, and gouge.

3. Tools whose cutting edges are under the direction of guides permanently attached to them. The spokeshave, and various planes, and cutting gauge, which last, however, is not often found in the carpenter's tool box.

4. Under this head may be classed those tools which have many edges or teeth—saws, files, and rasps.

5. Tools for boring holes, generally by rotatory motion of their edges, as gimlets, augurs, bradawls, and the variously shaped bits of the carpenter's brace. All these make circular holes only, no satisfactory tool

having been yet introduced for producing holes of square, oval, or oblong sections.

6. This class comprehends measuring and guiding tools and appliances of various kinds, as the two-foot rule, bevel, square, and mitring boards and boxes ; to which may be added sticking boards used in planing up sash bars, compasses and callipers, of which there are several kinds in use.

7. Clamps, holdfasts, and vices stand here alone, unless we add, as companion tools, the pincers and pliers, so generally useful in their respective departments.

The Axe.—Of these tools the first is probably one of the most ancient, as it is also that which accompanies the emigrant to all quarters of the globe. The axe is, in short, the pioneering instrument and most faithful ally of man in founding himself a home. He may for a time dispense with the chisel and plane, and even to a certain extent with the saw, but the axe is a matter of necessity. It serves, indeed, in a rough way as a chisel, plane and mallet, and for many reasons claims precedence for general utility.

There are several forms of axe in use, but the most general are the felling axe (Fig. 1), for cutting down timber, and the hand axe with double

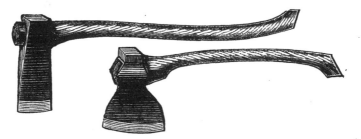

FIG. 1. FELLING AXE.   FIG. 2. HAND AXE.

bevelled edge (Fig. 2), for squaring and general purposes. There is also, in addition to the above, an axe with single bevelled edge, like that of an adze or chisel, intended especially for use in trimming logs and facing them more smoothly and evenly than can be done by the tool with double bevel or wedge-shaped edge, but this " side " axe, as it is called, is not in very general use, though well adapted for the special work for which it is intended.

The shape of the blade of axes is very varied, some preferring them very wide, and others liking them narrower and longer. They are also to be had of different weights, some being very heavy implements, fit only to split logs for the fire, and others light and elegant tools for use with one hand alone. Even to those acquainted in some degree with the lathe it would scarcely be credited that axe handles can be turned, especially those of the American felling axe which take the form of Fig. 3, and which are most beautifully finished. They are nevertheless frequently so made, and the latter, we believe, invariably. The lathe, however, is of peculiar construction, and is rather a copying or carving machine, a pattern handle of cast iron giving the to and fro movement necessary to enable the tool to follow the various curves required. The spokes of wheels, especially of field guns and of agricultural implements, are, it may be remarked, also made in great quantities in the same way, the work occupying only a few

FIG. 3. AMERICAN FELLING AXE.

minutes instead of many hours. The advantage is great where large numbers are required exactly alike; and now that labour has become so much more costly than it was a few years since, the introduction of machinery for all kinds of mechanical work will become more and more general. The use of the axe, simple as it may appear to a looker on, is not likely to be found very easy at first. It is one thing to split a log of wood, and quite another to square and trim it neatly. The tool having a

FIG. 4. SPLITTING AND TRIMMING WITH THE DOUBLE-BEVELLED AXE, A. AND B., AND SIDE AXE C.

wedge-like edge will do the first readily if sufficient impulse is given to it, but this very wedge-shaped or cuneiform edge originates the difficulty experienced in levelling a surface by its aid. Fig. 4, A. and B., will suffice to explain this, the blow being in one case directly downwards, and both bevels coming equally into use, but in the latter sideways, one bevel having to meet the full resistance of the heavy block of wood, while the other has but the resistance or support of the chip which is being detached. This gives the tool a tendency to fly off from the work, and it evidently has to be forcibly prevented from so doing, while being held at an awkward angle. This makes such work tiring to the arm and wrist, and it needs practice to overcome the difficulty. It will also be seen by the figure that the bevel next to the work must be kept parallel to it as nearly as possible, and that the inclination of the tool is much greater than would be probably given to it by a beginner. The side axe C, with one bevel, is free from this drawback, as it is held with the blade vertical—the position it naturally assumes in the hand—and when there is much trimming and squaring to be done it is a far more manageable tool than the first. Nevertheless,

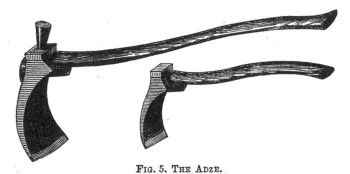

FIG. 5. THE ADZE.

practice, which makes perfect, soon gives the workman the necessary knack of using the ordinary axe, and as he never multiplies his tools unnecessarily, he makes this tool serve as his handmaid of all work.

The Adze.—Closely allied to the axe, yet at the same time wholly distinct from it, is the adze so generally used by the ship carpenter and wheelwright. In this tool the cutting edge is at right angles to the handle, and the blade itself is curved, forming part of a large circle. There is but one bevel, which is on the inner or concave side of the blade. There are two or three forms of this tool, of which the most common is that represented in Fig. 5, the long double-handed adze of the carpenter. The position of the work under the action of this tool is very commonly horizontal, the workman standing upon it and causing the edge of the adze to fall each time close under his toes. The unerring certainty of each stroke, and the perfection of the surface thus formed always strikes the beholder with admiration; the board or other work appearing almost as if it had been levelled with a plane. The edge of this tool is always kept extremely sharp, as it is never put to such rough jobs as the axe. Although a great deal of work is laid thus horizontally for the operation of the adze, the ship carpenter and wheelwright place it in other positions, and use this tool with equal facility. The edge of a cart wheel on which the iron tire is to be placed is always finished in this way, the workman placing it in an upright position, and striking directly in front of him. He will thus carefully trim his work exactly to line, correcting the previous inequalities caused by the saw and axe. The inside or hollow of the wheel felloes are first sawn out roughly with a sweep, or turn saw, fixed in a frame, and afterwards finished entirely with the adze, except that a spoke-shave, or plane with a convex sole, is run round the edges as a final touch.

The very form of the blade of an adze suggests the method of using it. It is swung in a circular arc; of which, when the work is under the feet, the centre is the shoulder joint, but when placed vertically the elbow. In the former case the handle is held nearer its extremity than in the latter, the weight of the tool being brought into operation as much as possible. When England's wooden walls of oak were the pride and glory of our nation some thousands of adzes were constantly at work, shaping ribs and stanchions and similar curved parts of those mighty skeletons.

But now that iron is so largely used, and steam giants do so much of the work, the use of this tool is somewhat more limited, though even now ample scope is given for its skilful application to divers constructive purposes. In addition to the large and heavy adze just described, there is one that is in constant use by the native carpenter in India, and which, in his hands, is perhaps one of the most efficient tools ever devised. It goes by the name

FIG. 6. BASSOOLAH, OR INDIAN ADZE.

of the Bassoolah (Fig. 6), and of late it has been brought into notice by more than one of our many amateur mechanics. Holtzapffel, too, in his valuable work on tools, gives it very high praise as the best tool for shaping wood for the lathe. It appears that the native Indian uses it on all occasions, whether the special work in hand be light or heavy—as one correspondent writes, "for house beams or toothpicks." It therefore claims by its own merits a place in the present series. The blade of this tool is, it will be seen from the figure, not curved like the adze of the carpenter or cooper, but straight; and the short handle is inserted at rather an acute angle. The action of the arm is chiefly from the elbow in using it, short quick strokes being given with it. We cannot claim in this case practical experience, but it has the strong recommendations of all who have given it a trial, and no doubt it will one day be more generally found than it is at present in the tool box of the workman and the amateur.

Whether the large adze is to be recommended to our readers as a matter of necessity, depends upon the character of the work to be done. If this demand the formation of curved surfaces, such as wheel felloes, it is indispensable; if not—and such is not very usual work of amateurs—the axe and the Indian adze at most will suffice.

The Hammer and Mallet.—Of hammer and mallet not much perhaps need be said in the way of description. We do not, however, recommend the claw hammer, one side of which is for drawing nails, but hammer heads without such claw (Fig. 7), fitted to handles passing through the centre, one heavy and one light—for a heavy hammer is not at all desirable for driving tacks or brads, being more likely to destroy than to assist in constructing light work. For work, indeed, of the latter description, the upholsterer's hammer is to be preferred even to the lightest of the other

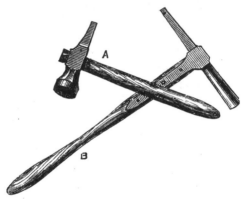

FIG. 7. HAND AND UPHOLSTERER'S HAMMERS.

form. It is made like Fig. 7B, much longer in the head than the first, so that it will reach into many an odd corner where otherwise it would be difficult to drive a nail at all. Perhaps it will be said that we are already adding tool to tool unnecessarily; but we are writing, not for boys only, with questionable mechanical ability, but for those who really wish to do good work, and if each tool, as it is added, is carefully preserved, as well as used, the prime cost of a few extras will be amply repaid. There is no doubt that tools are costly luxuries to many amateurs, but they are often rendered doubly so by being allowed to remain out of doors, or in various improper places in the workshop, from which they not unfrequently find their way to the dust bin, only to be replaced at a fresh outlay of good coin.

The mallet is usually made of a bit of dry beech, but box is also used for the purpose, and we have seen them also of mahogany, and even ebony; but it seems rather wasteful to use for this purpose any of the harder foreign woods when more ordinary material will suffice. There is, however, a very neat mallet of smaller dimensions than that used by the carpenter, which consists of a hollow flat socket or ferule of iron, into each end of which is driven a plug of box or hard wood, which latter can be renewed if it should become damaged or worn. For light work, and especially for driving wood into chucks for turning, these are quite the amateur's tool. But they are much smaller on the face than the ordinary mallet, and are not, so far as we have been able to ascertain, patronised by the trade. For anything like mortising, unless of the lightest kind, we ourselves decidedly prefer a mallet of solid beech.

The amateur is often guilty of using a hammer upon the head of his chisel, by which he invariably damages, if he does not actually split, the handle; and here, therefore, we say once for all, that however ready we may be in most cases to "make things do" by substituting, when possible, a tool we have for one we need but have not, the above must be always excepted. A hammer is not to be used in any case upon the wooden handle of a chisel or other tool. If you have, therefore, no mallet, buy at once, or make one; the latter is the best plan after all.

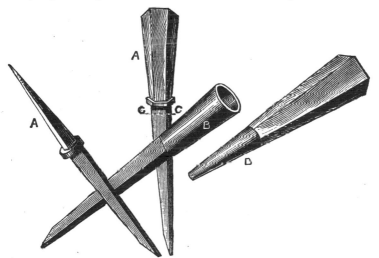

FIG. 8. MORTISING CHISELS.

The Chisel.—The mortising chisel, simply allied to tools of percussion from being generally made to penetrate the wood through the medium of the mallet, is either formed with a solid tang or a hollow socket (A and B, Fig. 8). In either case it is very strongly made, and that for narrow mortises is very broad in the other direction (C). For light work, however, in deal or other soft wood, the firmer chisel is often used, though less able to resist the blows of the mallet. Mortise chisels can be had from ¼in. wide, or even ⅛in. on the cutting edge to 2in., but a chisel of 1in. wide amply suffices even for large work. The practical use of this, as of the other tools sketched in this chapter, will form the subject of future remarks.

Of the cutting tools which do not work through percussive action, and which have no attachments for the guidance of their edges, the firmer chisel stands, perhaps, in the first place. This is made with a tang to fit into a wooden handle (Fig. 9), and is broad in comparison with its thickness. The paring chisel is merely a longer tool of the same shape. Firmer chisels are of all widths of edge, from ½in. to 2in., and possibly sometimes more when intended for special work. The more usual widths, however, are comprised within these two limits.

The Gouge.—The gouge may be considered as a chisel bent round until it assumes the form of about one-third of a cylinder. Some, however, are of greater curvature, and some of less according, to the special purpose for which they are intended. The carver's gouges are also bent in the shank so that they can be used in deep recesses and corners. This tool is nearly always ground on the outside or convex surface, and the car-

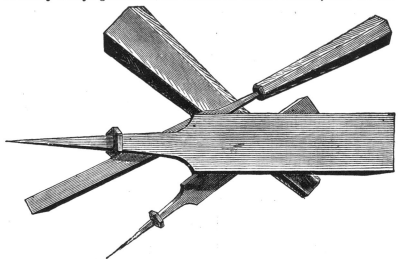

Fig. 9. The Firmer and Paring Chisels.

penter keeps the edge level from angle to angle, while the turner gives to his more or less of an elliptic form. We give here a sketch of the tool (Fig. 10), and show also by the lines below the varied curves given to these tools, the broadest being also generally least convex. We have to note also that the carpenter's gouges have a flange (*b*), against which the end of the handle abuts, so that it is not driven on further by the action of the mallet. The turner's gouge, on the contrary, not being subjected to blows or great pressure in the direction of its length, needs no such abutment for the handle, and is made without and with a long tapering shank or tang. Hence the turner's gouge must not be taken up, as we have sometimes seen it in an amateur's workshop, and used with a mallet, or its handle will most certainly be split. Although the gouge is usually bevelled on the outside, and ground on its convex side, this is as much as anything for convenience, as it is difficult to form and keep an inside bevel. In some carvers' gouges, however, the latter method prevails.

The Draw Knife.—We now come to the two handed shave or draw knife as it is often called (Fig. 11A), a tool of very general and extensive use, and, in skilful hands capable, not only of roughing out, but also of fairly finishing many articles. With this tool the maker of brush handles does the greater part of his work, taking off bark, and levelling down excrescences and generally preparing the rough poles for the hollow plane or

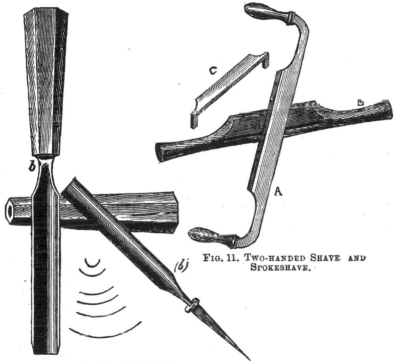

FIG. 11. TWO-HANDED SHAVE AND SPOKESHAVE.

FIG. 10. THE GOUGE.

lathe. The chair maker in the same way shapes his material ready for turning, and to the cooper, hurdle maker, and general carpenter this is a tool that is of the utmost value.

The Spokeshave.—This will be found an exceedingly useful tool (Fig. 11B), almost indispensable for smoothing curved surfaces, such as the inside edges of circles, and geometrical figures cut in boards by the sweep saw. It is, however, by no means an easy tool to use until practice has rendered the hand skilful in adjusting the cutting edge instantaneously to the various points of curvature in the work. The oval or ovoid form of its handles enables this tool to be held with a firm grip, and the whole action is from the wrist of the workman. The iron (C) is bevelled on the side next the wood, and is retained at any given distance from it by the two tangs which project at right angles and fit stiffly into the two mortices arranged to receive them. In the best spokeshaves, which are of ebony edged with brass, these tangs are cut with a screw thread, and the distance of the blade is thus regulated by wing nuts of brass. These, however, are costly, and of no great advantage over the common kinds.

It is, we would observe, very seldom that practical workmen purchase tools of the latter class. They are well aware of how little real value are ornamental additions of any kind; and, although it is true that an edge or border of brass may preserve the wood, the latter lasts generally as long, or longer, than the blade, and is durable enough for all practical purposes. It is the amateur who is so frequently captivated by glitter, and for whom are prepared the bright blue axes and smart tools which the workman does not even condescend to look at. The spokeshave is commonly considered a plane, because it has not only a blade related to the chisel, but is attached to a guide of wood which determines the thickness of shaving to be cut off. It has, however, no guide determining the direction of the cut, and is therefore the lowest sample of plane.

In grinding it, one side is kept flat, it having but a single bevel edge, and unless this is preserved the instrument cannot work properly. Young hands especially spoil many a good tool by grinding or honing it incorrectly. Scissors or shears with a partial bevel on the wrong side, or plane irons similarly ground are by no means unusual, and such tools as the first are absolutely spoilt, and the others seriously impaired, by being thus treated.

To take off the wire edge, produced by grinding a fresh bevel when the one first formed has become thickened by frequent honing of the edge, the tool must be laid quite flat upon the oilstone, and the handle not elevated in the least, as will be further explained when we speak of the uses and abuses of the grindstone.

Nearly all carpenters' tools are single bevelled, while those of the turner are very frequently double, his chisels especially being thus made to enable them to be used with either flat side uppermost.

The Saw.—The saw is a many-edged tool, which acts somewhat like a row of chisels clamped together, with their faces in one direction. Its size and shape depend on its special purpose: the long pit saw, for instance, for dividing logs of timber into planks; and the cross-cut saw, for cutting off timber across the grain into pieces of convenient length, made like the pit saw, with two handles, only these stand up at each end at right angles to the back, the timber always lying on the ground or horizontally when subjected to its action. A (Fig. 12) is the pit saw; B, cross-cut; C, pit frame saw, sometimes made with but one side to the frame; E, hand saw, divided into the largest or rip saw, intermediate or half-rip, and smallest, called generally a hand saw, of which many sizes are sold, some to fit into boxes or chests of tools, and therefore shorter, and some of greater length. Then we have also of frame saws, besides the large one used in a pit by two men, a smaller or chairmaker's saw; a turn or sweep saw, G; for cutting curved pieces; the buhl saw, N; the iron-backed saw for metal, and one or two others not generally used. In addition to these is the tenon saw, with metal back affixed to blade, H; the compass saw, I; key-hole or pad saw, J; the mitring saw, which is a small tenon saw; and the circular saw, K. of all sizes, from 1in. diameter, used by dentists, to one of several feet, and made of several pieces, for cutting veneers by steam. The pit saw does not come into the hands of the amateur carpenter; who can obtain his material in the form of quartering—i.e., strips sawn from a 3in. plank, each also 3in. wide, planks 3in. thick and from 12ft. to 20ft. long, or boards of any thickness desired, and up to 15in. wide. These can also now be had truly planed by machinery at a small increase of cost; but we advise good clean dry stuff rough from the saw, which will give the amateur very good practice in the use of the plane. As a rule the best wood for the amateur's purpose is clean deal or pine; but oak, teak, and mahogany should find a place in the workshop more often than they do, the mahogany being what is often called cedar, to distinguish it from the very hard Spanish wood. The softer and more common kind is from Honduras, and is always noted for its ready capability of being glued up. This and deal are, in fact, the two materials best united in this way.

The frame pit saw is used for the same purpose and in the same way as the long saw, of which one handle is fixed permanently, but the other or tiller, T, can be removed and replaced at pleasure, being secured to the blade at any desired place by means of a wedge. This is necessary to allow the saw to be drawn out of a cut, if desired, and also to provide means for regulating its length. The steam saws, for dividing timber lengthwise into planks, consist of a number of similar blades fixed side by side, and adjustable by wedges to any distance apart. The whole are thus united into one by a top and bottom bar, and the latter is moved up and down by a crank. In this way the saws work together, and the log of timber is cut at one operation into as many planks or boards as it will furnish. The timber is in this case placed on rollers level with the floor, and is moved forward by self-acting mechanism after each stroke of the saw.

Nearly all the heaviest work of sawing planks is now done in this way; while for lighter work the circular saw is most in demand. The latter is in extensive use for sawing stuff for packing cases, boxes for containing tin plate, and similar boxes of square or oblong section so constantly required for trade goods; and the amateur also very often attaches one to his lathe or has it mounted on a separate stand. This, for really light work, is a capital plan, but if it is for any stuff over two inches (one is quite enough) the leg has an onerous duty to perform to keep up the requisite speed. Notwithstanding this, however, there can be no doubt of the great service a circular saw renders to the amateur, if fairly kept to work of a light character; because, with a proper parallel guide fitted to it, it is easy to cut any number of strips exactly alike, and perfectly true from end to end, and the work is far more rapidly done than it can possibly be with an ordinary handsaw.

Among frame saws, *i.e.*, saws that are narrow in proportion to their length and consequently require either an iron or a wooden frame to keep them extended during work, the woodcutter's saw is one that the amateur seldom possesses, but which is very serviceable, especially for cutting

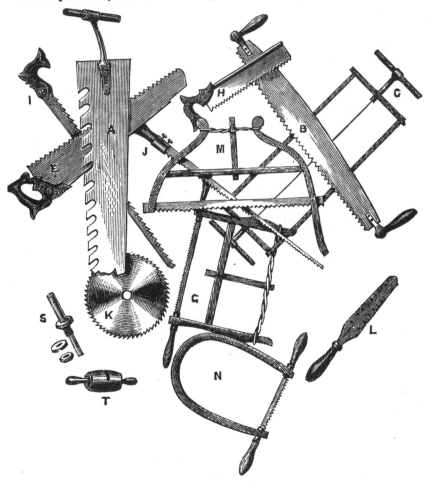

FIG. 12. GROUP OF SAWS.

small logs or planks across the grain. The teeth of this saw are upright, or nearly so, and it cuts freely and cannot double or buckle like the hand saw. It is represented at M of the set of saws delineated in Fig. 12.

The majority of saws being broad in the blade, are not calculated for cutting out curved or circular pieces, hence the sweep saw or turn saw (G) comes into frequent use, and a frame pit saw, with narrow blade, called a felloe saw, for cutting out the felloes (called fellies) of wheels. These will readily follow any curve of moderate sweep ; but for very fine work of this kind a still narrower blade is used, kept strained by a bow-shaped frame suffi-ciently large to include the whole width of the work to be operated on. This is the fret or buhl saw (N), which has come into general use by amateurs of late for carving perforated patterns. This saw, however, once used only by hand, is now fitted up in various ways to work by the foot ; a crank, cam, or eccentric giving it very rapid up and down movement, while the work, laid on the platform through which the blade passes, is shifted about in all directions as the saw follows the foliated or other patterns drawn upon it.

There are now several makers of these saws, which are sometimes made to fit on the lathe bed, and sometimes preferably fitted on a separate stand and combined with a circular saw and upright drill, making one of the handiest machines imaginable for the amateur or the professional. Moseley and Simpson of King-street, Covent Garden, are perhaps the principal makers of these machines, which have received various modi-fications, increasing their usefulness and rendering them applicable to drilling and sawing brass as well as wood. It is, however, not a very difficult matter to fit up such a saw, and detailed drawings are here given of a strong and serviceable arrangement.

A (Fig. 13), is a plank or board 1½in. thick and about 3ft. by 2ft., or 3ft. square, to form the bench or table of the machine. It should be of beech, nicely planed, although deal would answer—the object being to have a substantial and solid foundation for the various fittings. The logs (D, D.), must also be stout—not less than 2in. each way, and if of 3in. stuff it would be none the worse.

It is important to make this stand strong and firm, as it is applicable to many uses, and will cost but little extra if made stout and comparatively heavy. Amateurs generally are too much inclined to sacrifice solidity to elegance, which is a great mistake, if they mean to do real good work instead of toying and flirting with tools and machinery. E is a pedestal 3in. by 2in., and it rises 2ft. to 2ft. 6in. above the level of the table. It should be notched into the board, and made very firm with stout screws, or with two bed screws, the nuts being let into the table top from below. As it is proposed to use this also as a drilling bench, and a good deal of pressure will thus be brought upon the arm (F) and pillar (E), the latter may be further strengthened with a T shaped plate of iron at the back, or carried to the floor and stiffened by a cross bar running from one back leg to the other. Care, however, must be taken in such case to give room for the fly wheel by adding, if necessary, to the width of the table, so that the wheel [may not touch this back stay or bar. Thus made, another advantage is gained, inasmuch as the legs will not be made to spread by the pressure of the pointed screws carrying the crank shaft. The table is, of course, to be made in the usual way, with frame marked 1 and 2 mortised into the legs, the top being then screwed firmly down to this frame. G, is an indiarubber door spring, and it must be a strong one, its use being to draw up the saw after each cut. It is attached by a screwed eye, represented at U, which gives a power of tightening the saw when necessary. In the drawing of the whole machine, the lower end of the saw appears to go direct to the treadle, which it may do; but this has the drawback of only obtaining one stroke at each revolution of the flywheel, and of causing the saw to advance and recede as it is moved by the crank· This does not always matter, but at the same time is easily avoided in the following manner: Above the axle of the flywheel, but a little behind it, a second axle, X, with a small crank and pulley to take a strap from the large wheel, is centred on two pointed screws, and the saw is attached to this second crank by means of a crank hook and catgut band. Thus several strokes of the saw-are obtained at each revolution of the fly-wheel. To keep the saw vertical during the stroke it is not attached *directly* to the crank, but the catgut first passes over a pulley (Z) fitted under the table exactly in a line with the upper end of the saw, and then the catgut passes on to the crank. This is an easy and excellent method of obtaining parallel motion. To prevent the saw receding from the work, and to keep its edge in the right position, it is necessary to let its back rest in a block (Y), which for some work might fit into a mortise behind that seen at O. But with most kinds of work this block would be in the way, and the better plan is the following, because it not only acts as the guide, but prevents the work from rising when the saw is drawn up by the spring. Behind G is seen a round hole in the arm (F), in this is inserted the iron bar marked 6, carrying the block of hard wood (7), in which is a saw-cut for the back of the saw, including about half its width, to work in. The length of this bar allows it to reach to the table, and it is then raised, according to the thickness of the work to be operated on, which is free to pass under the block in all directions, while, as stated, it is prohibited from rising with the saw. The bar is fixed at the desired height by a clamping screw. The fly-wheel need not be large—18in. across will suffice; but the rim should be pretty heavy; plenty of speed, and consequently impetus, being the chief requirement. There is also no necessity for a long stroke, and a crank 1½in from centre to centre, giving a 3-in. stroke, will generally answer the purpose. A 2in. crank is certainly the longest we should advise. A guide for parallel motion can, if needed, be attached to the table similar to an ordinary parallel ruler, which will be referred to again presently. For the vertical saw alone this will be all that is needed, and the movement is in such short rapid strokes as to make it easy, with a narrow blade, to follow the most complicated curves by moving the material in all directions upon the saw bench or table. We have, however, designed the latter to take a circular saw as well, by adding the wooden poppets (K L) with their centre screws. The tenon of L fits into a square hole or mortise, and is fixed by a wedge underneath, but K slides in a groove, so that it allows an adjustment of a few inches. If both poppets

Fig. 18. SAW BENCH.

are similarly made, a little occasional job in the way of turning may be done, as in a pole lathe, the indiarubber spring taking the place of the bow or elastic pole. There are even cases in which this method is useful, although an ordinary lathe may stand in the same workshop. The main object, however, of the poppets is to support the spindle of a circular saw (R), on which a pulley is fixed to take the strap from the fly-wheel, a hole in the table allowing such strap to come up through it from underneath. The circular saw spindle, when in its place, is under the hinged cover of the box (V W), about one-third of the saw rising above this cover through the slit cut for that purpose. The cover being thus hinged, rests on the end of the screw seen in front, by which the height of the saw above it can be adjusted, so as to cut rebates and such like work. I have shown a parallel guide and fence on the box cover, and also at 4 a section of the fence with a screw and nut, which works in a slot at V ; but if this is used, which is the best plan, as it enables the fence to be clamped firmly in position, the parallel ruler system of guide must be of the double kind, like 5 of this Fig., because the single bars, although they give the fence a parallel motion, cause the fence to traverse in a direction parallel to the saw. The intermediate bar of the parallel arrangement prevents this, and such a clamp as shown is to be used. Even without the guide bars but with the clamp it is easy to set the fence parallel to the saw, and it is a good plan to mark the saw table with a scale of inches at both ends of the fence to assist in this adjustment. The box itself is made with a projecting tenon to fit the hole through which the fret saw when in use passes, by which it is secured at a proper height above the bench itself, and in the exact position required by the blade of the circular saw. If desired the slot in which the poppet slides can be carried quite across the table, but it rather spoils the latter for use as a workbench. There is on the whole no design of saw table which will prove so generally useful as the above.

It is true that we have also in these days a different arrangement called a band saw ; which (like the narrow reciprocating saw described) will cut out curved work with great rapidity, but it requires two pulleys of large size, and a good deal of power to render it of real service. It consists of an endless band of steel, from one-sixteenth of an inch wide to eight inches, which is respectively the narrowest and widest made ; the teeth being cut on one edge. This band is strained over two drums or pulleys, one above and one below the bench, in which is a slit through which the saw passes. There is also a guide or stop at the back of the saw. Nothing is needed to hold the work down, as the teeth of this saw work in one constant direction, so that there is no tendency in the work to rise as it does at the up stroke of a vertical reciprocating saw. From the reasons stated the band saw has not yet made its way in the workshop of the amateur, and therefore there is no need to enter into further details. It does not, however, appear to us that [any great difficulty would arise in arranging a narrow band saw to work in the lathe. A temporary band saw is not very difficult to make, with a length of good crinoline steel, an article happily less in demand for its original purpose than formerly and, therefore, not seldom to be found lying about disgraced and discarded.

The use of the tenon saw is sufficiently indicated by its name. It is of various sizes, but always made of a thin plate of steel with a piece of iron or brass doubled over the back to keep it rigid. The teeth are small, and at a greater angle, that is, more upright than those of the hand saw; this tool being intended to cut wood across the grain, and to leave a smooth surface, not needing the subsequent operations of the plane or chisel. Wood thus cut is, however, sufficiently rough to give a hold to glue, and in this state the corners of mitred work, as well as tenons, are securely held together. The mitring saw is in fact a small edition of that described, which is frequently made to take its place. These saws must be kept very keen, and when not in use should be hung up with the teeth protected by a guard, which is merely a slip of deal of the length of the blade and ¼in. or ⅜in. thick, in the edge of which a slit has been made from end to end by the saw which it is designed to protect.

The compass and keyhole saws are related to each other in the same degree as the above. The first is lettered I and the second J in the group of saws given on Fig. 12. The compass saw will answer for cutting out curves, though not so well as the sweep or frame saw. It is not set, but made much thinner at the back than where the teeth are cut, so as to clear itself readily. The absence of a stretching frame is in some cases an advantage, but the curve it will take is of large radius compared with what may be cut by the narrow saws with frames, and the compass saw is rather apt to stick fast and buckle or bend. It is not absolutely necessary to the amateur.

The keyhole saw, as its name implies, is used to cut keyholes and similar openings. It also goes by the name of the pad saw, on account of the handle in which it is inserted. This handle, or pad, after being turned, is bored quite through and is fitted with a long brass ferrule, the lower part of which is cast solid and then pierced with a rectangular hole or slot, a little larger each way than the blade of the saw, which is retained in its place by a couple of screws at the side. Thus the saw can be pushed down into, or even quite through the handle, so as to leave only a short portion projecting; or when necessary it can be used of its full length. By this plan it is prevented, as much as possible, from bending when the hole to be cut is small, and requires only an inch or two of the point of the blade for its execution. Thus shortened it may be used sometimes even for fretwork, of which we have seen some very fair specimens cut in this way. This saw, like the last, is made thicker at the teeth than at the back to keep it free, but needs to be used nevertheless with gentleness and care.

The carcase saw is only a small hand saw with fine teeth used to cut apart the cover and its counterpart in boxes and desks, made as a single deep box dovetailed at the corners, and afterwards divided; by which plan the parts are sure to meet accurately when hinged together subsequently. This is not the invariable plan, however, although in many respects it is preferable to making the cover as a separate piece, because it evidently saves a good deal of planning and fitting. A tenon saw, if long enough, will do almost as well, but in that case each cut has to be separately made, while a fine hand saw will do the whole at one cut.

The smaller piercing and buhl saws belong rather to the metal worker than the carpenter, and need not be detailed here. The amateur will require only a hand saw, a tenon and keyhole saw, with a sweep or narrow frame saw for circular and curved work. If, however, he intends to do much in the way of making picture frames, he should add a mitring saw, keeping it for the lightest work alone.

The Plane.—The planes proper may be divided into those which produce a level surface—as the jack, trying, and smoothing planes, and those which produce surfaces variously curved and moulded, as the beading and moulding planes. To the former class are allied planes for grooving and rebating, as the two or three surfaces thus formed are themselves level, although at right angles to one another. We shall treat of these in order.

The jack plane, Fig. 13, is the first used upon the sawn plank or board, to reduce it to a level surface. The iron, which is fitted into a kind of bed or mortise in the wood, is either a plain blade of steel, similar to a very broad but thin chisel, or is made up of two separate pieces, which is the plan universally followed in English planes. The wooden stock of a jack plane, generally of sound beech, is about 15in. in length, and of a width and breadth corresponding to that of the iron, the cross section being almost or quite square. The bottom is called the sole, in which is the mouth or narrow transverse slit through which the edge projects very slightly, the degree of its projection determining the thickness of shaving which it will detach at each stroke or forward movement. The Fig. 14 gives a section of a jack plane with its double iron A lying in its bed, the latter being at an angle of 45deg. to the sole. This is the angle called common pitch, suitable for deal and straight-grained soft woods generally. The bevel, however, of the cutting-iron itself, further reduces this angle to one of 35deg. Considered by itself, therefore, the iron is simply a paring chisel, the direction and depth of whose cut is determined and continually preserved by the wooden stock to which it is attached. The value of the latter will be readily perceived if an attempt is made to level a surface, by the ordinary broad chisel guided by the hand alone. In this the following drawbacks will be noted: First, the wood in advance of the tool will often split up, leaving a rough surface; secondly, the shaving will be of unequal thickness; thirdly, it will be detached from prominences and hollows alike, so that even at an expenditure of much time and labour, most unsatisfactory results will be obtained. It is in fact quite impossible to preserve the same angle, with the chisel thus held, for a single minute, nor would any amount of training enable the hand to effect this necessary "desideratum." Now let us see how the plane meets these several difficulties.

First of all, the tool or blade is securely fixed and maintained at the desired angle, from which it cannot deviate during its progress over the surface of the work to be levelled. This is effected by the bed of the iron on which it lies in the stock, and on which bed it is retained by a wedge D. Secondly, the cutting edge is set to project only a given distance beyond the level of the bottom or sole of the plane, and it cannot therefore penetrate the work more deeply at one part than another. The shaving will therefore be preserved of an uniform thickness. Thirdly, to prevent the splitting up of the wood in advance of the cutting edge,

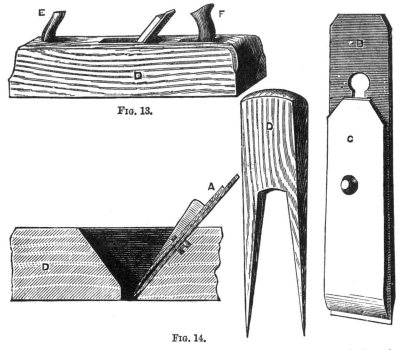

FIG. 13.

FIG. 14.

two forces are brought into action, the pressure of that part of the sole which is in front of the iron, and, secondly, the cleverly arranged break iron, the object of which is to break every part of each shaving as completely as possible the moment it is detached, by bending it sharply upwards towards the open mouth by which it escapes. The several parts are as follows: A, the double iron, composed of B and C, the first being the blade, and the second the break iron; D is the stock, E the toat or handle in front which assists in giving the workman a good hold. In smaller jack planes this is omitted, and only the handle F is attached for the right hand, the left grasping and pressing upon the front part of the plane. When in its place it must be noticed that the bevelled part of the blade is below, next the bed, for we have sometimes found a youthful amateur using it in a reversed position, and wondering why the plane would not cut. The position of the break iron is of great importance. The nearer its edge is to that of the cutter, the harder will be the work of planing, and the thinner the shaving, supposing the plane to be set " fine," i.e., with its edge projecting but slightly beyond the sole. Hence it is usual to set the break iron one-sixteenth from the edge for the first roughing-down process, and then to re-sharpen the blade and set the break iron but very slightly above the other, and thus to finish the work. This to the amateur whose jack plane is made to serve all purposes will be found essential to good work, but the carpenter uses this jack plane first, and, subsequently, his longer *trying plane*, and still longer *jointer*, to put the final touches, or, if it is a flat broad surface and not an edge requiring absolute accuracy, he will finish with his *smoothing plane*, made exactly like the others, but not above 6in. or 7in. long, and kept finely set and very keen. Planing is by no means an operation as easy as it appears. The beginner, finding that he does too little work, and that he cannot get the tool to bite, forthwith drives the iron further out beyond the sole. He then discovers that its bite is too great, and that the result is very bad rough work. But it arises from the very nature of the case that at the onset very little material can be removed, because the very object of a long plane is that it shall rest upon the several prominent parts of the work and not touch the hollows. Consequently such prominences only will be removed at first, and very probably they may not be very numerous, or of any considerable surface, so that the plane will bring away but very small shavings. The tool, therefore, will appear at the commencement to do but little work. The iron is not, however, to be further driven out if the shavings are not extremely thin; but the plane is to be pressed down firmly, and passed over the surface of the work steadily and patiently in the direction of the grain, and presently it will be found that as the prominences first attacked become broader, and others, which were at first below their level, successively come under the operation of the tool, the shavings will become more plentiful and larger, until eventually they will be of the full width of the plane iron, and may be taken off unbroken from end to end of the work. This is, however, under the supposition that the iron is accurately ground and sharpened, and that it projects equally its entire breadth below the sole of the plane. Thus to grind and set it, however, needs considerable practice, and it is seldom that the amateur succeeds in so doing until he has had some years' constant and painstaking practice. We shall, therefore, at once give the necessary directions for the proper performance of the work in question.

The common pitch at which the plane irons are set in the jack and smoothing planes for deal is not suited to harder and more knotty woods, and for these the angle is more obtuse, the iron being more upright, and approaching in its action more nearly to a scraper, like the turning tools for hard wood. It often happens, even then, that an even and smooth surface cannot be obtained in the ordinary manner, and it becomes necessary to use what is called a "toothing plane." In this the face of the iron is grooved or channelled, so that when ground it has a row of teeth, or very narrow edges, which score the wood, and thus cut the fibres in all directions, the plane being used across and with the grain, and working now in this direction, now in that, round the various knots and curls of the grain. The work is then finished with a scraper, or with the edge of a bit of newly-broken glass, and smoothed with sandpaper. Knotty and unequally-grained wood, however difficult to work, is of great beauty when polished, but is scarcely suitable for beginners. It will be observed that the harder the material the greater is the angle of the tool edges used to work it, whether such belong to the plane, chisel, turning tool, or saw. Before proceeding to consider the rebate and grooving planes, and others of a similar class, we must not omit to speak of those smoothing planes, constructed wholly of metal. These of late years have come into very general use, especially for work requiring great accuracy. The stock of these is of brass or gun metal, in the smaller sizes, and of iron in the larger, and the wedge is sometimes, but not always replaced by a screw contrivance to draw up or lower the iron. The intention is to supply a tool, not only capable of much finer adjustment than a common plane, but to obtain a sole which shall be subject to little appreciable wear from use. In the carpenter's plane the sole quickly deteriorates, and must then be planed off true again, by which the slit in front of the iron, or mouth, becomes wider, until the tool is only fit for very rough work. Then the workman has to let in a new piece to contract this mouth, and, of course, after a time the same defect recurs until the whole stock needs renewal. It may be well to tell the amateur that plane irons of any width can be bought without the stock at the various tool shops, and many workmen make the latter themselves. Sometimes, also, a metal sole is screwed under the plane, or a small plate is inserted in front of the edge, the object being, of course, the same as above set forth. Either plan considerably improves the plane as a finishing tool, but the cost is considerably increased. In the planes with metal stocks, which are as perfect as can be made, the double iron is not seldom replaced by a single one placed at a very acute angle, and with the bevel of the edge uppermost instead of below. The mouth in these cases is an exceedingly narrow slit, admitting only the passage of a very thin shaving, which is therefore so easily bent upward as not to need the action of the break iron ; but the tool is, of course, set accordingly, the iron projecting only a hairsbreadth or so below the general level of the sole. Some of these tools are literally pocket planes, but they work beautifully if kept in good order.

A rebate, always called *rabbet*, is a rectangular recess, such as is seen in sashes for the reception of the panes of glass, or at the back of picture frames, and also in door posts. To produce it a special plane is necessary, because the iron or cutter must be so contrived as to reach close into the angle. This the ordinary plane will not effect because the wood or stock projects on each side of the iron. The rebate plane is therefore made as follows. Fig. 15 : A is the stock, in the upper part of which a narrow mortise is cut, which, however, will not, as in the smoothing plane, take in the whole width of cutting edge, but only the thin part of the iron which is represented at B. The broad part, which is of the full width of the sole, rests upon its bed and is retained by a wedge as before, but the shavings escape at the side of the instrument. The iron is sometimes set at right angles to the sole of the plane and sometimes at an acute angle, when it is called a skew iron. This facilitates its cutting, as it not only more directly turns the shavings sideways, causing them to curl out at the side more freely, but it also cuts across any chance knot in the wood or inequality in the grain with greater ease. This plane is intended to work only with the grain, although, if finely set, it may answer fairly well across the grain, and is, in fact, often thus used. For the latter

FIG. 15. REBATE PLANE.   FIG. 16. MOULDING PLANE.

purpose, however, a different tool is made with a sharp point or cutter to cut across the fibres and make cleaner work.

The moulding planes are in general appearance similar to the one last described. The iron is thin, and its entire form like that of a rebate plane, but its edge, and the sole of the stock, are hollowed out to various patterns, each of which has a special name. The simplest plane of this kind is the beading plane, which is used to cut a rounded surface only, the plane iron being made with a concave edge. This is used to plane not only a bead as an ornament to any work, but also such strips as pencils, handles of brushes and brooms, and round rods for various purposes. Fishing rods, for instance, are thus planed from sawn strips of ash, hickory, and other woods, the lowest joint or butt only being turned on the lathe. It will be gathered from this that the beading planes are made of various widths, and can be bought in sets. As we have by chance spoken of fishing rods, and are addressing that jack-of-all-trades, the amateur, we may here mention that fishing rod ferules are bought in complete sets, ready fitted, and also that it is by no means a very difficult thing to make a rod. Unfortunately, crooked pieces are straightered very frequently by being baked or held to the fire, and it is pretty certain that after use will bring back the original bends. They should be fairly planed up, of well-seasoned stuff, carefully and very gradually tapered; the splices well glued, and then replaned or scraped before being bound, and the whole thoroughly varnished. We have seen home-made rods of great excellence.

The ordinary mouldings made by planes are named from similar ones common in architecture.

When, as is frequently the case, a moulding several inches wide is required, it is not the work of any single plane, but is made up of smaller mouldings. It may consist, perhaps, of a heavy roll, which is made by a large beading plane, or hollow, and below this may come ogec and fillet, and perhaps a smaller bead, or flat, each being cut with its own special tool. Mouldings are now cut in immense quantity by machinery, the plane iron being replaced by saws and revolving cutters of various kinds working at a terrific speed. The strips of wood lie on a level table

below these cutters, and are made to traverse automatically. Such machines are daily coming into more extensive use. Sash bars, door frames, hand rails, and other joiner's fittings can be bought by the foot, and only need to be mortised and fitted together. It was the Exhibition building of 1851 that first developed

FIG. 17. SIDE FILISTER.

this kind of machinery, all the sashes and woodwork generally having been sawn, planed, moulded, mortised, and fitted by the aid of steam power. Many of the machines of this class have been invented and first made in America, where, owing to their extensive forests, woodwork is more generally used even than here, where iron often replaces it.

The side filister is a rebate plane of more complicated and expensive construction, being fitted with shifting guides or fences regulating the depth and width of cut. It is represented in Fig. 17. The stock is similar to that of the rebate plane, but is much thicker, because it has to be itself shaped as here seen. A great part of the stock, it will be seen, is taken up with the fittings and various parts of the fence and guides, the projecting part only receiving the iron. Besides the latter there is fitted a second iron, which is, however, only a cutting point, projecting slightly below the other, to cut across the fibres. A, the stock, B, the fence, regulating the width of the rebate, C, the screw of the brass plate or stop, which regulates the depth, and which is sometimes attached to one side of the stock instead of being placed in the middle as here. The practical use of this tool will be explained in a future chapter. There are other patterns of filisters for special work, but the amateur need only obtain the above.

We now come to the plough (Fig. 18), which, true to name, is intended to cut grooves or furrows either across or with the grain, but generally in the latter direction. Indeed, no plane will make good work across the grain, unless there is some kind of point or knife edge at the side of the plane iron to cut these fibres cleanly across. It is very seldom, however, that it becomes necessary to use this plane at all across the grain of the wood, the plough serving more especially to make a longitudinal groove in the edges of boards in order to connect them by a strip or feather of thin wood or of iron, so as to make an air-tight joint. It is also used very extensively in cutting grooves to lay in panels in doors and wainscots. The plough is a very complicated looking plane, though it is not so in reality. It consists of the stock (A) mortised to admit the iron with its wedge, a stop (B) to prevent its going deeper than required, and the fence (C) to regulate the distance of the groove to be cut from the edge of the work. This fence can be placed either nearer to or further from the side of the stock by means of the two projecting arms attached firmly to it, these pass stiffly through holes in the stock and are secured by wedges. The stop regulating the depth of the cut is connected with a screw and nut on the top of the stock. A plough is fitted with irons of various widths sold in sets; these are thin above, but gradually

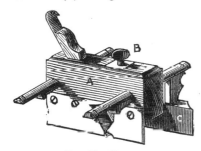

FIG. 18. PLOUGH.

become much thicker towards the lower part or cutting edge. The width of the groove depends therefore solely upon the breadth of the particular irons selected, and not upon any adjustment of the guides or fences.

As the process of uniting boards edgeways is a very common one, and the boards run in certain standard thicknesses, a plane has been contrived of a far more simple form than the plough, and may be had for 1in., ½in., &c., boards. They are sold in pairs, one cutting a groove and the other a tongue exactly to fit it. These are called match planes. The plough will make a similar groove, and also the tongue, which latter, however, is generally the work of the rebate plane, used first on one side of the plank, and then on the other, or of the side filister, and the range of the match planes being very limited, it is not worth while to buy both. There are a great number of other planes of strange names and shapes, but they will not be required by the amateur, and, indeed, are very seldom found in the tool chests of the professional carpenter. They will, therefore, not be described here, but should it become necessary to mention them in speaking of some special work in a subsequent chapter, we shall take the opportunity of setting their peculiarities before the reader. Flooring boards are now to be bought, grooved by machinery. In this case no plane is used, but a cutter like a thick circular saw, which attacks the edge or edges of the boards as they are carried along by self-acting machinery. We may note here, because we suppose our readers not only amateur carpenters, but mechanics, that, as a rule, hand tools are moved while the work is securely fixed; but machine tools remain in one position, except, it may be, that they revolve on an axis, while the work is carried to and fro, so as to be brought under their action. It may readily be conceived that it is easier to obtain the necessary automatic action of a cutter in this way than if the latter had itself to traverse in various directions over the work to be operated on.

Boring Tools.—Of these the simplest is the bradawl (Fig. 19A); it is not a cutting tool in the sense of being a tool that removes the material by cutting action, but it makes a hole by pushing aside the fibres of the wood. It has indeed a double bevelled edge which is sharp, but this is only that it may cut across the fibres in commencing its operation, and it is to be always placed so as to do this, and then pressed down and moved to and fro in a half revolution by the hand and wrist. It is a very handy little tool, but is only used for deal and soft woods. If made to penetrate harder stuff, like beech or ash, the handle will probably come off and the awl remain fast in the wood, a mishap by no means, however, uncommon, even when soft wood is operated upon. There is an awl

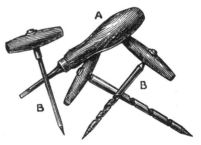

FIG. 19. BORING TOOLS.

used by birdcage makers which has three flat sides instead of a round shank, this cuts its way more freely, with less chance of splitting the wood, but it is not found in the tool chest of the carpenter and joiner. A convenient little handle is now sold in which the shank of the awl is squared and fitted into a brass ferule, being retained by a screw nut. The awl cannot be pulled out of the handle accidentally, and the latter is generally hollowed to form a receptacle for a set of these tools of different sizes.

Next come gimlets, or gimblets (B), of which little need be said. Some are made with twisted shanks, which allow the dust and little chips to escape more easily, and some have only a gouge-shaped channel with a pointed screw below. These tools cut away the material as they go, the screw point only serving to give a hold at first, and gradually to draw the tool deeper and deeper into the work. The shell or gouge-shaped ones are generally preferred by carpenters as being stronger and more suited for rough work in various woods, but they are more likely to split the work, especially if the latter be at all thin or slight. In such case it is best to use very little pressure, and to give a quick movement to the handle.

Gimlets are seldom made sharp enough in the shell, but they are fairly satisfactory in their action. A set of all sizes should be had, some being as small as a thin bradawl, and some almost requiring two hands to work them.

Allied to the gimlets, being in fact the same tool of gigantic size, are the augers, also of two patterns, shell or twisted. The first have a turned up edge or lip, which is filed up very sharp. One pattern of twisted auger is very beautifully made with a double cutting edge, and cuts out the wood with great ease and rapidity. For rough work, however, the shell auger alone is used. In the drawing of augers (Fig. 20) I have endeavoured to show the different kinds in use. A is a shell augur, which, if made smaller and used with a brace, goes by the name of a nose-bit. B is the twisted augur, and C the American, to a larger scale, which is the one specially alluded to as doing such excellent work.

The carpenter's brace and bits (Fig. 21) is one of the most useful boring tools in use. It consists of a stock of wood of a cranked form, Fig. A, in the lower end of which is a socket into which the bits are fitted; they are retained from falling out by a spring catch, which can be released by the pressure of the thumb. The set of bits is generally forty-eight, but each can be bought singly. The knob on the upper end of the brace is attached to it by a pivot, on which it turns easily, and in use this knob is held against the chest with one hand, while with the other the brace is rotated. There is consequently a good deal of leverage in favour of the workman, and holes are bored easily and quickly. Among the bits used with this tool the various-sized centre-bits (A) are of extensive service. The central point penetrates the wood, and, while the other edge or point cuts

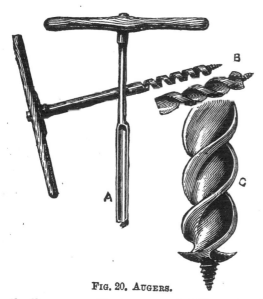

FIG. 20. AUGERS.

the fibres across, the flattened chisel-like part on the opposite side scoops out a shaving, which curls out as the boring proceeds. There are expanding centrebits in which the cutter can, by a set screw, be made to stand nearer to or further from the centre point, so that a set of three only suffices for holes from ¼in. to 2in. These, however, are not very strong, and the ordinary solid bits are preferable, although a large number are required to make up a complete set. In addition to centre bits the brace is fitted with a few sizes of nose or augur bits, and plain shell or gouge bits. The screw augurs are also made to fit, and are, in fact, much more suitable for this tool than for the ordinary cross handle. The brace is also fitted with a screw-driver, and sometimes with gimlets. It should be in every workshop, as it is a tool of extensive use. The more costly braces are hand-somely got up in ebony, and ornamented and strength-ened by bright plates of polished and lacquered brass. All this is unnecessary, and adds to the cost without in-creasing the real value of the tool. Carpenters seldom buy these as they care far more that the bits shall be well made and carefully tem-pered. The common shell augur, it must be remem-bered, although it will bore a hole very well even in oak and hard wood, will not enter the wood at first without a recess having been first cut by a gouge. This need not be deep, as it is only to give an entry to the tool.

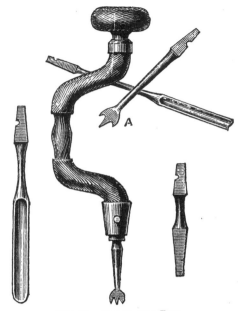

FIG. 21. BRACE AND BITS.

Appliances for Sharpening Tools.—In the first place, it is absolutely

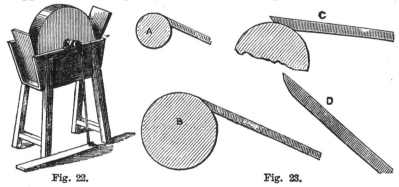

Fig. 22.   Fig. 23.

essential to have a grindstone, and that in good condition. It should be heavy enough to be driven by the foot, and arranged accordingly in a manner similar to the sketch (Fig. 22). This is from one of Fenn's, and for excellence and cheapness cannot be excelled. There should, however, be a handle on one side, removable at pleasure, in case of any extra heavy work. To be wholly dependent, however, on an assistant to turn the stone every time it may be needed is not only very impolitic, but absurd; yet we find crank and treadle very seldom attached to this indispensable machine. A stone over 2ft. diameter will answer very well with a treadle, but the larger and broader it is, in reason, the better. It must in all cases run very truly, and the face must be quite flat; and if it should get out of round, it must be refaced—in fact turned—by means of a hard steel bar. If very much out of truth, however, it may require to be first dressed with a hack hammer. The stone may, of course, be mounted as usual with a square spindle, rounded at the ends, or it may be rigged up on a turned axle, resting upon friction wheels, which is far better; but at the same time the ordinary fitting is sufficiently good, as is proved every day by the working carpenter. We should say do not spend too much in this way at first, but save such extra cost to add to your stock of tools. When you are master of these same tools, spend as your fancy dictates.

It is a good plan to keep a smaller grindstone, about 9in. in diameter —such as is to be had for 7s. 6d., fitted in a neat iron tank, with lugs to allow of its being screwed to a bench—besides the large one, if you have no room for the latter in your workshop. It will answer well for all kinds of small tools, but not for axe, adze, or plane irons, because you have but one hand free to steady the tool. A little consideration will make it clear that upon a small stone it will be more difficult to grind a perfectly flat surface than on a large one, and that if a tool is held steadily, as it ought to be, in one position, both stones, large as well as small, will grind a hollow or concave, of the same radius as the stone. This, however, is no drawback, but quite the contrary, the very worst bevel you can grind being a convex one (the usual bevel seen on the tools of amateurs). In Fig. 23 we have shown the results of good and bad grinding, the thickness of the tool exaggerated to render the matter more evident. A is a tool seen edgewise, ground on a small stone; B, the same, ground on a larger one; C the same tool with the additional bevel, which the hone ought to make; D, a tool ground and set badly, the bevel formed by the grindstone uneven, and no second bevel at all, but the two run into one convex surface. Such a tool can never do good work. C looks sharp, and is so; D is blunt and useless.

We have now spoken of the grindstone, and casually, also, of the oil-stone. Of the latter, however, there are several kinds, and nearly every year new ones are exposed for sale in the tool shops. Foremost of these comes the old-fashioned Turkey oilstone. This is hard, durable, and does its work well and rapidly. It is probably still the favourite with professional carpenters, having satisfactorily stood the test of many years' experience. It is, however, not always of equal excellence. Some pieces are too hard, and others have here and there hard places like knots, over which the tool glides without being ground. These hard places, therefore, soon stand up above the general level of the stone, which becomes practically useless. A good piece of oilstone, though it may be somewhat dear, is most precious, and there is no other stone so entirely satisfactory.

Arkansas is a white tolerably hard oilstone, but gives scarcely so fine an edge, perhaps, to the tool. It depends on the piece selected, however, because some are much finer than others. It cuts rapidly if of rather coarse quality, and is then very useful for general work. We often find it a good plan to rub down a tool on a bit of Arkansas of coarse quality, and finish with a few strokes on a very fine piece of the same. This puts a very keen edge to the tools.

Washita is very similar to the last in colour and quality, and may be used instead of it. There is no other stone which is satisfactory for the present purpose except perhaps what is called " Charley Forester," a corruption of Charnley forester. This is a native oilstone much used by travelling knife grinders and cutlers, though it is certainly inferior to the kinds above named. The slaty hones, of which there are several, including the German hones, used to finish off the edges of razors, are of no use to carpenters, being much too soft. We should advise the reader to purchase either Turkey or Arkansas oilstone, and either should be let into a block of wood and fitted with a cover to keep the surface clean. The oilstone, like the grindstone, must be kept in first-rate condition. It will always wear most in the middle, so that the two ends will become its highest points ; but when this occurs it must be at once rubbed down on a stone slab with water so as to level the surface. The oil to be used must not be one expressed from vegetables, as it quickly thickens and prevents the stone from cutting. It is far better to use the best sperm or neatsfoot oil for this and for lubricating machinery. Salad oil is nevertheless very generally substituted. The main difficulty likely to be experienced in setting a tool upon the oilstone after it has been ground arises from the natural movement of the arms which tends to round the bevel. Practice alone will wholly overcome this, but the thing to be aimed at is to raise the tool to a somewhat more upright position as it reaches the end of the hone furthest from the workman. Naturally, as it recedes in that direction it will take up more and more of a horizontal position. A chisel, or plane iron, sharpened by a workman, will be found to have a beautifully bright and perfectly even bevel, making a slight but decided and well-defined angle with that produced by the grindstone. It is formed in a minute or less by a few well-directed strokes, whereas the amateur unused to this work will not only expend several minutes in the same operation, but will find, as the result, that he has only rounded off the bevel, which, with labour and difficulty, he produced by means of the grindstone. We know well all such failures, from experience ; and it must be remembered that no one ever became a good carpenter from reading books on the subject, but only by constant and patient practice. Books are necessary to direct his efforts, unless he can obtain lessons from a practical workman, but that is all they can do. Even a carpenter's apprentice, however, has to work too much by rote and rule of thumb, and afterwards is left to find out for himself the way to do his work. It ought not, indeed, to be the case, but in old days it was impossible to obtain books which should set the true theory of work before the aspirant, and a sort of rule or set of rules sprung up which were extremely faulty, but have been handed down from father to son, and have stood much in the way of real advance in these and cognate trades. Happily in our time theory and practice can go hand in hand.

The Bench.—Upon the carpenter's bench (Fig. 24) and its fittings, depend, not only to a great degree the accuracy of the work, but to a still greater degree, the ease and rapidity with which it can be done. The ordinary bench is of very rough construction, and for such a purpose it is certainly not necessary to use planed material, and still less, mahogany or other expensive wood. In certain parts, however, accuracy is by no means unimportant, and a badly made work bench is a perpetual source of trouble and annoyance. It is essential that the top of the bench be level (which is very often not the case), and also that the whole shall stand quite firmly and steadily, and that its several parts shall be securely fastened together. It is not usual to mortise the several joints, except for amateur's benches intended for sale at the tool shops, but merely to nail the broad boards to the legs, to make up the frame, and then to attach the top. Cross-stays (K L) are essential, the strain during the operation of planing being in the direction of the length of the bench. At M we have shown the mode of framing the end, the opposite one being, of course, precisely similar.

These ends should be made first, the legs being of 3in. quartering at the least, and the board 1in. thick. The bottom rail may be partly notched in, but will do without, if firmly nailed on. The width of these ends may be from 2ft. 6in. and upwards, according to the size of the workshop. Having prepared the two ends as here directed, they are to be set up at the required distance apart, and united by the front board (A), and a similar board at the back. These latter may project beyond the legs, and should do so at the left hand or vice-end of the bench, because the board (M) of the end will then act as a stay and support to the planing stop (H). This is generally only a squared block of wood sawn off a piece of 2in. or 3in. quartering, into the top of which are driven two or three large headed nails, the heads of which projecting a little are filed into points to hold the work securely while it is being planed. This stop is fitted into a mortise cut in the top board of the bench, so that it will move stiffly up and down by a tap from the mallet or hammer. The end projecting below rests against the inside of the end plank (M), which holds it steadily against the lateral pressure caused by planing. There is another bench stop of iron advertised, which appears to be serviceable, but we have not had any opportunity of testing its merits. As a rule iron or metal is objectionable where a slip of the tool may probably bring the edge into contact with it, creating to a certainty an ugly notch or gap. The vice

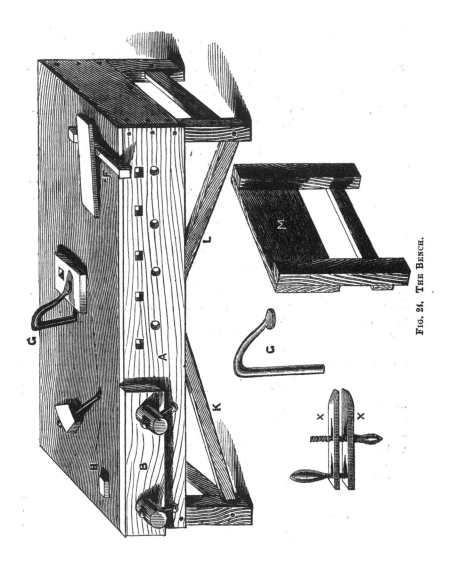

FIG. 24. THE BENCH.

(B) is a simple affair, but absolutely necessary, although we have known it replaced by the expedient of a wedge and block of wood. Very often only one screw is made use of, and a squared bar of wood in place of the other is fixed into the vice board, and slides in a mortice cut in the plank which forms the front of the bench. A second screw is, however, very much better, and as they are not expensive, and are easily obtained at tool shops, two may as well be used. A single screw would, indeed, answer sufficiently well, if the object was merely to hold a board while its edge was being planed ; but frequently it is desired to hold a short thick piece of wood in an upright position while it is being sawn off, and it is difficult to secure such a piece with a single screw and guide. The front, or movable piece of the vice, must be made of sound wood 2in. thick, two holes being made in it to allow the free passage of the screws. The nuts of the latter are blocks of thick beech, with the necessary threads cut in them, and are attached to the back of the front board of the bench by a couple of stout screws or nails. The strain of the vice does not tend, it may be remembered, to draw these blocks from the board, and therefore no other attachment is needed. It will be noticed that the front board has in it a number of round and square holes, which are intended for the insertion of pegs to support the ends of planks, and are convenient also at times for other purposes.

There is sometimes added an additional vice or cramp at the end of the bench, acting lengthwise ; but, though convenient, it is hardly necessary. We never, in fact, see it in the ordinary carpenter's workshop. The bench hook or holdfast (G) is, however, a very useful contrivance for holding work flat down upon the surface of the bench. This it effects by having its shank or tail passed through a hole in the top board, which should be, if possible, 2in. thick, but at all events 1in. or 1½in.; and if only of this thickness, it should have a piece screwed on below, where the hole for the holdfast is to be made. When a piece of wood is placed under the end of the hook, and the latter is struck on the top with a mallet, it jambs against the hole through which it passes, and holds the work very tightly, because, from its peculiar shape, its tendency is not to rise, but to press backwards against the hole in the bench. It is loosened at once by a tap on the back, which throws it into a more upright position. There is a similar cramp made, which, instead of being fixed by a blow, is caused to grip by a screw, the head or hook being made movable on a central pin. We do not, however, like these so well as the more simple kind, although they are used in many carvers' workshops. They are, of course, more expensive, yet, in our opinion, do not hold the work so tightly. They bruise it less, but then a piece of thin board can be easily laid on the surface of work to protect it, if any damage to a nearly finished article is likely to ensue.

The sawing stop (F), simple as it is, will be found a very convenient adjunct to the fittings of the work bench ; it is simply a double hook of wood, and when laid flat upon the bench so that one hook overlaps the edge, the other standing up a little forms a block against which any light strip of wood or board can be held and pressed while being sawn off. This little contrivance is, in fact, of far more extensive use than may at first sight appear. Then there are the wooden cramps, X, X, which can be made by the amateur if he has a lathe and a screw-box of ½in. or ¾in. size; they are intended for holding glued work firmly together until dry, and should be had of various sizes. We have spoken of the necessity of having the top of the work bench as level as possible, because it is impossible to plane up work truly which rests upon a curved or irregular surface. If it be absolutely necessary to use an imperfect bench, as may sometimes be the case when working at a distance from home, get a good plank, an inch or two in thickness, and lay it upon the bench, and place upon this the work requiring to be planed; such planks may generally be had very level, being cut by machinery. It often happens that boards have to be accurately planed and squared up on their edges, especially when it becomes necessary to glue or dowel together two pieces to increase the width. The vice is specially meant to hold such pieces, but

there are also two or three other contrivances well worthy of mention in a series like the present. The front part of the vice itself, it may be observed, should have its upper edge exactly on a level with the surface of the bench, or else, if a narrow strip is to be planed, it will not stand

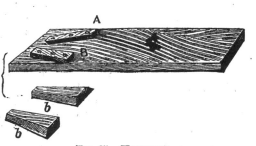

FIG. 25.   HOLDFAST.

high enough to allow of this operation. We have found the defect, in a country-made affair, of the vice board being an inch or two below the general level of the bench, and a very great nuisance it proved to be, for the reason just stated. It is evident that in many cases it will be preferable to set the whole strip on one of its edges while the other is being planed, and it becomes necessary to devise a method of holding it in this position. The simplest device of all is to tack to the bench a forked bit of wood, an inch or more in thickness, so that the piece to be planed may project slightly above it. The end of the latter being pressed into the fork, the angle of which should be small, the strip will be held on its edge tolerably secure. Still, with this contrivance, which simply holds the extreme end of the work, the plane needs to be used very carefully, or the piece will move from side to side under the action of the tool, and will not easily be planed up with sufficient accuracy. Hence it is better to be provided with a separate plank, the surface of which is planed level, and which is fitted near one end with the following simple but ingeniously contrived holdfast. It saves the necessity of tacking to the surface of the bench strips and wedges of some kind to hold the work to the detriment of the bench itself.

The Holdfast.—The holdfasts, A. B. (Fig. 25) are strips of mahogany, beech, or other hard wood, 1in. thick at the least, and they are better perhaps if made of 1½in. or 2in. stuff. They may be from 6in. to 9in. in length, and must be chamfered underneath, so as to be in section like the figure. These are screwed firmly to the plank by means of three ordinary wood screws, but are not placed parallel, their ends converging somewhat, but not too suddenly. Two wedges, also of hard wood (*b b*), and chamfered, slide in the groove formed by the two fixed pieces. The sides of these, opposite the chamfered part, are planed up true and square to the flat sides; between these the strip to be planed is placed on its edge, and the wedges are tapped gently until they grip the work between them. The pressure of the plane at each stroke has the effect of still further tightening the grip of the wedges. By this arrangement the work is held, not at its extremity, but at any part of its length, so that the plane can pass over its whole surface. By the slightest pull in the contrary direction the work is immediately loosened, and can be shifted and refixed in a moment. Of all the plans devised none can exceed this in simplicity and practical effect. It will, however, readily be seen that unless the sides of the wedges between which the work is held be planed truly square, they will not hold the piece perpendicularly, and will render accurate planing not only more difficult, but almost impossible.

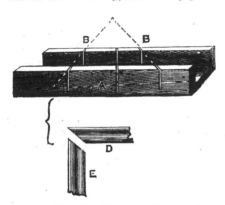

FIG. 26. MITREING BOX.

As bench fittings we may here mention the shooting boards and mitreing boxes, simple contrivances enough, but of absolute necessity, if good work is to be done, especially in picture frame making and similar jobs.

The Mitreing Box.—This (Fig. 26 A) is used to cut pieces of moulding at the right angle for picture and other frames, so that when glued together such frames shall be truly square. The box is simply made of mahogany about 3in. wide and deep and 18in. or so in length. It has no top or ends, but is merely a rectangular trough or tray. Two saw cuts are then made with a tenon saw at an angle of 45 deg., or half a right angle with the side, one in each direction, either meeting as seen at B, or a little apart. The piece of moulding that is laid in this trough, and cut by placing a tenon saw in these saw-cuts or guiding slits, will appear like D and E, and consequently can be glued together at the sloping part, forming a square. But how shall we measure these 45 degs. if we have nothing already made of the same kind as a pattern or guide? There are two or three ways of doing this; the following is perhaps the simplest : Plane up a thin bit of board, or take a sheet of tin, the corners of which are already, in all probability, truly square or at right angles. Test the corners, however, by your square (if one only is correct it will suffice, because you only require one); measure off C D, D B (Fig. 27), exactly equal, and, joining C B by a line, cut the piece off at this line. The angle at D will be a right angle of 90 deg., and both the angles C D will be 45 degs., or half right angles. You have therefore only to lay this tin upon the edges of the box, so that one of its sides coincides with one side of the box,

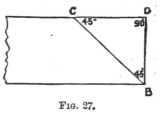

FIG. 27.

and mark the place for the saw with a pencil; then mark from this down the side of the box with your square, and make the cut. The size of the mitre box depends, of course, on the width of moulding to be used, and sometimes when an angle of 45 deg. is not desired, or there are any peculiar circumstances of fit to be attended to, a special box is made on the spot; but, the principle being understood, nothing can be easier than to make this to any required design. It is almost impossible to make mitred frames or boxes without some contrivance of this kind to guide the saw.

The Shooting Board.—This (Fig. 28) is another arrangement of a similar nature to the last, but intended to be used with a plane, whereas the mitre box is only for sawing, and the joint is left rough from the saw, as it holds the glue more readily. The shooting board can be used with the saw alone, however, as well as the mitre box, and it enables the workman to cut a piece straight across, or at an angle of 45 deg., as will be understood by a reference to the figure. The foundation is a sound 1in. board 2ft. 6in. long, by 18in. wide, or of any other convenient dimensions. Upon this is screwed another piece an inch thick or more, so as

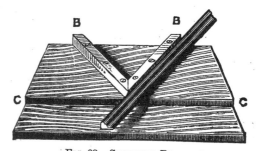

FIG. 28. SHOOTING BOARD.

to make a step (CC). Both pieces must be dry, so as not to be liable to warp; upon the higher part are screwed two strips of hard wood (BB) about 1½in. or 2in. wide, forming a right angle where they meet. The whole must be very accurately made, and although deal will answer the purpose, hard wood of some kind will be more satisfactory—mahogany will do very well.

To render perfectly clear the use of this shooting board, we have supposed the piece of moulding to require mitring. It has only to be laid as shown against the guide bar (B), and sawn off on the line (CC), or laid on the other side against the second guide bar, and similarly cut off. It will be necessary to use both sides in this way, because, although the piece cut off has also an angle of 45 deg., it would need to be turned over and applied to the other, which could not be done without reversing the moulding. In a plain unmoulded strip, this of course would not signify. The strip lying as it now does close to the step or rebate of the board, can be trimmed by the plane by laying it on its side, but care must be taken not to plane the edge of the step itself. The plane must be set very fine, and must cut keenly. Joints cut, however, with a mitring saw are generally quite smooth enough for glueing, and are better unplaned. To saw off a piece at right angles, and not with a mitre, we have but to lay it against the bar (B) and saw it off in a line with the other, when it cannot fail to be cut correctly, BB forming two sides of a square. It is evident that this shooting board will serve a number of purposes, and, being of simple construction, should certainly be among the first fittings of the amateur's workshop. If the edge of the step were of very hard wood there would be less danger of cutting it with the plane in the act of trimming strips of softer material. It is, however, generally made by the carpenter of ash or beech, and not unfrequently of deal.

CHAPTER II.

FIRST LESSON.

PREPARATION OF MATERIAL — SQUARING UP — MORTISING —
GROOVING — REBATING — PANELLING — PANELLED DOORS —
LIGHT MORTISED FRAMES.

WE may now pass on at once to the actual work of the carpenter. This
includes light and heavy work, the former being specially designated
joinery and cabinet making, while the heavier work, more properly called
carpentry, is such as is required in building and engineering operations.
Without doubt, the first essential in either case is the proper squaring of

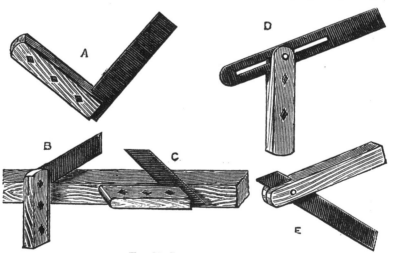

FIG. 29. SQUARE AND BEVEL.

the material, because, if this be not done, the work must necessarily be
crooked and awry. And this is by no means the easy thing it appears
when it is seen done by a practised hand. In larger works, indeed, where
the stuff does not require to be planed up, but is left rough from the saw,
the squaring is done by the latter tool, which, cutting to a chalk or pencil

line carefully drawn by rule and compass, secures the correctness of form. This sort of work, moreover, scarcely falls to the amateur, and need therefore be but partially treated. The square, whether wholly of wood or with a wooden handle and thin metal blade (Fig. 29, A), is absolutely essential to the amateur; not even a rough unplaned box should be attempted without its use, nor, for a long time, should a board or bit of quartering be sawn off, even for the most trivial purpose, without a ruled line being made by help of this instrument to mark the path of the saw. The mode of applying it will be readily understood from the figure. In A the square is shown by itself; B is its application in testing the accuracy of a squared bar, on which it should be applied at intervals; C, its position in order to mark a line by which to saw off a piece of board or plank. If the latter be thick, it should be marked on both sides and on the edges, and during the operation of sawing it should be turned over occasionally, and so cut from both sides.

We will suppose a strip required to be cut and planed up perfectly true and even on its sides and ends, 2ft. long by 3in. square. We can always procure planks 3in. thick, as this is a common standard size. Let such a plank, therefore, be taken, and a 2ft. length be marked off as shown, by the aid of the square, the measurements being carefully taken, and a little extra allowed for the saw cut and necessary waste. The piece in this case is to be marked on all sides, and, be it observed, the extra size allowed is not to be marked, for reasons that will appear presently. The exact width should be taken with the compasses applied to the two foot rule and pricked off upon the stuff. Then the saw is to be used to cut out the piece, and although the lines marked will be the guide, these are not to be sawn into, or in the least obliterated, but the allowance for waste is to be made by cutting on all sides ⅛ of an inch outside them. The lines, therefore, remain upon the piece which is to be used, and not on that from which it has to be taken. It is rather difficult at first to cut a piece correctly to a guide line; if it were not so, we should allow only one-sixteenth for waste instead of ⅛, because the more that is left the greater labour remains for the workman in planing down the useless part, although the value of the stuff may be too small to make it an important consideration whether or no we waste a little more than is absolutely necessary. In squaring up such a piece as this, the amateur will encounter his first great difficulty; but he must be content with nothing short of perfection, because to conquer in this special operation is to lay a sound foundation for all future work. In the first place, the jack and trying plane must be used, and not the short smoothing plane. The outside of the wood, whether newly sawn or otherwise, but especially if it has been lying about for any length of time, is sure to blunt the plane considerably; so that if the jack alone is to be used it must be re-sharpened for the final touches. The iron should also be set out at first to take a tolerably thick shaving, and after re-sharpening it should be set much more finely. In either case, however, it must project equally at all parts of its edge, because, if one

angle should project, it will score the work with deep grooves or channels.
In sharpening a plane, the extreme angles of the iron should be very
slightly reduced, especially of the jack plane, the edge of which may form
part of a very large circle, being made slightly convex. The trying plane
and jointer must not, however, be so treated.

Commence work by planing up one side to a perfectly level surface.
Try this by setting the square edgewise upon it in various places. Hold
it up also on a level with the eye, and look along it to see whether it
appears twisted or winding. When it is level and straight, use it as the
foundation from which to square the remaining three sides, beginning
with that which is at right angles to it. Plane this level, and then test its
squareness to the first. Probably, it will not at first be correct; but if
not winding, it will be, nevertheless, more or less out of square, one angle

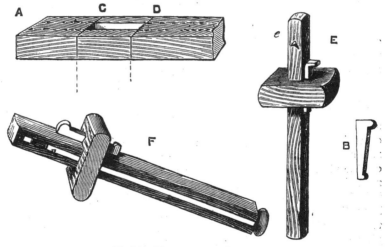

FIG. 30. MORTIC AND GAUGES.

being greater than the other, so that the surface appears to be inclined.
Set to work again with the plane, taking care not to over-plane the high
side, but work as if you felt you could not afford any waste of material,
and do not hurry it over as if you were obliged to work against time, for
this no amateur has occasion to do. Follow the same course in working
up the third and fourth sides, and, if necessary, mark and saw off enough
to trim the two ends, using the tenon saw, or a sharp and well-set handsaw. You cannot, of course, plane the ends, but if not left sufficiently
smooth, you may very carefully pare them with a chisel : a sharp tenon
saw will, however, generally suffice for this work. Now, when the
amateur can really square up a piece of wood like this with ease and certainty, he will find no serious difficulty in the performance of other
work.

Of course, although we have suggested cutting off a piece of plank wood of a certain size, it will be as well to make it of some use, the sole object being to give the amateur a first lesson in planing and squaring up pieces of wood. We may for practice go a step further with the strip already squared by cutting a mortice in it. Mark it, as shown in Fig. 30, using the square in pencilling the ends C and D, and the gauge or mortice gauge for the sides in the direction of the grain of the wood. These gauges may be made by the amateur, or purchased, beautifully finished in hard wood plated with brass. They consist of a stem of about ½in. square and 6in. long, on which slides an oval, round, or square block, which can be fixed at any point by a small wedge. This wedge is shaped like B in Fig. 30, so that it will not fall out and get lost. It is of course placed in position before the sliding piece is put on. In the stem of the instrument near the end is fixed a small point of steel, e, or often a brad driven in and filed off.

Simple as this tool is, none is of more use, especially for such work as mortising. Determine how wide your mortice is to be, i.e., how far from each edge of the wood, and then set the sliding head of the gauge so that the marking point will be at that distance. You have only to rub the instrument once or twice to and fro upon the work, and it will make a mark to guide the chisel. But you must, with this kind of gauge, also make the opposite or fellow mark, measured from the other edge of the piece on which you are working. When the mortice is to stand centrally, of course this second measurement is no special trouble; but if, instead of being central, it has to be more on one side of the piece than the other, the sliding head must be set anew. For this reason a somewhat different tool is made, called a mortice gauge, which has two points instead of one, and enables the workman to mark the mortice complete at once, measuring only from one side of the work. The movable head is made as before, with one fixed point set in a brass plate. A similar plate or strip of brass carries the second point, and both are set together and filed up as one conical point, the part of each which touches the other being flattened. The plate in which the second point is fixed slides in a dovetailed groove in the stem of the instrument, and, [in the best, is moved by a thumb screw at the end of the stem, which extends the whole length, and passes through a nut at the back of the strip of brass, such nut being concealed in the stem. The second (Fig. 30, F) gives this mortice gauge as it generally appears. The slide, however, may be moved by a projection or knob almost equally well. The stem is often graduated in inches.

To use this instrument, determine the distance the mortice is to be from either side of the piece in which it is to be cut; and set the head as before, fixing it by means of the wedge. Then, by the thumb-screw, separate the points to the desired width of the mortice and mark it. You have then only to mark its ends with a pencil or steel point. If the mortice is to be cut quite through, which, especially if made for practice, is the best way, carry all the marks round to the opposite side, which is easy enough. Using the square, mark the ends of the mortices quite across, as C. D., Fig. 30, then down the side and similarly across the bottom. The mortice gauge will then mark the other lines at the same distance as on the first side. When it is thus marked, the wood is to be cut partly from one face and partly from the other, so that, when the sides and ends are carefully pared with a sharp chisel to the several lines, you will have secured a mortice whose sides are parallel, and which passes truly and perpendicularly through the wood from side to side. It is less easy to keep the sides of the mortice perpendicular when it does not pass through the piece, and has therefore to be cut from one side only. To remove the substance of the wood from a mortice is, of course, if it be large, a somewhat laborious process, and to relieve the workman in this respect there are now to be had machines made for hand or steam power; but these are wholly unnecessary for an amateur, though he should, if possible, see one in use, for they do the work very easily and quickly.

In the case of soft wood, a centre bit is not unfrequently used to remove the chief parts of the material, which it will do very well. It should not, however, be used until the chisel has cut the fibres across so as to commence the mortice, lest this tool should spoil the edges of the mortice by tearing out the stuff beyond the intended boundary lines. The main-work of mortising, however, is done with mallet and chisel, the material being laid on a strong stool or block, so as to give it plenty of support, and prevent any jarring of the work as the opera-tor proceeds. Very gene-rally the workman holds the piece firmly by sitting astride upon it. If it be a piece of soft deal, care is to be taken to lay it on a smooth surface, so as not to damage it more than can be helped. Care-lessness in this respect will produce bruises not to be effaced; but, in spite

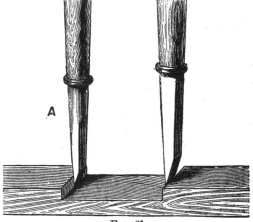

FIG. 31.

of all care, it will be generally necessary to plane up the face again after the mortice is complete. Another item of necessary instruction is not to begin near the boundary lines, but near the middle, and not to hold the chisel perpendicularly, but so as first to cut out a wedge-shaped piece, and then to work on each side of the cavity, but never, even at last, to obliterate the marked lines. Moreover, the chisel must be well sharpened, so that it effects the clean cutting of the fibres, instead of breaking them, as a blunt tool will do. In cutting away the wood on the side of the mor-tice furthest from the workman, the bevelled face of the chisel is generally towards him, the back lying on the solid work; but, be it observed, that a chisel is inclined to draw into the work on the plain or unbevelled side, so that, as the final cuts are taken with the tool in the above position, there will be a tendency to hollow or under-cut the face of the mortice against which the back of the tool is resting. Thus, in Fig. 31 the chisel A would incline to draw itself deeper in, under-cutting the mortice, whereas B, with its bevel towards the side of the mortice, would draw outwards into the hollow already cut. An experiment will soon render this clear, and it is worth noting, because, in finally trimming the mortice, it would often fatally ruin an otherwise accurate fit to under-cut it. The reason for beginning at a little distance from the guide lines at the commencement is, that in raising the detached chips the chisel is used as a lever, and the fulcrum is the solid wood against which the tool is forcibly pressed. The fibres, therefore, would soon be crushed, and the mortice damaged or spoilt; but by beginning in the middle such damaged parts are gradually removed as the work proceeds, so that, when it is completed, the whole is nicely squared, with clean flat sides and sharp edges. In such a hole the tenon, if well cut, fits with the greatest accuracy, touching it at all points, and giving a large surface for the glue to act upon. If it be under-cut or otherwise hollow in places, the glue will only act upon the pieces here and there where they chance to touch, and the joint will never be firm.

We now pass on to the tenon which is destined to fit into this mortice. The wood is marked as before by square and compass at A B (Fig. 32), and

with the gauge at *e f*, the lines being made on both sides and on the face or end. The pieces are then removed from each side with the tenon saw alone, or sometimes the saw is only applied to cut across the grain, and the cheek pieces are split off with a broad chisel. This, however, is not a safe plan, as—unless the wood be of very even and straight grain—the cut does not always run straight,

Fig. 32.

and the tenon is thus cut into and spoilt. It must be remembered in this case also that the guide lines are not to be obliterated—a point of great importance in all operations of jointing and fitting. In speaking here of fitting, let it be understood that a tenon must not be so tight as to need much force in driving it into its mortice; the result of which, very frequently seen, is to split out the latter; but it must fit so as to slide in stiffly, accurately touching at all points. This will need some little experience on the part of the amateur, as, in spite of measure accurately taken and guide lines carefully drawn, it frequently happens that the fit is not at all such as was expected or hoped for. But from the very first operations in carpentry—from the simple cubical box unplaned and nailed together—accuracy in fitting must be considered a *sine quâ non*. Carpentry is something like writing, the letters must be accurately formed, and the pen held in precisely the right manner in learning its rudiments, and then, and then only, ultimate success may be expected. In each case, the more haste the worse speed.

We will now advance a step further in the same direction, as grooving, rebating, and panelling almost of necessity include frames fitted together by mortice and tenon joints. We will describe the method of making a small door for a cabinet with a single panel. These small cabinets, moreover, are very convenient, especially if fitted up with trays or drawers, as will be hereafter described. The strips of deal, mahogany, or birch, either of which will answer well, and have a good appearance if varnished, are to be correctly squared up as before, and, if possible, worked as a single piece. Let it be 2in. wide and ⅜in. thick before being planed ; fix it with one edge or one side upmost in any convenient way upon the bench—

the edge if it is to be grooved, the side if rebated—either will do for the reception of a panel but the latter, if it is to lie in a rebate, will have to be secured with a strip of plain or moulded wood, whereas the groove will hold the panel securely with no such addition. It is, however, rather easier to make a rebate, and sometimes, a plough not being obtainable, the other plan of

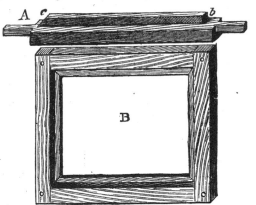

FIG. 33. REBATED FRAME.

arranging a panel will answer very well. In Fig. 33 a rebated strip is shown at A, and this work is done with the plane already described. But this tool has, it will be observed, no guide to determine either the depth or width of cut, and very often a temporary guide is therefore made by tacking on a narrow strip of wood, covering as much of the sole and edge of the plane as is not required to cut ; at the same time this is not absolutely necessary, and the same effect is produced by so grasping the plane (until it has made a few cuts), as to prevent its passing a given distance. This will not be found difficult, if the fingers are made to overlap the plane, and rest against the side or edge of the work. To make a very clean and smooth rebate, the plane should be reversed, to give a final cut on both sides, or rather, to speak correctly, the position of the wood must be changed, and laid first on its side and then on its edge. The mortice is to be cut before the strip is rebated, at least it is better to do so, because it is difficult to set up the strip firmly to stand the action of the chisel with the edge of the rebate resting upon the bench, neither can it be cut from both sides as directed. But after the mortices are made, and the pieces cut to their several proper lengths—the rebate having also been made—it will be found on fitting together the tenoned and mortised ends of the pieces, that the projecting rebates prevent their close union. These must either be cut away on the alternate strips, as shown in the Fig. at b, to a depth equal to their width, or these parts of the rebates must be sloped off on all the pieces alike to an angle of 45 deg., as seen at c, so as to form four mitred corners. If this be carefully done, it will make very neat and close joints, and the completed frame will appear like Fig. 33 B. Upon the ledge thus formed by the rebate, the panel of board ⅜in. thick is to be laid, and upon this a strip of narrow moulding or beading, neatly mitred, is to be attached to the frame by small sprigs or glue, to retain the panel in its place. But observe this, in all panelled work whether large or small, that the panel itself is not to be glued or fixed immovably to its frame, or else, when it shrinks, as it generally will if the article be placed in a warm room, it is quite sure to split; whereas, if it be left free, the utmost damage will be a white line of wood appearing beyond the painted or varnished part; or, at any rate, an unvarnished edge will show—a defect easily remedied. To make the work look well, the moulding by which the panel is secured should not come quite flush or even with the frame, but a little below it, so as to let the edge stand up clear and sharp. This, we may observe, has more to do than might be suspected with the handsome appearance of all work, whether in stone, wood, or metal. It is the contrast of rounded moulding and sharp edges which lends it beauty and refinement; and the fault of amateurs' work is generally utter want of attention to such details. With them it is often difficult to say whether edges were meant to be sharp or rounded off. They are often neither the one nor the other. This results probably from a blunt plane, or not unfrequently from bruising the edges of the work which have been originally well defined, by rude contact with the bench or perhaps even by careless use of mallet or hammer.

The side fillister, as we have already explained, has a fixed stop and guide, and it will therefore plane a rebate exactly of any desired width and depth; but the rebate plane in good hands will answer as well for a great deal of such work as that described, and is of course a far cheaper tool to buy.

We may now pass from this to grooving, which is effected by means of the plough. It is, remember, absolutely necessary that a strip or board to be grooved shall have its edge planed exactly square to its side, or else the groove itself will not run straight into the edge, but have a tendency to one side or the other; and if a board thus grooved be united length-wise to a tongued board, the tongue of this will be split off in the attempt to make the two lie in one level plane. Nothing is more common than to see tongued and grooved boards thus split up at the point of junction. Supposing the piece, however, nicely planed up; the plough, with the iron of the intended width of the groove inserted, has its side fence arranged so that when it presses flat against the side of the board the iron or cutting edge falls as desired, either in the middle of the piece or a little beyond the centre, which is the usual practice in panelled work. The brass fence is then lowered or raised to give the desired depth of cut, and the plane thus arranged is taken the whole length of the board at once, so as each time to carry out a long thin shaving. The fence must for this be kept very firmly against the side of the board by means of the left hand, which for the purpose grasps the fence, while the right drives the plough steadily forward. The reason that, in grooving or in rebating, the plane should be taken at once the whole length of the cut is, that if it be not done there will presently be a high spot where it has ceased to cut, against which it is apt to stick, and it will then frequently split off a chip rather

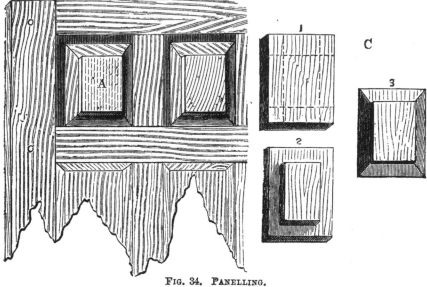

FIG. 34. PANELLING.

than a shaving. All work like this should be steadily and gently done, and though after the groove is fairly commenced the plane iron may be set out to take deeper cuts and thicker shavings, these latter will, if too thick, only clog the tool and endanger the work itself.

In panelling grooved frames the panel is generally thicker towards the middle, and is sloped off so as to thin it at the edges; but it must be remembered that as this makes it wedge-shaped all round, it is apt to split out the frame unless the groove is wide enough to take it easily. Generally speaking, it will not matter if a panel be somewhat loose, because it is usual to finish the work on the outer side with a moulding or beading of some kind, as can be seen by looking at the panelled doors of a room. If this is not to be done, more care must be taken in fitting the panels with accuracy. It will give a handsome appearance to such work to follow a plan in use in old days, but not so often practised now—viz., to leave a central nicely-squared part of the panel thick, like A (Fig. 34), either sloping it off from that point, or, better still, leaving an edge standing, as

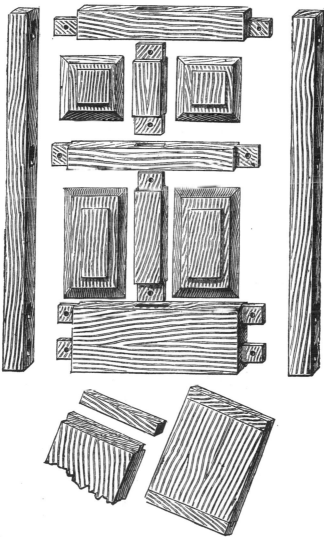

Fig. 35. Framing of a Panelled Door.

shown. For the latter work, which is difficult to do well, the side fillister can be used to form the edges of the central square, and the top and also the sides will then be finished by the smoothing plane. In Fig. 34, at C

D 2

this work is shown in its several stages; first, the board marked out; secondly, planed with the side fillister; and thirdly, finished. If the panel be small, the tenon saw used on the two edges which have to be made across the grain, will assist the plane, which, of course, cuts best with the grain; but a side filister is specially made to act across grain by having a second point or lancet edge to cut the fibres across as the work proceeds. In Fig. 35 (p. 51), which gives the framework of an ordinary door, the whole arrangement of panelling is sufficiently shown, and also the mode of clamping a board (such, for instance, as a drawing board) to prevent it from warping. The grooving for the panels is not shown in the drawing of the door panelling. No description of either will now be necessary except to state the way of putting the parts together. The cross centre rail, and two vertical central styles, are first fitted, glued, and pinned; then the panels are slid into their respective grooves; next the top and bottom rails, and last, the outer styles. These last must also be well glued and wedged or fixed by pins of wood driven through the tenons and mortices, which is the best way of securing heavy work. Of wedging we shall treat separately.

We may now proceed to lighter articles in tenoned and mortised work, such as a frame to be covered with canvas for an oil painting. The nature of the several operations will of course be precisely similar to those required in works of large dimensions, yet are not in all respects quite so easy to accomplish successfully. In the first place it will prove more difficult to square up the material of, say, 1in. wide by $\frac{1}{2}$in. or $\frac{5}{8}$in. thick. The flat sides will be easy to manage, but not the edges, because the surface is so narrow that no support is afforded to the sole of the plane, which, unless carefully managed, will roll from side to side most provokingly. There have indeed been several guides invented which can be fixed to the plane and rest against the side of a board so as to keep the plane in position, and insure the edge of the strip being planed truly at right angles to the side. We do not, however, recommend their use in any case, and we never see them adopted by the trade, the only guide used by professionals being the hand, which acts as a kind of stay, and prevents the oscillation of the tool. Let the strip be held in the chaps of the vice, and lie horizontally. Take off a few shavings and then test it by the square to see if it is being cut as it ought to be. Probably you will at once notice that the plane has had a tendency to lean over to one side or the other, and therefore, when you return the piece to continue the operation, you will try and give it a slight bias in the opposite direction, which will probably make matters right. Practically, we have generally found a tendency to plane such narrow work, and indeed broader pieces, lower on one side than the other. Supposing the strip to be held in the vice at the left-hand end of the bench, the workman will, of course, stand with the right side towards the latter. The tendency will probably be (as it is with the writer) to make the nearer side the lower. By trying to make the farther side lower instead, we find the work usually becomes true and square to the side. Now, remember not to cut off the piece to the intended length until after the mortices have been made, so that, there being plenty of wood beyond it, the mortice may not split out in cutting, if ordinary care is used. After the tenons have been glued in, and the work become quite dry, the superfluous ends are cut off, and the plane run over the whole. The following figure (Fig. 36) shows a frame of this kind (but made of thicker material than specified above) in course of construction. The pieces A, are planed up generally in a single strip, to be afterwards cut to the desired lengths. The measurements are usually taken inside, so that the size can be reckoned from the pencil lines, between the tenons, as e, f, and also on the mortices, (g, g, h, h). The latter, like the other strips, are cut longer than required, so as to project, and are sawn off with a tenon saw when the whole is complete. Attention is called to the

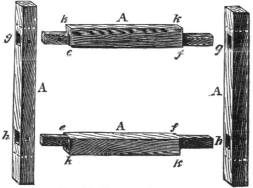

FIG. 36. MORTISED FRAME.

shoulders, k k, on the outside of the pieces, these being necessary in order to bring the outsides flush with the ends of the cross pieces. The parts of the latter, which have to be cut off, are marked by dotted lines in the drawing. If the parts of a small and light frame, such as that described, be nicely fitted, wedging will not be required, as glue alone will hold the joints firmly together. In the description of panelled work, the method of securing by wedges will be explained.

To hold the strips of only $\frac{1}{2}$in. or $\frac{3}{4}$in. stuff on edge while cutting the mortice, either the bench holdfast or forked piece of wood, already described, may be used, or the vice, which will aid in preventing the material from being split. But the latter is not a good plan, as it ties the chisel somewhat, and it is also better to have a firm basis on which to work. If one can be had, the holdfast is the best; if not, any little odd bit of stuff, cut into blocks, and attached temporarily to the bench on each side of the strips, will suffice to keep it steady. Remember to mark all sides where the tenons and mortices are to be cut, and to chisel them first from one side and then from the other, and only at last cut to the lines with a sharp chisel, not using the mallet, or only using it with the utmost gentleness.   A mortice and tenon should just slide into place stiffly.   If it need to be forced with a mallet, you are almost sure to split out the mortices.   Take, therefore, from the first all possible care, and do not be content with anything like a bad fit, in the hope that by means of a wedge here and a lump of glue there, supplemented by putty everywhere to hide mistakes, you will deceive yourself or your friends into the idea that your work is sufficiently good for the intended purpose.   Take, in short, as your invariable motto (you had better stick it up in good legible characters in your workshop) that

What is worth doing at all is worth doing well.

CHAPTER III.

SECOND LESSON.

Wedging Tenons—Open Mortice—Dowelling—Dovetails —Tool Box—Gluing—Mitring—Mitre Keys—Secret Dovetails.

WE must now call attention to the simple but useful operation of wedging tenon and mortice joints, because this is the general way of securing all but the heaviest work of this kind. Fig. 37 shows a mortice

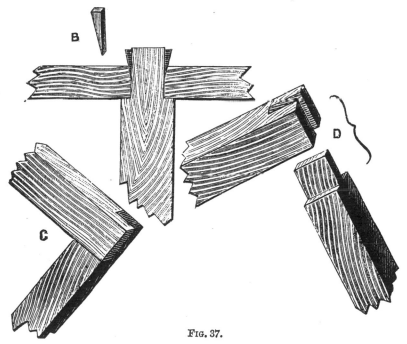

FIG. 37.

cut as usual, but part of which after the tenon is made to fit is sloped off on both sides (or rather ends, the slope being cut on the narrow part). Two wedges are now cut to fill up the space thus created, the form of the wedge being that shown at B, with one side perpendicular to the end, this side coming in contact with the tenon. When the latter is glued and driven into its place, one wedge, also glued, is inserted on each side and hammered down so as to bed fairly. It is evident that the tenon and] its two wedges will now form a dovetail; and, the latter being firmly glued to the tenon, the pieces cannot be separated except under the influence of a force sufficient to break the material. When the pieces of wood to be framed are too thin to allow tenoned and mortised joints to be made, they are often united by the half lap, shown at C in Fig. 37, half of each being cut away, so that when glued up the joint shall be even and flush on both sides. Sometimes a dovetailed form is given to one of the pieces, which increases the hold in one direction, but there is little strength in a joint of this kind. An open mortice is better like D, which being made almost wholly by a mitre or tenon saw, can be cut in very thin pieces, and by careful fitting and gluing a tolerably good junction may be effected between the parts.

In many common articles made thus, as, for instance, slate frames, the open mortice is wholly cut by a circular saw or rotary cutter as thick as the required mortice, no chisel being needed; and often, in work that falls to an amateur, a thick saw, like a compass saw, will answer in a similar way to remove wholly, at one cut, the piece of wood that has to be taken out to form the mortice. Where the pieces to be united by tenon and mortice are broad, two tenons, or even more, are preferable to one.

There is another way of uniting such pieces, which is called dowelling. Instead of cutting tenons and mortices, holes are made in each by a nose-bit or small centrebit, and pins are glued and driven in, first into one piece so as to stand up about an inch, and then the other piece is driven on and the two hammered up close, glue being previously run along the joint. Boards are thus frequently joined lengthwise, and chairmakers use this joint extensively. It is not so strong as a tenon and mortice, but the holes, not having to be cut with a chisel, are made in a few seconds, and the work proceeds consequently much more rapidly. The position of the centre of each hole is easily determined by making a line on the edge of each piece with a mortice gauge, and pricking off in this line, by the aid of a rule, the distances from the ends of the pieces. Great care must be taken to keep the holes perpendicular, so that the pins may stand upright; and these should not be of deal, but of beech, ash, or other tolerably hard wood.

We now come to dovetailing, which specially belongs to the joiner's art, as distinguished from that of the carpenter and builder. This, to make good work, requires the greatest care, both in marking and cutting out, and it is hopeless for anyone to attempt it who cannot plane up pieces of board quite true and square on all sides. Supposing this, however, to be the case—which, if our directions have been followed, it ought to be after a fair amount of practice—the work is to be done in the following manner: First, the pieces are to be accurately planed on all sides, care being taken not to thin them at one edge more than another. When fairly squared up, a line is to be made with a marking gauge at the same distance from the edge as the thickness of the sides. We will suppose half an inch— allowing, however, an eighth in addition, which can be subsequently cut off and planed smooth. To make the whole plan clear, we will suppose the present work to be a tool box of deal, the stuff of which when planed should at least be of the thickness named, and even with advantage rather more, but there is no need to make it heavy and clumsy, and the various partitions will give it stiffness and strength. As to dimensions, if 3ft. long it will take easily a hand saw, and it may be 18in. wide and 2ft.deep. This will make, be it remembered, quite a large chest for a good stock of full-sized tools, and will give depth for a tray and nest of drawers.

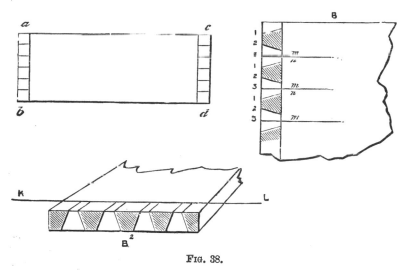

FIG. 38.

In Fig. 38, A is the front board marked for dovetails, allowing for the latter ⅜in. at each end, which will make the full length of this board 3ft. 1¼in. It is sometimes preferred to have the ends of such a box thicker than the front and back, to which, if preferred, there is no objection, but then more width must be allowed to these dovetails. Mark, therefore, by gauge or otherwise, a b and c d, and with compasses prick off the spaces, as shown, of 3in. each, and draw lines at each, which will divide the board into six equal spaces, each of 3in. (see larger scale at B). Now prick off on the outside edge a space of 1in. on each side of each line, and on the other line spaces of ½in. (m n), and join these points to complete the dovetails, of which there are five, and two half-dovetails at the top and bottom. There is no particular rule for the sizes of these, which often are made to slope less than the above; and this can be effected, if desired, by taking spaces of ¾in. each side of the first lines, instead of 1in., or $\frac{3}{4}$in. on the second line, which will come to the same thing. If too much sloped, and the material is deal, there will be danger of the points splitting off, especially in the case of the two outer ones, which are weaker than the rest. If not tolerably sure of your powers, you may so mark out your work as to make these half dovetails of extra width, or you may wholly cut them off, and let the pins on the sides fill up the space thus created.

We have now to speak of these pins, as they are called, and which some prefer to cut first. Supposing the pieces which will form the ends of the box squared up, set one of them in the vice, edge upwards, after you have cut out, by tenon or dovetail saw, the pieces between the dovetails, and taken care with a sharp chisel to cut all clean to the line a   b, which must be drawn on both sides of the board. Now hold the dovetailed part exactly in its place upon the end of the board in the vice, and with a steel scriber or sharp hard pencil trace each dovetail carefully on the end of the wood. This will now appear like B². The line K L shows the inner edge of the front or back, drawn as before according to the thickness of material, and the dotted lines are drawn on both sides by the square from the corners of the pins to the cross line. We forgot to say that the square is to be used on the tops of the dovetails already described, accuracy being absolutely essential in every detail of the work. Not a single cut of chisel or saw is to be made without first, with square and pencil, marking every line which is to be followed by the cutting tool. Observe also, especially in such work as dovetailing, never to cut into or efface these lines. If this be done, there will no longer be a guide to work by, and the dovetails will be so loose, or so badly fitted as to give no hold; whereas, even without glue, they should be so secure as not to fall apart nor even shake. This joint is, in fact, a very cleverly designed one, and when the amateur can make it in a satisfactory and workmanlike manner, he may congratulate himself upon having made a decided advance in his apprenticeship. If there be need of special caution, it is upon the following points, which we give in order :

1. Take care to square up accurately the boards to form the front, back, and sides, allowing the pins of the latter to project an eighth, when cut, beyond the dovetails.

2. Mark out the pins and corresponding dovetails on all sides by help of the square and compasses.

3. In cutting these out, take care to leave the lines marked on the extreme edges, but on no account cut into or obliterate them.

4. In cutting the pins and dovetails, take care to make the end of the board between each quite level or slightly hollow, using the chisel alternately on both sides of the boards, so that the cuts meet at the centre. If this surface be at all convex the joint cannot be made close and firm, but if a little concave it will not signify.

5. Do not make the dovetails with too sharp angles, or they will soon get broken off in putting the work together. Let the fit be tight, but not

so tight as to need much force to drive the pins home, lest the top and bottom dovetail be split off.

In making a tool box of the dimensions given, it will become necessary to join edgewise two pieces of board to get the desired width. This will give good practice in planing and squaring up edges, and also in gluing, which though simple in itself, is very often one of the many stumbling blocks which amateurs have to encounter. The boards to be joined should be set up together in the vice, if only $\frac{1}{2}$in. or so thick, because it affords greater width of surface for the sole of the plane to rest on. The latter is to be carefully sharpened and finely set; the long trying plane is the best to use, but for so short a joint as the present one a well-set jack plane will suffice. With this go to work steadily and slowly, until you get a level surface square to the sides of the board, which should be first planed, but not cut exactly to the required length. Now see if, on being placed edge to edge, as they lie flat on the bench or table they be in close contact. Probably they will be found convex, or higher in the middle than at the ends, so that the latter are apart and only the middle in contact. Try again until you get all nice and level. Now you may dowel these boards with a couple of pins inserted as already directed, because it will keep them together while drying, but this is not absolutely necessary, for they will be quite strong if well glued without such pins. By *well glued* we do not mean thickly glued, but quite the contrary.

The following is the proper way to glue up this or any other work : Buy the best glue, which is *thin* and clear, and not tough and thick like some that is made. Break up a small quantity, and put it in the inner vessel of the glue pot with cold water, and let it steep for twelve hours. Then add cold water in the outer vessel, as much as it will hold without spilling when the inner vessel is inserted, and set it on the fire to boil and simmer until the glue is dissolved, and is, when stirred, about as thick as cream. It must not be thicker, or it will only clog and be useless. Now set up one board in the vice, but first warm the edge, and have the glue boiling hot ; quickly brush over both edges, clap one on the other, and rub them together a few times till you feel them begin to stick ; then leave till quite dry. Remember always that the less glue in a joint the better. You want to keep the edges in close contact, not with a thick cake of glue between them. The standing rule is, to have the glue moderately thick and boiling hot, to work quickly, and let the materials to be united be also hot, especially in winter. Do not disturb, when once in position, until dry. The result will be a union so perfect that the wood will split off rather than the glue give way.

When boards are thus joined for the sides of a box, take care that the joint so made falls in the middle of a dovetail or pin, because, when the work is put together, it will itself form a clamp to keep all close. In the present case, if possible, and if the workman be a sufficiently good hand with a plane to shoot up true the necessary length, it will be as well to glue up, as one, a piece long enough for the two ends, and a second piece long enough to form the front and back of the box, and subsequently to divide each across into two pieces.

We must now, before putting the box together, consider the proposed arrangement of its interior, as all such matters ought to be decided in case we require to cut any grooves in the inside of the sides or ends to receive partitions. The plan is given opposite in Fig. 39. A is the appearance looking down from above, when the nest of drawers, *a*, is in its place, *b*, *c*, *d*, *e* being the several compartments. B is the same with the drawers removed, showing partitioned places below for planes of various kinds and for saws or long tools. C is an elevation in which it will be noticed that the nest of drawers, which is complete in itself, rests on two narrow slips of deal nailed to the ends of the box, so that the whole can be slid from front to back at pleasure, as the nest is only half the width of the box. This enables the lower part to be reached, which is intended for such tools as should be kept together, like sets of beading and moulding planes, with the plough and fillisters. Saws may be placed as shown, or secured inside the lid by studs, straps, and buttons, as will be described; and the squares and bevels, rules, and such like thin tools, liable to injury, may be also similarly placed. The nest of drawers is intended to hold screws and nails in assorted sizes ; bradawls, gimlets, and any small tools. A couple of nail trays may also be added in the front corners of the box, but these should be movable, for convenience of getting easily at all below.

We can now proceed with the details of construction. An inspection of plan B shows one division (*f*) reaching across from end to end. This will hardly need to be taken out, and therefore may be slid in from below into grooves, before the bottom of the box is put on. A groove has to be made, therefore, in the lower half of the ends. Two others will be required at *d*, *e*, plan B, and in *f*, to take the short divisions, a third being added at *g* if desired. For exact distances measure the planes, &c. There are grooving planes for this work, but it is as easy to mark and cut with a tenon saw, and then to remove with a narrow chisel the part between the saw cuts. By removing the fence the plough will finish these, or the fillister when once deep enough to guide the tool. If it be preferred to make all the partitions movable from above, they may slide in between two strips tacked on to form grooves. The latter can, indeed, be planed up quite to the upper edge, but the strips tacked or glued on will answer, and be neat if nicely planed and fitted.

Having got out all the stuff to exact measure, and cut all dovetails and pins, proceed to put the box together. Stand up in the vice one of the ends, pins upward, have glue boiling hot, and brush on quickly; put on the side, and at once hammer down all close. This end must be removed from the vice and stood on the bench, and the other quickly glued, placed in position, and closed up, so that the three sides will be now united and standing on the bench with the side upwards, the ends forming legs. Now lay on the bench two strips of quartering, or a board, on which to place the side already fixed, when inverted, as it is now to be. You need this

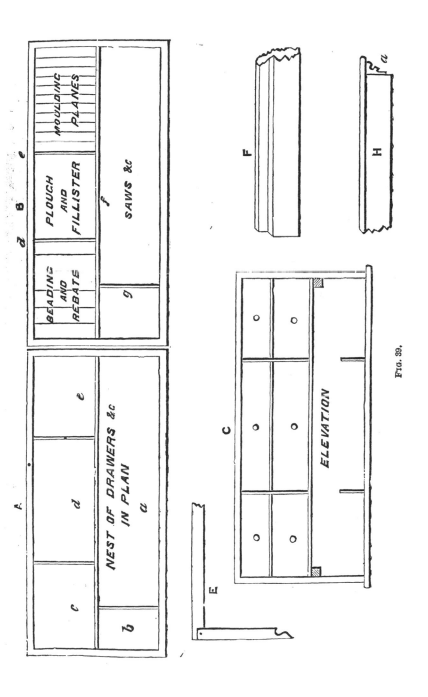

FIG. 39.

because the pins project, and you must not let the work rest on these, or when you hammer on the other side you will shake the work apart which you have already glued up. Resting the finished side, therefore, on a bit of wood, to raise it from the bench, brush over the other pins now uppermost, put on the other side, hammer up close, and leave all for a day to dry thoroughly.

In the meanwhile you have to see about the bottom board, and also the cover. In both of these you will require, as before, the width of two pieces glued together, but neither need be dowelled, as the bottom will be nailed on so that the pieces cannot possibly separate, and the top will be made as a carcase lid, or shallow box, for the purpose of making room for saws inside it. Glue up and plane the pieces for the lid, and also plane up carefully a strip 2in. wide and as thick as the material of the box itself. Take the inside measure of the latter accurately, and mark off the side and end pieces on this strip, or cut them at once near the length, and accurately set them out afterwards. They will be the exact lengths of the front and back of the box, and of the ends, and will have one dovetail at each corner, so that, when glued up as a frame, it will be the exact size of the box, as if it were a narrow piece sawn from it. You can notch in the corners, like E, as it cannot get out of place when the top is nailed on, and a brad will hold it; but it is by no means as good or workmanlike a way as the dovetail, and will be as troublesome in the long run to finish satisfactorily. When this is dry, nail on the top board, letting it project a little all round. In very good, neat work, the top is often let in by ploughing away or rebating, which hides the edges of the top board. But this you need not do; the other method is easier and as good, and a light moulding will be subsequently run round under the projecting cover to give a finish, as H a. We may now suppose all dry, and proceed with a fine saw to cut off all the pins projecting from the dovetails, afterwards running over them a sharp plane, and rendering them smooth, and level with the surface of the box. The same is also done to the cover, which may perhaps, when hinged and also locked, need to be further faced a little to make it quite true with the box itself. Nail on the bottom, leaving a projection all round, but first place the divisions or partitions in their grooves, if so arranged. Do not round off the upper edge of these, but only the edges of the top and bottom boards. The square edge should always be preserved, except where the hands would be liable to be hurt by contact with them, or rather, where it will be necessary to handle the article, whatever it may be. Sometimes also a rounded edge is made, to form a contrast with a sharp one adjacent to it, which gives more or less of the effect of a moulding to the part.

Now let us go on to the nest of drawers, which needs a little special description, and which will, perhaps, prove a somewhat more difficult task to the amateur than the more simple process of making the box itself. We will suppose two rows of drawers, of three in a row, the middle one wider than the other two; the material of the case or nest itself, as of the drawers, will be quite thin—½in. deal before being planed, but the front board of each drawer should be thicker, say, ⅜in. But first we must set about the case or nest itself, in which are to be fitted the several drawers. This consists practically of an oblong box, open in front and divided off into six parts by partitions. This may be made of ¼in. stuff at the top, bottom, and back, but the ends should be of ½in., or at any rate ⅜in. stuff, which will add to its strength and enable it to be dovetailed at the corners. If, indeed, it be not desired to dovetail this part of the work, the extra thickness will still be necessary to take the nails (brads) by which it is to be secured at the angles. As regards this case, therefore, it is unnecessary to go into details of the work so far as it

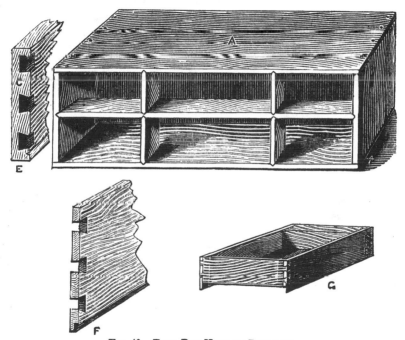

FIG. 40. TOOL BOX NEST OF DRAWERS.

resembles, on a smaller scale, the large box itself, into which it has to be fitted. In Fig. 40 we give a sketch which will be sufficiently explanatory. In whatever way the outer case is fastened at the corners the divisions or partitions should slide in, angular grooves being cut in the case for the upright ones, and in these for the horizontal ones, which are generally thinner than the latter. These partitions are seldom carried to the back of the case, as there will be sufficient support without if they reach about two-thirds of the depth, as here drawn. The drawers are not exactly like shallow boxes, though somewhat resembling them. True, they are not unfrequently so made for such uses as the present, but only because they are designed for common purposes, and are made with but small expenditure of time and trouble. There is no need for the amateur to work thus, and the proper method is altogether more satisfactory. The front, as stated, is always of thicker stuff, because the dovetails are not allowed to appear in front, but are cut as shown at C. Only two or three need be made, and these can be shallow, because the sides are thin. Cabinet makers, whose chief work is furniture, do not often make broad dovetails, as they make the pins narrower and further apart in general than joiners; the pins, too, are not much sloped or bevelled. This is the neatest way of working, especially if the material be thin, say $\frac{1}{4}$in., and less. Two or three such pins are ample in a light drawer, such as we are supposed to be making, the depth of which will not be over 3in. As we are making the whole box 18in. deep, we may allow one-third of the depth for the nest of drawers, exclusive of the thickness of stuff used in the construction. The actual drawers can be from 2$\frac{1}{2}$in. to 3in. deep, and from front to back 6in., or thereabout, so as to leave for the open part of the box in front of them a width of 1ft. The backs of the drawers are to be dovetailed to the sides, but must be rather narrower, because the bottom of the drawer is to be slid in two shallow grooves, cut in the sides at $\frac{1}{8}$in. from their lowest edge, and secured by a small brad or sprig to the back In the front it falls into a rebate, F., or a groove, E., securing it completely; of course it is nailed if a rebate be used. The object of this arrangement is to allow the drawer to rest, not on the bottom, but on the edges of the two sides, on which it will slide much more readily, the bearing surfaces being then very narrow. These edges, in large heavy drawers, may with advantage be rubbed with soap, or with blacklead, either of which will be found to reduce the friction very materially. G. shows such a drawer seen from the back and from above.

In the figure of the exterior of the finished box (Fig. 41) is seen a strip nailed round it after the bottom is attached to conceal the edge of the latter, and give a finish to the whole; it is mitred at the corners and sometimes beaded or moulded at its upper edge. To cut such moulding, plane up the whole strip at once long enough to go quite round the box. Make it quite square and true. It may be 2$\frac{1}{2}$in. to 3in. wide, but only 1in. or 1$\frac{1}{4}$in. need be moulded. The only difficulty in the latter work is to start it correctly. For a narrow strip of light moulding, such as the present, the hand overlapping the work will probably suffice to keep all straight until the cut is deep enough to become itself the guide of the tool. But if this be found difficult, work as follows: To the sole of the rebate plane attach a piece of wood an inch wide or so, with countersunk screws working in two slots cut across the piece, near its ends. It will thus become like a sash fillister as regards its guide, and will be handy for cutting rebates at any time. Suppose the section of moulding to be as in Fig. 41, you see that as a good deal has to be cut away, you can run a rebate at $a\,b$, which will guide the moulding plane at once, and insure its straight run; or the same can be done at c, as is evident from the drawing.

A straight edged shooting board is also used for the purpose of running a straight course. Of course when once the pattern is fairly started, little difficulty will exist in continuing the work and bringing it to a satisfactory issue. The final strokes of the plane should be made with the tool held neither vertically nor horizontally, but on a slant, so as to be perpendicular to the face of the moulding. Sometimes, however, the pattern is such as to preclude this, as, for instance, when *a* and *b* of Y have one face at right angles to the surface of the work and the plane iron is not so shaped as to effect this when it is held at the above angle.

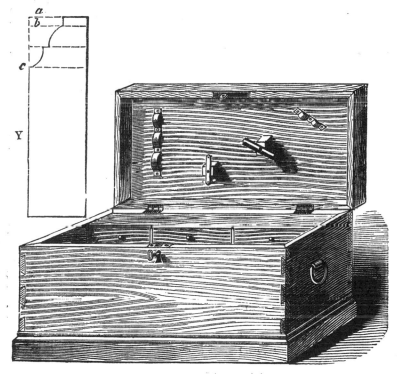

FIG. 41. TOOL CHEST.

As we have had occasion here to speak of mitred corners, and our tool box is also practically finished, requiring only its cover to be made and attached by hinges, and its lock to be put on, with here and there a final touch from the smoothing plane, we will describe at more length the various kinds of mitres which belong to the carpenter's (and not the episcopal) bench, and the mitring boxes and boards convenient for such work. We have already shown one kind of shooting board and one mitre box, but neither will do such work as mitring up a box, as they are only fit for picture frames and similar articles.

E

In Fig. 42 A is a mitring and shooting block, that will enable us to shoot up with a sharp plane the edge of a board at an angle of 45°, the two pieces thus united forming a square; and a box like B can be readily made, or like C, wherein the corners are mitred and also the lower edge and bottom on the line D D. The short corners, however, being cut across the grain, cannot be so easily shot with a plane, and are generally cut in a mitre box. The principle of all such guides is, of course, the same, all being so contrived as to enable an angle of 45 deg. to be easily cut. The sliding bevel is often used (figured at E, Fig. 42), set to an angle of 45 deg. By this a little distance at each corner of the strip of wood is accurately formed, and then a plane can be run from one to the other to complete the bevel. This mode of framing up a box or drawer is very neat, and extensively used for desks, glove boxes, and light articles. The joints are glued up, and clamped or bound till dry, and then little bits of thin, hard wood are let into saw cuts, as seen at K, these also being glued, and when dry they are planed off even with the sides of the box. These saw cuts should be made not horizontally but one sloping up and the next down, alternately. They go by the name of mitre keys, and look well if of white wood in a dark box and *vice versâ* of course. If not intended to show, they are made of the same wood as the box, but they are difficult to conceal because the grain is always in a different direction to that of the side of the box, since they are fitted in at an angle, as stated. If on any occasion it should be necessary to form a mitre, and no guide be at hand for the correct angle, it must be remembered that, if a piece of wood be squared up, as, for instance, the side and end of a bit of board, and a line be drawn across it as A, B (Fig. 43), at a distance from the edge equal to the thickness, a line, C, D, from this line to the corner will make an angle of 45° (see also Fig. 31) so that such a corner can be cut off correctly by a chisel or mitre saw without any further guide. Lines again connecting the opposite corners of a square also make angles of 45°, so that a mitre joint is by no means difficult to make. One piece of advice we may here give the reader, viz., to make even his nail boxes neatly, instead of, according to the general custom of amateurs, nailing up pieces of rough material not even planed, nor very often cut true by the square. It does not take much longer to do such jobs well, and the result will always give satisfaction.

The mitre joint is specially used for light work, and, in making a mitred box, trouble will be saved by forming box and cover as one, and then, marking round with a gauge at the required distance from the edge, sawing off the top. The whole box, be it understood, is thus made, top, bottom, and all complete, before it is sawn apart. The plan saves the trouble of planing up and mitring such narrow strips as the cover alone would need, a broader piece being far more easy to work than a very narrow one. This is the special object of a carcase saw, but a tenon or mitre saw carefully used is as efficient. It is easy to see that, instead of marking and sawing on a horizontal line, it is as easy to cut the work apart on a slope to form

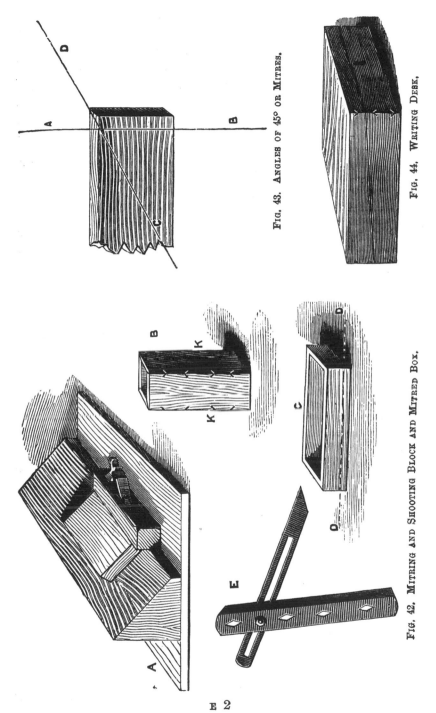

FIG. 43. ANGLES OF 45° OR MITRES.

FIG. 44. WRITING DESK.

FIG. 42. MITRING AND SHOOTING BLOCK AND MITRED BOX.

E 2

a desk like Fig. 44. Great care has to be taken, in planing up such work to remove saw marks, not to destroy the evenness of line, else the desk will not shut closely in some places, while in others the parts fit well. Corners and edges of brass for boxes can be bought in the larger towns, especially London and Birmingham, but not often in other places. The amateur must not expect for some time to do work equal to or even bordering on that produced by the trade. To make only an ordinary nailed box, true and even, nicely planed with sharp or rounded edges that will bear close inspection, is not the easy job it may, at first sight, appear. It must be remembered that much depends on the acquired power of using the plane successfully both on flat surfaces of board (so as to reduce them to a true level), and on the edges. A very little deviation from absolute correctness in this respect will produce open joints, or throw the whole cube out of square, as will be evident on inspection of the exagge-rated defects in question in Fig. 45.

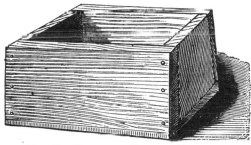

FIG. 45. RESULT OF UNEQUAL PLANING.

We must now return to dovetailing of another kind, in which the pins and dovetails are so arranged that one or both are entirely concealed. This variety of work is far more difficult to execute than the more simple kind, and is not very often attempted by amateurs. Nevertheless, like all else, it can be done by careful manipulation, if the tools be sharp, and in that perfect order in which all tools must be kept for the execution of really workmanlike jobs.

Blind or concealed dovetails are either wholly concealed, so that nothing is observable but a line at the point of union, or the pins alone are seen, or dovetails only. We have already described the method of uniting the front of a drawer to the sides, and in this case no joint appears in front, but only at the sides. Suppose that instead of working exactly in this way the dovetails themselves were only cut half through the side pieces, we should see neither pins nor dovetails, but there would be a single line only, at a little distance from the corner, on the side piece. Such a joint taken apart is shown in Fig. 46, in which A is the piece containing the pins, and C that of the dovetails; the latter must be of the thickness of A to B. To make a joint of this kind proceed as follows: Plane all pieces true with exceeding care. With a marking gauge set off a distance on each, equal to the thickness of that which is to be united to it, as shown by the lines B B, and a b, in the figures A and C. Then on the edge and side, as seen at D, gauge about half the thickness of the pieces, and mark n n, a b. This line will mark the depth (in the thickness of the wood) to

which both pins and dovetails are to be cut. A little consideration, however, will show that the piece A, with the pins, must overlap the ends of
the dovetails, by which lap they are concealed, consequently half the
length of the pin must be cut away, or the piece must be rebated to that
depth before the pins are cut. It is better, however, to make them the
full length and then to reduce them, as otherwise it will not be possible
to trace their shape on the piece in which the dovetails are to be cut ;
whereas if they be made of full length first of all, they can be stood upon
the other piece and a sharp-pointed pencil run round them. Great
accuracy will be needed in cutting the dovetails, and neither these nor the
pins can be sawn at all. It is all chisel work, but the joint is, if well made,
beautifully close, and such as is only seen in the best style of cabinet
work. It is evident that, after such a joint has been put together and
become dry, the edge of the lap on A may be rounded off if desired, without

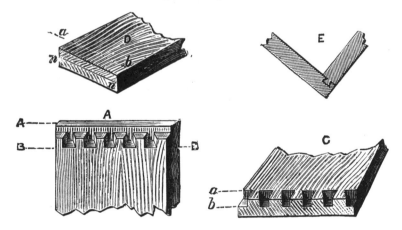

Fig. 46. BLIND DOVETAILS.

in any degree impairing the firmness of the junction. In all these joints
there is, it is plain, a very large amount of surface for the glue, which
tends to make dovetails particularly firm.

There is yet one other way of making this joint, the object of which is
to throw the line which betrays it exactly on the angle, as in a morticed
joint. It is in point of fact a morticed joint, with dovetails and pins
added. As, however, it is scarcely likely the amateur will care to increase
his difficulties to gain so little, we shall not enter into details of its construction, it being practically similar to the last described, but instead of
there being a lap on one piece only, each projects beyond the pins or dovetails in an equal degree, and the two laps being mitred, meet accurately
upon a single line at the angle.

Mention may here be made of a mitred and dovetailed joint, recently
patented in America, and cut by machinery, which, though not suited to

deal or other wood which splits easily, is, to say the least, very clever and ingenious. In this, which is shown in section only at E, the dovetail is cut in one edge the whole width of the piece, and the groove in the other, and the two are united by sliding one into the other. Thus there is but one long dovetail and one groove to be cut. This may be done by hand if the joint be not above two or three inches long, but there is danger of splitting off the piece outside the groove, either in the process of its formation or in sliding in the dovetailed piece, if it should chance to be a little too tight. It is in fact simple, though it may seem a difficult joint to make, and if attempted at all, it is better to leave plenty of stuff outside the groove, and to cut it off after the whole is glued up and dry.

Of the above methods of uniting pieces of wood at the corners, the half lap dovetail A C of the last figure has this one advantage, that if any one of the pins or dovetails should fail to be accurately cut, the lap will conceal the defect, while the glue on the lap itself will make up in some degree for the slightly weakened condition of the joint caused by such misfit. It is, nevertheless, on the whole, more difficult than the open dovetail, and extra care spent on the latter is better than to work badly and conceal defects.

CHAPTER IV.

THIRD LESSON.

WASHSTAND—CHEST OF DRAWERS—INDIAN WARDROBE—BEDSTEAD.

HAVING now gone through in detail the essential operations of carpentry so far as regards the method of uniting pieces of wood together, it will perhaps be as well to describe the formation of a few articles of daily use, upon either or all of which the amateur may satisfactorily try his powers. If possessed of a simple lathe, moreover, for wood turning, such as is now found in the majority of workshops, he may add a certain degree of decoration to these simple objects, and frequently also work more speedily.

We will begin with a small washstand, and this should not only be made, but painted by the amateur; for we have had to pay as much for the latter operation as we could have bought the whole concern for—painted, varnished, and complete. The front legs ought to be turned, and all four may be thus treated with advantage. If, however, no lathe be at hand, they must of necessity be formed by the plane alone. Fig. 47 represents the affair complete, the several details being also given. We shall not now give dimensions because they depend wholly upon convenience or taste and often have to be modified to suit the materials that chance to be at hand. The first consideration will be the legs, which are of 2in. to 2½in. stuff, according to the proposed size; they should not be too slight, and at the same time need not be clumsy. If 2in. square when completely finished, they will probably be large enough, as the framing tends to stiffen them.

The pieces, whether they are to be subsequently turned or not, must, as in other cases, be carefully squared, and then they are to be marked for the several mortices. Where these occur the wood must be left square, but the intermediate parts can be turned, or, if desired, have the angles taken off with a plane. If to be turned let this be now done, before the mortices are cut. Of these there will evidently be two sets in each face of the legs, one to take the bearers of the top board, the other to receive the supports of the drawer. The upper ones are merely simple mortices,

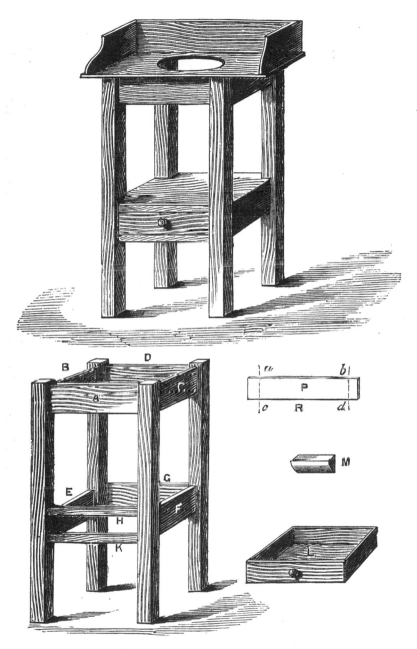

FIG. 47. WASHSTAND AND DETAILS.

which should not be through the front legs, but *may* be if the whole is to be painted; it is not, however, in this case the |proper way ; and the work will hold together very well if they are cut deeply, but not quite through the pieces. These bearers must be of board not less than 3in. wide and from ½in. to ¾in. thick, according to the size of the proposed stand. Those marked A, B, C, D, if more than 3in. wide may have two tenons at each end instead of one; as also, E, F, and G, all of which it will be observed stand edge upwards, but H and K, between which the drawer is to slide, are of half width only, and are fitted to lie flat side upwards, their edges coming to the front. None of these bearers should be quite flush with the legs, as they will give the whole work a better appearance if they stand in a little distance. They are, moreover, more easily fitted thus, as the mortice will fall more in the middle of the wood and be stronger. Under the strips or bearers E F a narrow strip must be glued or tacked on with brads, to form a support to the drawer, and upon which it will slide. Their upper surface must, of course, be level with the top of the front piece, K.

The drawer is represented at L, and is made with half lap dovetails, like those of the tool chest, the slides also coming below the level of the bottom, that it may work easily upon its bearers. To fit a drawer so that it may slide smoothly and yet without shake is not an easy matter, as is unfortunately easy to be proved in the case of cheap furniture. The famous Gillow was noted for his chests of drawers, and some of the first-class London makers are very expert in this matter, but we suppose most people have experienced the irritation and annoyance caused by a drawer that defies all efforts to run in straight, as it ought to do, and which sticks and jambs and goes in first this side and now that side, playing fast and loose, till the owner wishes the whole concern at the bottom of the sea. A cheap washstand of the form given here usually has the worst fitting drawer it is possible to conceive; but as in all else, if you want good articles, you must pay for them, and then possibly you will get them, and quite as possibly not in these degenerate days. It is like the Glenfield starch, if you want it, *see that you get it.*

The last thing to be done to the washstand is to put on the top board, with its back and side pieces. The board may or may not be cut out to allow the basin to drop into it, which is the best way. In any case, cut some pieces to form blocks like M, with two flat sides, one of which is to be glued inside A, B, C, and D, so that the other flat side comes up exactly even with the edges of these bearers. The top board, which is made large enough to project a couple of inches on each side and about one inch in front, is to be glued to the surface of these blocks. In this position it will act as a stay to the stand as well as serve its own special purpose. You can also, if desired, put four screws through the board into the legs, countersinking their heads, so that they shall be slightly below the surface, and hiding them with putty, to be subsequently itself concealed by the paint. Another board is also to be fixed to the upper edges of E, F, G, H, but no blocks can be placed here because of the drawer. It will suffice to attach it with sprigs to the bearers. This board will require to be notched out to allow it to pass the legs, as it should be flush with the bearers or extend a little beyond them. The back and sides which surmount the top board should be framed with dove-tailed joints at the angles, and may then be attached by screws passed in from below, or, if the stand be small and these sides thin, it may suffice to nail with brads. In either case let this be done before the top is fixed on.

To cut the hole in the top board it must be first glued up from two pieces to make it sufficiently wide, and it may have strips glued underneath to strengthen the joint, taking care to keep them beyond the limits of the hole. Then, if a sweep or turning saw is at hand, bore a hole at any part within the above limits, and near the circle inscribed; detach one end of the saw, and put it through the hole; attach it again to its handle by re-inserting the pin, and, having set up the board in a bench vice, cut out the circle by quick short strokes. If no turn saw is obtainable, use a keyhole saw, which will do almost as well if carefully used; the work should be kept as much as possible towards the point as being the narrowest part, and, therefore, the more easily turned about in following the curved line. It will be the safest plan to allow but 3in. of the saw to project beyond the handle or pad. After the hole is thus cut it can be smoothed with a spokeshave. Cut *from* the face which is to form the upper side, *i.e.*, let that be facing you as you work, as the saw will make the opposite side the most ragged, owing to the direction of its teeth. With the above details there should be no great difficulty experienced in making such an article of useful furniture as is here delineated; nevertheless it may be found that when finished there is a degree of instability or lop-sidedness which should not exist. If so, it will probably arise from the fact that some mortices are deeper than others, or the pieces not well squared up at the onset. To avoid the first error gauge your bearers, taking inside measure from *a* to *b* in R. If all the bearings be then let into their mortices to these several lines, it is no matter if one mortice be a little too deep, as you can drop in a little chip before glueing up. To avoid the second error be more careful.

A chest of drawers is, perhaps, scarcely as likely an article for an amateur to undertake as others of a less bulky character. There is, moreover, a good deal of work in it, all needing accuracy, if the whole, when finished, is to be of permanent use in the household. At the same time, it is but right that the usual method of construction should be understood. The work may be divided into three parts: (1) The outer case; (2); the divisions between the drawers; (3) the drawers themselves.

As regards the first, there are two ways of making it. It may be constructed as a dovetailed box, without top or bottom, to be afterwards stood on one end and fitted with a back, legs, and a wider top with moulded edges attached to the first, so as to overhang it on three sides, or this overhanging top may be nailed at once upon the upper end, there

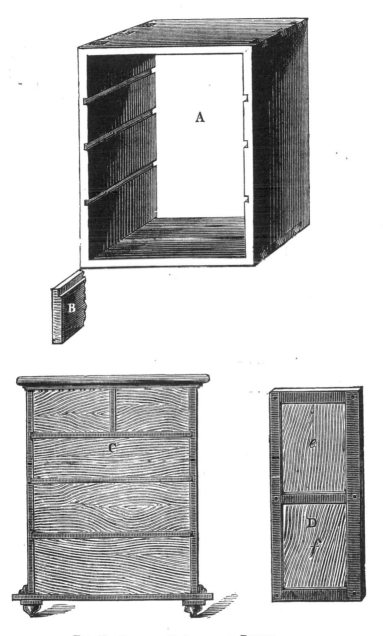

FIG. 48. CHEST OF DRAWERS AND DETAIL.

being dovetailed joints only at the lower corners. If the top is a single board only—a strip must be added below it from side to side to match the divisions between the drawers—so that the top drawers shall not be close under the overhanging top. In cheaper work there are no such dovetails at all, but the case is simply nailed up at each angle, the divisions slid in, and the back, of much thinner stuff, fixed into a rebate by glue and brads. Of course the nail holes are subsequently filled with putty, and the whole well painted, and then it will be impossible, without very close inspection, to determine whether dovetails have or have not been used. It is evident that when mahogany is used nails will be inadmissible, and dovetails a matter of necessity, as there will be neither putty nor paint to conceal defects; for though by mahogany dust and glue a nail hole may be partially hidden, it is sure to show subsequently.

Taking into consideration that the best construction will prove in every way the most satisfactory, as well as the most durable, we shall commence as follows :—Determine and draw to scale—which is in all cases the workmanlike way—the exact pattern, in elevation, plan, and detail, of the chest which is to be made. Let the first be a small one, of deal, as it will be somewhat easier to manage, and a failure will be of less importance. The front elevation will be like C, Fig. 48. The perspective view of the case before the divisions and top are added is seen at A. This is dovetailed neatly at the four corners, but the boards are first grooved, as shown, and at the edge which is to form the back they are rebated as B, because the back is to be let into this rebate, and lie flush with the edges. So far, at any rate, there is nothing to be done of great difficulty if each of the boards has been carefully planed and squared up accurately. A tenon saw will cut the grooves, aided by a narrow chisel, to remove what lies between the saw cuts, and a rebate plane will level the bottom as well as any other. The divisions that are to slide into these grooves are not merely planed boards, because these are liable to warp, but are specially framed up for the purpose, as shown at D. The pieces forming the frame are all grooved with the plough, and are then tenoned and mortised at the angles. The cross piece in the centre is also grooved on both sides, and the panels e f, of lighter stuff, are of course inserted before the frame is finally put together, so that the whole is very similar in workmanship to an ordinary panelled door. As, however, the outer case will keep it secure, not much trouble is generally taken about glueing it up. It is, nevertheless, better to glue and pin the angles as carefully as if it were of the utmost importance. In cheap work these are put together in a disgracefully rough manner, simply because it occupies less time. Of course, such articles are made to sell and to tumble to pieces as speedily as possible. The concealing power of paint, friend as it is to the maker of cheap work, is a terrible foe to the buyer; and not long since we had a chest of drawers in which, after a few weeks' ordinary use, a large piece of the front of one of the drawers fell off.

exposing, of course, a very ancient crack in the wood, which putty and paint had successfully hidden from view. In all cases unpainted articles of furniture are the most reliable, and for elegance and beauty nothing can exceed the pine furniture inlaid round the edge and simply varnished. Such work is nearly always of first-rate quality. The amateur is unfortunately inclined to resort to paint for the same reason that the makers of cheap furniture use it, viz., to conceal imperfections which care and patience would have wholly prevented. We must not, however, be too severe upon this point, because earlier attempts cannot be expected to equal later ones, and, in a difficult job like the present, a little putty and the necessary paint may be considered perfectly allowable, and if, on the whole, fair success be attained, so that the chest stands firmly on its legs, and is square in outline, and the drawers slide easily and fit well when closed, a great deal of credit will have been justly earned by the amateur, for this is not an easy job.

Each of the panelled divisions, as it is slid into its place, is secured with a brad or two, or, which is better, with glue ; care being taken to make the outer edge of each exactly level with the front of the case. This edge will look better if it be moulded ; but in that case each drawer should also have glued on to its front edges a similar strip. This may, therefore, in the present case be omitted. It commonly happens in cheaper work that these intermediate divisions are not carried across more than half way, the back panel being wholly omitted ; but this allows the hand to get at any drawer if the one above it is drawn out, which is by no means generally desirable, keys becoming thereby almost useless. If it were not for this, a mere strip, 2in. wide, running from front to back, and a 3in. strip across between the drawers, would suffice as bearers, and we have seen a chest made exactly in this way.

The drawers, after our former description, need no special directions, but the ultimate appearance of the chest will mainly depend upon the accuracy with which their front boards fit the spaces allotted to them.

As regards the top, it may be added upon the upper board of the chest, and a neat moulding run round below to form a connection with the lower board, giving the whole a more massive and handsome appearance. It is, however, as stated above, a very common practice to nail or screw on the top to the lower part of the case at once.

The back is of thin panelled work, let into the rebate in the side boards, and secured by brads, or it is of false panels—i.e., the frame is made but not grooved, and this being fitted into the back, thin boards are glued on outside it quite flush. We may here observe, as regards panelling, that the panel itself is sometimes made purposely flush with its frame, either on both sides or on one. In the latter case the panel is rebated ; in the former tongued ; the tongue being in the centre of its thickness, the rebate being of course near its edge. False panels are also made by first constructing a framework, and then nailing on a strip of moulding so as to form a rebate on one side. The panel is laid upon this and secured by a second strip of moulding. Not much time or trouble is really saved by these makeshifts, which are allowable only when the amateur has no plough for cutting the grooves in a proper manner. If the outer shell or case be made with three sides, and the top is to be attached as the fourth, projecting in front and at the ends, blocks must be glued on, upon which, as well as the edges of the sides, it may rest, and to which it can be attached by glue, or by screws passed from below into it, holes being quite inadmissible, unless the chest is to be painted.

The legs are, of course, to be turned in the lathe, and made with a projecting pin to glue into a block of wood at each corner underneath the chest. If a screw box be at hand, a still better job can be made by making the pin of beech, and cutting a thread upon it, tapping the block, also of beech, to receive it. The whole is to be finished by running a good solid moulding round the lower edge.

For screwing wood there is a special tool in addition to those used in the lathe, and described in our little work on the subject of turning. This tool, called a screw box, is made of various sizes, from ½in. to 3in., the latter being constructed with two handles, for cutting bench and press screws. First of all a block of wood, hard beech or mahogany, or other close grained stuff, is taken and squared up, and then it is tapped with the screw thread required (Fig. 49). At A is cut a recess to fit the cutter of steel, which is made of a V section, B C, to match the thread, and is kept very sharp. The edge of this is, in fact, so fitted as to take the place of one of the threads in the box, which is cut away to permit of this.

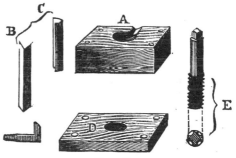

FIG. 49.

A top plate of wood, D, with a hole not tapped, of the exact size of the screw blank, is then attached by a couple of screws. A tap, E, is sold with each box to cut the requisite thread inside the nut. The amateur will find one or two of these tools of great use, but unfortunately they are rather dear, 4s. for a small size.

We have introduced them here because it chances that a screw cut on the legs of our chest of drawers will be of decided advantage; but in making footstools, music stools, and various articles of furniture, screwing the parts together will be often far better than using glue. It will be convenient also to make many articles in such a manner as to enable them to be taken apart, so as to be more easily packed, and in this case the screw box will be found almost indispensable.

There is another, and a very simple mode of fitting drawers that is specially applicable when no division is intended to be shown between

F

them on looking at the front of the chest. This is often the case in microscopic and other cabinets, and it is by no means difficult to make them in this way. The two sides of the shell, or outer case, are grooved in parallel lines, as far apart as the proposed depth of the drawers, and to the latter are attached strips of hard wood on each side, carefully planed to fit the grooves easily; but without shake. In this case there is no need to let the two sides of the several drawers overlap the bottom, but each is made like a shallow box. The bottom itself of each drawer may overlap the side, and slide in the grooves instead of a slip being added to each. A little care will be needed in attaching the strips in the right place so that, when completed, the fronts of the drawers shall accurately touch each other, and, together, fill up the whole open space in the outer case; but, to effect this, each drawer should be put in its place and held up while the position of the strip is marked opposite the groove, and, as soon as the first (the top drawer) is fitted, it should be put in place, and the next held up so as to touch it, and similarly marked. Then, to ensure perfect fit, the strip should be nailed on a little lower on the drawer than necessary, so that it will not quite run in, owing to its contact with the one above it. With a finely-set plane, the front of it (left purposely higher than the sides) is to be planed down until an exact fit is obtained. This will be found the surest way of securing accuracy, for the beauty of such a chest consists in the perfect fit of each drawer, so that the whole front shall present an even polished surface, marked with horizontal parallel lines, but with no open spaces whatever. It may be readily seen that instead of grooving the outer case the operations can, if preferred, be reversed, the grooves being made in the drawers, and the strips nailed to the shell. Practically, however, the easiest and most satisfactory method is that which we have given above, and which, being so simple, will be readily understood without any special illustrations. For chests of drawers of all kinds there is now ample choice of handles and other fittings made of china, either plain white, or black, or figured and inlaid. This not only saves a great deal of time and trouble, but the contrast produced is of a very pleasing character, and gives the whole a handsomer appearance than if wooden handles are used.

There is a simple mode used in India of making a wardrobe which, with the modification of using deal or other wood instead of bamboo, will be found very convenient, because the whole affair is capable of being taken to pieces in case of removal. The original consists of frames of bamboo bound at the corners and strengthened with cross pieces similarly fastened. Upon these, when built up in the desired form, are stretched pieces of muslin, chintz, or other suitable material forming altogether a light and not inelegant piece of furniture. We have made several similar wardrobes by using frames of deal morticed at the corners, all of one size, say 6ft. long by 2ft. wide, with one cross bar in the centre. Each of these is covered with chintz, either independently or all together, after being set up and united by screws where necessary. Two of the frames are to be united by hinges to form the door, and one frame will form the top and another the bottom. The whole structure is to be placed against a wall, as usual with such pieces of furniture, and it is as well to connect it to the wall by a couple of light stay nails driven in near the top, and screwed to the upper part of the side frames. To make one of these wardrobes, 6ft. long by 2ft. deep and 6ft. high, there will be required seven such frames —one for the top; a second for the bottom, to lie flat on the ground; three for the front, and one at each end—two of the front ones being united by hinges.

Begin by laying down the bottom frame, and screwing it to the floor. The wood may be 2½in. wide and ¾in. thick. Then set up the ends, screwing these to the bottom frame by two 1¼in. screws inserted near the corners. Next put in the top frame, and unite in a similar way to the tops of the end frames. One of the front frames has now to be screwed on at one end, and one at the other, leaving the third central one already hinged as a door, and the framework is complete. When the screw holes are ready made and countersunk, the whole may be thus erected in a few minutes. It has now to be covered with chintz, and if panelled out with red tape tacked on with ornamental brass nails, a very neat wardrobe will result. The top frame should be covered in one piece, and so also should the two end frames respectively. The whole front cannot be so covered on account of the door, but whenever this can be done it should, because the dust will be not only kept out more effectually but the frames can be folded up zigzag fashion, for packing, just as well as if each had its own separate covering. Hanging wardrobes are so costly that a substitute made in this way, although less solid, has its advantages. There are strips of deal sold as SLATERER'S battens of very nearly or quite the same measure as that given, and, as they are sawn by machinery to these standard sizes, they will be cheap and sufficiently good for the purpose. They should be planed on one side and on the edges; the other side will be concealed by the chintz. We have not thought it necessary to detail the making of the frames, as we have already given precise directions for similar work.

It ought not, indeed, to be now a matter of great difficulty to panel the whole with wood, instead of chintz, making a solid desirable wardrobe, the several parts of which may still be made separately, and united by screws, for the sake of portability. This, however, would be a much longer job, and we have described the simpler plan, because it will be within the powers of any amateur, and can be made and put together in a day. These makeshifts are, in fact, frequently of great value, especially in homes which are likely to be but temporary.

Making use of a modern (revived) plan of ornamentation, the chintz may be replaced by canvas, which can be then covered entirely with coloured prints, such as those which appear from time to time in the illustrated newspapers. These are afterwards to be varnished with the same varnish used upon wall papers. If the pictures are well arranged so that the colours harmonise, so as to give some degree of unity to the whole, this method of ornamenting cabinets or screens is sufficiently satisfactory. On the whole, however, we prefer chintz, and this material is of such varied colour and pattern that it can be easily selected to agree with the general tone of the furniture and hangings. It should not, however, be of the same pattern as the curtains. A wardrobe of the above construction may be somewhat improved by attaching strips of moulding along the top to form a kind of cornice, which may be repeated at the floor line. This should also be put on with screws and not nails, so that it can be easily detached. It must be put on outside the chintz, after the whole wardrobe has been put together and covered.

Another way to vary the effect is to stain the framework or varnish it, and then to nail the chintz on the inside of the frames, so that it may appear in panels. This is more effective than to hide the wood.

As we have described the construction of a wardrobe of simple design, a chest of drawers, and also a plain washstand, we shall add a few words descriptive of making that useful article of furniture—a bedstead. The details are almost identical, whether the form is the old-fashioned and well-nigh obsolete four-poster or the half-tester or stump. The first question to be decided is the material, and here we have free choice between the various woods obtainable for the purpose. We have made them once or twice of deal, but it is a bad wood to use, being too soft and not sufficiently rigid. The bolts, by which the framework is fastened together, sink into it, and, if sacking be used, it will be found that the nails which secure it draw out, or, as sometimes happens, the whole strip along which the nails run will split off. Let this wood, therefore, be set aside as unfit for the purpose, and make choice of mahogany, beech, birch, or ash, either of which will answer, and, if well managed, will make a handsome and durable article. First come the legs, of which the front pair, at any rate, ought to be turned, as giving a better finish to the bedstead. If there be no footboard the length of these will not exceed 3ft. allowing from 1ft. to 18in. from the floor to the frame work, and 1½ft. to 2ft. for the depth of the bed clothes. If made, however, to stand up as high as the latter, it will be as well to add a footboard, though it may be omitted. In the latter case the two legs may just as well rise only so far above the frame as to give sufficient strength to the mortices, and the bed clothes will then fall over them and conceal their tops altogether. The two posts for the head of the bed will also depend for length on the proposed pattern. They may be precisely similar in form to those at the foot, and the footboard be nearly as high as the head, which is the pattern of French bedsteads; or they may run to a height of 5ft. or 6ft., and carry a half tester. In the latter case they are seldom turned, but are planed up, their size gradually diminishing towards the upper part, and this may be also done where no lathe is at hand to turn the short legs at the foot. The work of framing the parts together consists wholly of making mor-

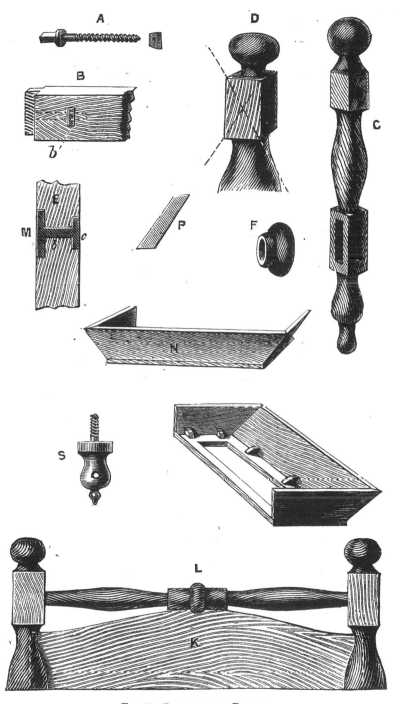

FIG. 50. BEDSTEAD AND DETAILS.

tised and tenoned joints, but these are held by bed screws (Fig. 50 A), each with its own nut. The frame is to be made of wood 4in. wide by 2in. thick, or, if only for a small bedstead, 3in. wide will be sufficient. The squared part of the bed post must not be less than 3in., and therefore the raw material is to be 3½in. thick, previous to planing and turning. It must be accurately squared, and, where it is to be rounded in the lathe, the angles are first to be taken off by means of the spokeshave or draw knife. First of all, therefore, square up the pieces, and, laying them on the bench side by side, set off and rule the several divisions and the mortices, but do not fail to have your design sketched, as a guide, however roughly. Next cut the mortices, which it is better to do before turning the pieces, because they will rest more steadily on the bench than when a part of their length is rounded. Then turn these pieces as accurately as possible, using the callipers, as directed in our work on the lathe. The mortices, remember, will require to be cut in two adjacent sides of each, and marks should at once be made on all, designating their intended position. They must not be deep, and should not run into each other. Three-quarters of an inch will be deep enough, unless the bed is to be of very large size. Next make the holes for the bolts, which must run accurately at right angles to the other face of the work, and should be well in the centre of each mortice. To insure this, draw diagonals, as shown at D, upon the side of the mortice, and also on the opposite side; this may be done with advantage, and also the holes made, before cutting the mortices.

First, on the side opposite the mortice, placing the point of a large centre-bit on the point of intersection of the diagonal lines, cut a recess for the head of the bolt, so that when in place it shall not project beyond the level of the post. Now, with a shell or spoon bit, carry a hole through from the centre of the recess, just large enough to admit the bolt easily, and, to insure its direction, bore it half from one side and half from the other; this was the object in view in marking diagonals on both sides. Next plane up the pieces of frame work to support the sacking or boards. Have them sawn out of the desired scantling, and rather longer than needed, viz., two of about 6ft. long, and two of 5ft. or less, according to the desired width of the bedstead; 6ft. by 5ft. is full size, 5½ft. by 4½ft. is often sold as a double bed, and 6ft. by 3ft. 6in. makes a good single bed. Of course, for a child's cot, any smaller size that may be preferred can be substituted, and a cot is a good article for a beginner, before a larger size is attempted.

Now cut the tenons, fitting them nicely to the mortices, and having put them in their respective places, so that they cannot shift their position, use the shell bit again, passing it through the holes already bored, and carry the hole rather more than the length of the bolt into the side and end pieces. These holes will be in the centres of the several tenons; the dotted lines in B illustrate their position. Now proceed to let in the nut. This is done by cutting with a narrow chisel a deep but small mortice at *b* of B, in which the nut may rest, so that its centre may lie in the centre of the hole already made. The recess must fit the nut as nearly as possible, and this has to be secured and prevented from turning round with the screw by means of a plug of wood fitted into the hole above it and glued into its place. E represents in section the squared part of one of the legs ; M being the mortice, *b* the bolt-hole, *c* the recess for the head. This recess is subsequently concealed by a turned and hollowed plug of wood made to fit tightly into it, like F. It is hollowed to allow the squared part of the iron bolt to lie within it. The bolts can be had from any ironmonger and are made of two general sizes, or perhaps more, but this is not of much importance. They are screwed up by help of a bed key, of which there are two or three patterns, but those of wrought iron are the best, as the cast iron, though cheaper, is brittle, and often breaks under the strain of tightening the bolts.

If there is to be a footboard between the posts it will be better to leave, just below the upper end, a squared part like that at D, through which a bolt may be passed into a turned rod which stretches from post to post. As, however, the foot of the bed, including its board and framework is seldom or never taken apart, this turned rod may be simply inserted in two holes and glued into its place instead of being secured by screws. Its object is to prevent the foot posts from spreading wider apart, so as to suffer the footboard to fall out. L is such a rod, K being the top of the footboard. This latter is supported in a groove cut in each post, and by two iron pins fitting into holes in the lower framework. The grooves cannot well be marked until the legs have been turned, but may be thus contrived. Stick a bradawl into the post at the intended end of the groove, to which attach a piece of string well chalked or blackened with charcoal. Strain it tightly, holding the other end down so that its course marks that of the intended groove ; then, by raising its middle part slightly with the finger and thumb of the other hand, and letting it go suddenly, a perfectly straight line in black or white will be made. Another may be similarly made parallel to it, and the groove chiselled out. Probably the line will not be marked in the deep recesses, but the board will hardly be let in so deeply as to reach these, and even if it be, the line can be drawn along its edge after it is in its place, and lying in the grooves cut in the more projecting parts of the posts. The footboard, however, if preferred, may be held between the lower bar and the upper, instead of being fitted into grooves in the legs, and it is a common practice to attach it securely to the upper bar, which thus forms a top moulding, and is itself mortised into a squared part of the legs, just below the upper knobs.

If the head and foot of the bed are not thus alike, the former may be made of unturned posts, and far less trouble need be taken. Generally speaking, the iron bolts are not recessed in the wood of the legs nor concealed in any way, and the head board is slipped into a groove formed by strips of wood nailed inside the posts. The latter may be carried up to hold a tester, or rather half-tester. To make this part is by no means a very difficult task, unless heavy moulding be desired, which the amateur will hardly be likely to attempt, nor should we advise him to try his hand at veneering, although we shall describe the process in a later page. First decide the size of the tester—about one-third of the whole length of the bed will be wide enough—then make a frame of this outside measure, and let it be of ⅜in. stuff, 3in. wide, well and strongly mortised at the corners. This is to be supported on the top of the two posts by a couple of bed screws passing through it into the posts, in which the nuts must, of course, be imbedded as before. The strain, however, when the curtains are added, being great, it is as well to put on the frame a small iron plate at the two corners, with a central hole for the bolts to pass through ; the plates being attached by wood screws. At all events broad washers should be placed for the bolt head to rest on, and it is a good plan to add two brackets or diagonal iron bars to aid in supporting the tester. These can be made ornamental, if desired. The easiest plan is to leave this plain frame, and merely decorate it by means of a valance and frill of chintz or other material, attached by small black tacks. The proper way is to raise a bevelled frame upon the other, as shown at N. The corners, remember, of the bevelled part are right angles and are to be mitred as usual, but owing to the inclination of the boards, the top and bottom edges must, by means of a bevel, be sloped off, so that the section of the pieces will be a rhomboid like P. This bevelled part is attached to the lower frame by means of blocks (R) glued inside both pieces, and the lower frame, upon which in fact it stands, serves to hold the valance, that is subsequently nailed to its edge. The mitred angles can also be strengthened with blocks glued inside them, as of course these cannot be seen when the tester is in its place. The usual mode of supporting curtains on these half testers is to turn a couple of ornaments similar to S, and screwing them into the flat part of the frame at the angles, so that they form pendants, a hole is made halfway through these, which supports one end of a wooden curtain rod, the opposite end of which rests in a similar hole or recess made in the upper part of the bedstead. These pendants give a neat and handsome finish to the bedstead, besides affording a support to the curtain rod ; and, being very simple and easy to turn, are preferable to any hook or other appliance by which sometimes a rod of iron is supported. Wooden rings can be turned or bought at pleasure.

CHAPTER V.

FOURTH LESSON.

Hot Water Plant Case—Lamp Heated Plant Cases—Garden Frames—Greenhouses.

WE shall now try to turn our newly-acquired knowledge of carpentry to the construction of cases, frames, and greenhouses for indoor and outdoor use. Of the first are contrivances to be used with a lamp or with hot water— some of which are patented—but as the *principle* of obtaining heat in this way is as old as the discovery of lamps and kettles, and cannot, there- fore, be made the subject of a patent, we shall set to work in our own way, and construct such cases of any pattern that may suit our present purpose. It will be found convenient to have the stand of an indoor case for plants quite distinct and separate from the case itself. The simplest form is that of the framework of a table (Fig. 51, A.), with neatly turned legs, which should be strong but not clumsy—stained deal, mahogany, or any other wood will answer. This should not be of less size than 2ft. 6in. high, 3ft. long, and 18in. or 20in. wide; the legs of 2in. stuff, after planing, the frame of ¾in. stuff, and the mortices must be well made, so that the whole frame may be stiff and substantial. To render the stand even more strong, it may be wholly or partially boarded at the bottom. We prefer to board this entirely, and then to lay sand upon it, which will catch any accidental drippings of water from the pots, and preserve the carpet. This, however, will chiefly depend on the details of construction.

The front of the frame is constructed to receive a drawer, which drawer is a rectangular zinc tank for hot water, 2½in. deep. Now, in order to keep this really hot, we may advantageously make use of the principle of the Norwegian cases, viz., surround it with non-conducting material on all sides but the top—the tank, be it understood, is made quite close, with only one screwed hole by which it may be filled. For a first-rate case, therefore, nail inside this frame a lining of half-inch (or less) board, attaching it to the squared part of the legs, so as to leave an intermediate space, which is to be closely packed with coarse wool. A layer of felt is to be attached to the inside of the lower board, upon which should lie a second or lining

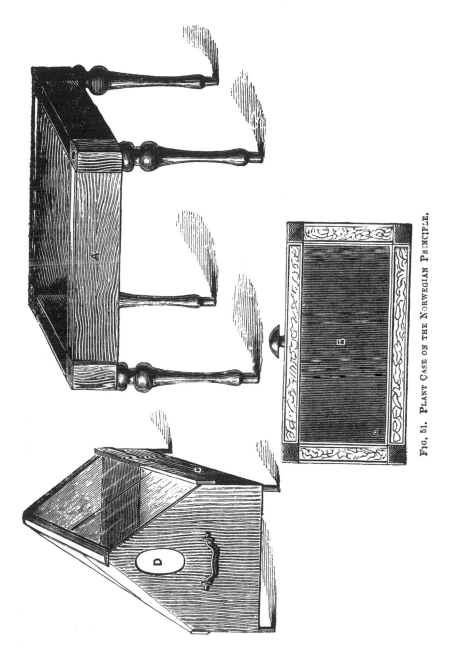

FIG. 51. PLANT CASE ON THE NORWEGIAN PRINCIPLE.

board, to enable the water tank to slide in with greater facility. If preferred, or thought easier, a wooden drawer to fit the tank, but with room at the bottom for a layer of wool, and also at the front, sides, and back, can be substituted for the above, the object being simply to have plenty of non-conducting substances round the tank, to sustain its temperature so that it shall not require to be filled more than once in twelve, or even twenty-four hours, by which the necessity for a lamp—a manifest advantage—can be avoided.

The unscientific reader may be told, in order that he may thoroughly understand what he is about, that the woollen coverings we wear, and in which this hot water case is to be enveloped, are not designed to keep out the cold, but to keep in the warmth; that substances, if bright, reflect, and if dark or rough, radiate heat on all sides, and this radiation we want to prevent. So fully is the prevention carried out in the Norwegian cooking stoves, that a joint partially cooked and transferred to one of them will actually complete the process by means of its own already acquired heat, without being exposed to the action of any fire or lamp. Suppose, for instance, that we have a joint of meat boiling "fast and furious" in a saucepan, if we could insure the continuance of the heat after removing it from the fire, the joint would go on cooking as before. Now by placing it in a case in which, on all sides, is a very thick layer of wool, sawdust, or other non-conducting material, the boiling heat can thus be retained. The Norwegian cases are made double on all sides, with 3in. to 6in. of non-conducting material—including a close-fitting cover, also double, and similarly fitted, and by their means it is easy to keep soup, meat, or any other food, quite hot for many hours together. This principle we are now applying to the plant case, and, if we cared for a patent, we might, so far as we know, lay absolute claim to the application, for we have never, ourselves, seen such an arrangement, although common sense would suggest it.

In the continuance of our description, we shall suppose the lining inside the lower framework, as well as the front of wooden drawer—the plan of the whole being shown at B, in which the tank is shaded. The drawer, it will be seen, is made as usual, but with a partition running lengthwise 2in. or so from the front. As the requirement is not so much great heat as constant warmth well sustained, we should even lay a piece of flannel over the top of the tank, when it is in its place, as sufficient warmth will still rise from its upper surface. Lying upon cleats attached to the inside of the stand, above the drawer and tank, a shallow tray is to rest, the bottom of which consists of merely one or two bars, on which is attached a piece of wire netting of the smallest mesh obtainable; this is to support the pots. Thus the tank can be removed for filling, and replaced without moving any of the plants. It is not absolutely necessary to make this frame movable, a stiff trellis of wire may, instead, be nailed on the top of the stand, but, if so, there should be a light framework standing up— merely such as a couple of wires, strained on upright pillars, to prevent any accidental capsize of a pot when the glass top is lifted off in order to water or prune the plants.

The construction of this glass covering now demands attention. It may be made as ornamental as the capabilities and taste of the maker may avail to accomplish, but it must, at all events, be sufficiently strong and light—the latter quality enabling it to be lifted off entire, which, in a case of the size given, is the better plan.

To begin with, a frame the size of that forming the upper part of the stand, not less than 3in. deep, will be required, and this should be dovetailed together and then secured with long brads, in case the glue should be affected by moisture. If not firmly put together, there will be a smash of glass some day. The material must be the same as that of the stand, and at least three-quarter stuff when planed. Handles should be attached at each end. This frame is marked C. The ends are to be carried up in the form of a gable, and a strip must be fastened on the top of each, as shown. These gables must also be rebated on the inside, and a fillet, by preference moulded, must be attached by sprigs to the upper edge of C., so as to stand up and form also a rebate. Sheets of glass—three on each side —will now form the double span roof resting in their rebates and against the upper bar. Practically this is by far the best plan, as it is also the easiest to manage for a plain case of this kind. Ventilation is readily arranged by partially lifting one or more of the glasses out of contact with the upper bar, and inserting a small wedge of cork. But, at the same time, a sufficiency of air is generally insured by the very fact of the glass being left quite loose, instead of being puttied into the rebates. The handles should be attached as high as possible, so as not to make the frame with its glasses top heavy, or it may topple over when lifted off. It is, however, but seldom that it will be necessary to do more in this respect than lift out the sheets of glass, as every plant can thus be reached quite easily. As regards the slope, the peak of the gable may be 9in. above the top edge of the frame. The easiest way to secure the latter is by four pins at the lower corners made to fit into holes on the top of the legs of the stand, or the latter may have a moulded fillet running round it to form a rebate inside which the upper frame will fit securely. It may then be further secured by brass hooks and eyes. This case will hold about seventy 3-in. pots, if made of the dimensions given (inside measure); viz., six rows of twelve, supposing them to be packed tightly; but one or two less will be found more convenient. Cuttings will strike readily, and seeds of tender annuals will rapidly germinate in such a case as described, and the whole will furnish a most interesting and profitable source of pleasure when there is little that can be done in the way of outdoor gardening. As regards appearance, one or two additions not difficult to carry out will decidedly improve matters. The upper bar of the gable, for instance, may be moulded on each side, and thus brought to a sharp or rounded edge above, and to this can be attached a strip of zinc or very thin wood cut into an ornamental shape to form an elegant ridge. The sides, too, of the gable may be of glass, instead of being made of wood. Rebated bars will, of course, in that case be needed at the angles, and the various difficulties of bevilled framing must be encountered. The end glasses should in such a case be considered fixtures, and secured in their respective rebates by putty. To avoid having to make the framework, this plan may be varied by cutting out an oval piece in each gable, and inserting a sheet of glass like D. It may, nevertheless, be remarked, that the object of the whole case is use rather than ornament.

To show what a very simple contrivance will answer as a heated case for plants, we may describe one from which we obtained all our verbenas last spring. We first hunted up an old box about 2ft. 6in. long, and half as wide, or less ; the depth being 9in. Into this we put a false bottom of wire netting, leaving the lower part 3in. deep ; the upper part 6in. Then with a knife, keyhole saw, or some such instrument, we cut in front a little doorway, into which we could barely get our hand. On the wire netting we laid a few crocks, and then a layer of cocoa-nut fibre and moss, upon and imbedded into which we set our little thumb pots filled with cuttings. We then laid pieces of glass all over the top of the box clear of the cuttings. Now for the heat—a simple night light ! one of those which stand in a saucer of water. This was put in at the little door and safely shut up. Our only difficulty was, that exactly above it the heat was too great and scorched the cuttings, but we simply left over it a blank space, and that small source of heat sufficed to warm the air throughout the lower part of the case, and the cuttings grew marvellously well. As to moisture, we had quite enough from the damp earth in the pots, so that there was a constant dew over the under surface of the glass. The cost of fuel was of course infinitesimal, and we were at liberty to double the " grate surface," as engineers would call it, by inserting a second night light.

We will now describe a better class of lamp-heated case. The lower part or stand is made much as before, but the frame above the legs is considerably deeper. It should be not less than 1ft. The front is solid like the sides, but is made to take out, or at any rate a part is so made for the insertion of the lamp by which it is heated. This need not now be made double, as the supply of heat is continuous ; it may, however, if cost is no great object, be preferably lined with tin, because this will aid the powers of the lamp by reflecting the heat which it produces on all sides, and thus warming more effectually this air space below the pots, represented in Fig. 52 by the letter A—the drawing showing the case in section. The upper part B., is, as before, a tray with a wire bottom, over which is to be placed a few crocks, and then moss or cocoa fibre, into which the pots can be plunged, and which can be made damp at pleasure by watering from a very fine-rosed watering pot. Running across the bottom of this tray, from side to side, is a strip of wood 3in. wide, and in its centre, towards the front, is bored a hole 2in. in diameter, into which is fitted a chimney of zinc or sheet iron, with a folded or riveted seam made without solder, and in which are punched a number of holes for the escape of heated air ; through these the sooty fumes will *not* escape, because the current of hot air through the glass chimney of the lamp will suffice to carry them clear of the case and its contents—for this metal chimney is to go through the glass roof entirely, because the fumes of a lamp are fatal to the constitution of all plants. This is, indeed, the grand difficulty of using lamps to obtain heat. In all cases such lamps must be stood under a flue or chimney, and by the latter it happens of necessity that a great deal of heat escapes and is wasted. If the flue be bent, as in A., so as to lie horizontally as it passes across inside the case, the bulk of the heat is saved, but in that case it sadly interferes with the plants, and takes up room which is too valuable to be sacrificed. If the flue be painted a dead black, it will radiate a considerable amount of

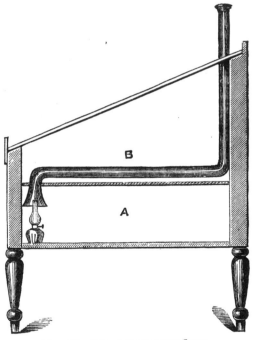

FIG. 52. PLANT CASE WITH LAMP.

heat into the case, and this is the utmost we can compel such flue to do towards heating our miniature greenhouse. We have, indeed, devised a plan in which the lamp passes through an annular cistern of water, keeping it at a tolerably high temperature, but experience proves that such compound and complicated contrivances cause more trouble than they are worth, and although in certain particulars they are a source of gain, it is on the whole better to sacrifice a certain amount of heat, instead of resorting to them on the score of economy.

This case which, it is intended, is for practical work, and not a show case for the drawing room, had better be constructed of the form shown, *i.e.*, with

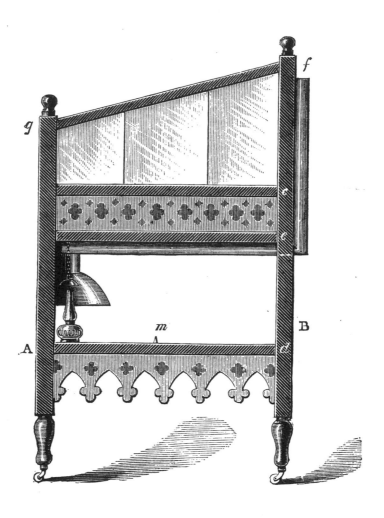
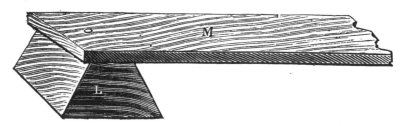

Fig. 53. Lamp-Heated Plant Case.

a simple lean-to roof of glass, and the sheets of the latter should be puttied into their beds, with the exception, perhaps, of the central one. To supply air for the lamp, a bit of perforated zinc should be inserted near it in the back of the case.

In Fig. 52 A, we have sketched the best position for a horizontal flue, namely, along the bottom of the plant tray, from which it turns up the back of the case, being surmounted by a little cap where it passes through it. In this way all the heat possible to be gained will be saved—the flue, nevertheless, will take nearly the room of one row of pots. It is hardly worth while to make a case of this sort so small as that in which a hot water tank is used, and, consequently, it will be better to give it at once the form of a schoolmaster's desk, carrying up the back legs to the ridge, and panelling the triangular space above the tray with wood or glass. The front had also better be made as two separate frames, each capable of being lifted off or raised at pleasure. If they are hinged, let it be in front, and then they can be raised at the upper part, and wedged open when it may be necessary to give more air to the plants. In this case let the hinges be such as will allow the lights to hang down entirely in front of the case when it is required to change the pots, water them, or do any extensive work among them. A case 4ft. long by 2ft. wide, carefully constructed, will be found of great practical use; and if sufficient depth be given to the lower part, the horizontal flue may be made to lie altogether below the plant tray, where it will increase the bottom heat and be out of sight, as well as out of the way of the pots. Smaller cases can only have a plain vertical flue.

Fig. 53 is another design somewhat different in arrangement, and in which is an attempt at decoration, by means of perforated zinc panels and cornices. The construction is as follows, and will be understood from the drawing of one end only of the case :—A B, the legs, the front pair 3ft. 6in. high to 4ft. ; the back pair 5ft. 6in. to 6ft. A good proportion for a case 3ft. wide will be 4ft. high in front and 5ft. at the back ; this will not give too sharp an angle to the glass top, which will slope as in the drawing. A case of this height will be large enough for a good collection of plants—will, in fact, be a regular window conservatory if made in front 4ft. 6in. to 6ft. wide. Exact proportions will depend upon the space to be afforded to the case in the room or hall in which it is to stand, and the best plan is to measure such space, and then draw a rough plan to scale, making the whole of elegant proportions. It will then be at once seen whether the case is likely to have a good appearance, as also whether the slope from back to front is too sharp, or otherwise. The front legs, at least, should be turned as shown, and it will be all the better if the others are decorated in the same way, but the amateur may possibly have a lathe too short in the bed for work of this kind ; we ourselves, however, in such a case rig up a couple of bars of wood as an extra length of bed—at any rate it is easy to get the work done, and it is not costly.

At d, e, c, f, and g, cross bars or rails are to be mortised into the legs all round, so as to build up a kind of framed cage. On these bars will rest, first at the level of d, a plain board, on which the lamp is to stand. This will only be required to extend a few inches, at any rate not more than half across, e.g., from A to m, the rest being open, so that the hand and arm can enter to adjust the lamp under its hood and chimney. At the level of e, is to rest, as before, a wire frame, or bars of iron. If wire be used, two or three stays will be needed to keep it stiff and level. Between e and c will be the crocks and moss for the pots to stand on, and to conceal these a narrow panel of zinc, perforated with ornamental holes is to be placed. A similar panel, not shown in the drawing, is to be inserted between e and d. The lamp flue is to be carried across the upper part of this division, and thence to the upright tube at the back. Immediately over the lamp a piece of tinned iron is to be suspended, to which a slightly cupped form has been given like a very shallow scale pan, or saucer. This will prevent the more intense heat from rising direct into the case above, which will not be much warmer just over the lamp than it is elsewhere. This hollowed disc is to be suspended by a link of iron wire, and must not be so near the lamp as to cause it to smoke. A disc of talc, to be had of any lampmaker, will answer even better than tin. The arrangement is shown at L on a larger scale. The flue should preferably be flat and shallow like M, to extend the heating surface in a horizontal direction. It must be merely folded and not soldered, and should be painted dead black.

The case described, if of the full size here given will require a lamp at from 3s. 6d. to 5s. to heat it *thoroughly* in mid winter, but one at 1s. will impart warmth enough for most purposes, as it is well not to overheat and thus cause the plants to grow up weak and delicate. If a narrow panel similar to that between e and c, be inserted along the upper part of the back of the case, which may otherwise be panelled with board, there will always be plenty of ventilation. Below the line A, d, is represented a hanging cornice of zinc, cut into any desired pattern. This can be replaced by a strip of gilt or lacquered brass cornice, to be had of any upholsterer, and which will give a handsome finish to the case if the rest of it be painted green. Gilt knobs can be also placed on the tops of the four legs, and castors will be convenient below; in fact, the various cornices now made of stamped and gilded brass, of all widths and patterns, will enable a case of this kind to be made handsome enough for any drawing room, and at a very small cost. If the stand, instead of being painted green, be carefully got up in white, with merely green lines here and there, and borders of stamped brass as stated, it will be even more elegant, and the rich green of the plants will then give more effect to the whole. The panel e, c, may also be made deeper to hide the pots themselves, showing only the moss.

We now pass on to outdoor cases or frames and greenhouses, on which the amateur may exercise his art with great satisfaction. We have ourselves built a greenhouse, even to the laying the bricks, and speak from experience. First, as to size. Of course, in regard to this item, all depends upon the number of plants to be accommodated, and whether or no the proposed house is to fit a given recess. We will, however, suppose a small

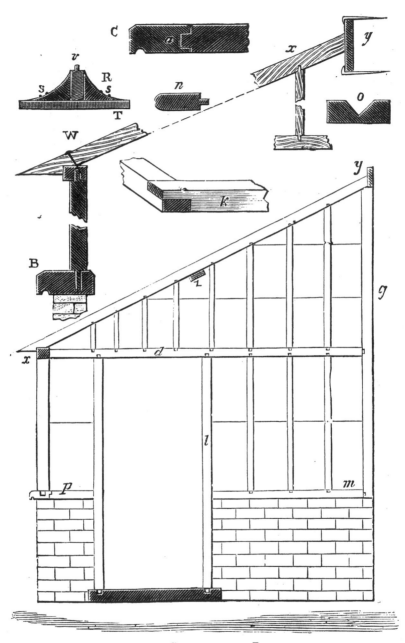

FIG. 54. GREENHOUSE AND DETAILS.

house sufficient, 12ft. by 8ft., and that it is to be a lean-to, advantage
being taken of some available blank wall to form the back, which will
effect a considerable saving of cash in its construction. Now if it be
wished to make the house sufficiently high in front to enable a person
to stand upright close to the windows—i.e., 6ft. high—a back wall 10ft. in
height will be needed, or the roof will lie too flat. If, therefore, such a
wall cannot be commanded, you must be content with less head room in
front; and if there is to be a wide stand in that part for pots, 6ft. will not
be needed, though it can still be obtained in one way, viz., by lowering the
floor and stepping down into the house. This, however, we do not
ourselves like. If you are much restricted in this way make the house
narrower, and at most go down but one step into it, taking care that there
you have efficient drainage, so that the house shall not be damp.

In the plan, or elevation rather, of the end in which the door is made,
and which is drawn to scale, the general arrangement is shown. The
width is thus divided: front shelf, 14in. wide; door posts, each 3in.;
doorway, 2ft. 6in.; leaving a width of 3ft. 10in. beyond the door. The
front and back upright are included in this measurement. This will allow
280 6in. pots on the shelves, of which there will be four, the length of
the house, on the main stand, each 14in. wide, and forming a flight of
steps, besides that in front. Each such shelf will take two rows of pots
of the size named. Then there is left the floor space, and in addition, if
required, a single or double row of narrow shelves may run along the front,
and similar ones at the sides of the house. Three hundred pots will give
a great deal of work—quite as much as most people would care to do single
handed—and a much smaller house, say 8ft. by 5ft. will allow a sufficient
store for many a small garden, such as we commonly meet with in towns.

However, we shall go on describing a greenhouse of the size first named,
viz., 12ft. by 8ft., 6ft. high in front, and 10ft. at the back. First of all a
brick wall will be needed, 2ft. 6in. high, and one brick thick, which will equal
9in. These should be laid with good mortar, or even cement. The space
for the doorway—3ft. in all, must be left—and unless local reasons exist
for a different arrangement, that shown will be the most suitable. The
first bit of carpentry necessary is the preparation of the wall plates, which
lie upon the top of the brickwork, and into which are mortised the
uprights between the sashes. This wall plate is to be not less than 4in.,
and may be preferably 5in. or 6in. wide, by 3in. deep, and should overhang the brickwork, and be planed up to section, B, Fig. 54, a groove being
ploughed under the over-hanging edge to cause the rain to drip clear
of the wall. It may thus, if required, be conducted by an open iron trough
to a pipe at one corner, saving, what is of great importance, the bed outside from the incessant and deleterious drip of the rain. Into this plate,
taking the front one first, will have to be mortised five uprights, each of
3in. stuff, to complete the front frame in which the swinging lights are to
be fitted. As we have a wall 2ft. 6in. high, a wall plate 3in. thick, and
there will be another 3in. plate above, the inside measure of the window

frames will be 3ft. in height, by 2ft. 8¼in. in width, and there will be four lights of this size. This front should be fitted complete in the workshop, the mortices cut quite through and pinned with oak or ash pins.

Leaving the sashes for the present, we may proceed with the framing of the house. Let the wall plate of the front part overlap slightly at each end, in order to allow the side plates to be notched a little way into it, as shown at a of figure C. Leave a similar projection also in the upper plate. The framing of the side in which the door is placed may next be made. The upper bar d, of 3in. stuff, must be planed up truly, and mortices cut for the door posts. It will lie upon the top plate of the front frame, but each must be half lapped like k, so as to lie flush with one another. If this should cut the tenon of the front corner upright it will do no harm, provided it is pinned securely, because no part can shift at all after the house is once fixed. The other end of d is to be mortised into the high upright g, which is to be clamped to the wall by two or three wall hooks. The bottom of this will be mortised into the wall plate m, and this in turn into the door post l. p is to be mortised into the other door post, and notched into the front plate, as seen at C, or let in with a very short tenon. At the bottom of the door posts should be a sill of oak, into which they must be mortised to a short depth. m and d above it, have also to be mortised to support three sash bars of section n, to receive the glass. m can also be rebated, but it will be easier to attach strips. Even these are not essential — many houses being glazed so that the sheets of glass have no lap,—any chance air way being left for ventilation. Sometimes d and m are, however, grooved instead of being rebated, so that the glass is slipped in at the top and bottom. There is no real necessity for this. The easiest way to make the bar n is to take strips of clean deal, free from knots, 1in. thick and 2in. wide, plane them up parallel, rebate each side, and then bevel off as shown, or mould if preferred. For a job of this kind lay on the bench a plank 2in. thick, on which the strips can be secured by little blocks cut out with a V-shaped notch, like o. The moulded, bevelled, or rebated strips can be set on edge in these, and thus be retained sufficiently to permit the plane to work upon them. They may with equal facility be blocked up on each side with separate pieces tacked to the plank. This is shown at R, s, s, being the supporting blocks, v the sash bar, T the plank to be laid upon the bench. Such a plank will often be found useful, and a nice level one should be set aside for the purpose. The opposite end of the greenhouse will require no special description, as it will be identical with that of which details have been given, except that it will need no doorway.

We may now, therefore, proceed to the roof, bars, and sashes. The long bar at each angle, marked x y, should be strong, and likewise one or two of the intermediate ones; the rest may be lighter. A tie bar or stay (z) should run across from side to side, to give stiffness to the whole. W x y show on a larger scale the method of arranging these rafters; y is a wall plate, 2in. thick and 5in. wide, held by iron hooks to the wall; W x is the rafter abutting against the plate, to which it is securely nailed. The other end is notched, as seen at W, over the front plate, and secured by being nailed to it. The larger rafters may be 2in. thick and 4in. wide. The others are 1½in. thick and the same width or depth, as we prefer glazing at once upon these rafters to having sliding top lights. The section of all these rafters should be the same as n, the rebated part being, of course, placed on the top to receive the sheets of glass, which in this part of the house must lap over each other half an inch to keep out the rain.

In order to fit rafters either in this or any similar case, they have evidently to be cut at the ends to a particular angle dependent on the respective height of the front and back walls. This is best done by first of all cutting out as a guide, a strip of half inch board, for instance, about 4in. wide and the exact length of a rafter, the ends of which are bevelled as required. This can be laid on each rafter, which can then be marked and sawn off. To get the right angle for this guide the bevel A, Fig. 55, can be used, the back set against the wall as shown, while the blade rests upon the edge of the board. This will be the angle, therefore, at which the end is to be cut. The bevel can then be used at the other end in a similar way. The square will do equally well, if the piece of board be held in position while being marked. Allow length enough, however, so that if on trial the strip does not seem to bed fairly on the wall plates it may be trimmed more precisely with a sharp paring chisel. The upper end of all rafters is a simple slope, but the lower end is notched out like C, in most cases, so that the rafter may project any required distance beyond the front wall plate. In a greenhouse, however, it is better to let each rafter end on the plate like D, and as this plate projects slightly beyond the face of the front wall and sashes, an open shoot below it will carry off the rain water. The plate, however, must be grooved out underneath like the lower one, or the water will not escape in this way, but will have a tendency to run back on the under side of the plate. Great care should be taken to keep the rafter level, or the glazing will be more difficult, and when it is done it will be up and down, and thoroughly unworkmanlike. The length of each rafter may be stated at 11ft. or thereabout, and they ought not to bend, "sag," with the weight of 21oz. glass (i.e., 21oz. to the square foot) with which the roof should be glazed. To insure their stiffness, nevertheless, it is better to put a cross stay, as indicated, about the middle, securing it to the main rafters at each end of the house, and to the larger intermediate ones. Two uprights may then be placed underneath it, and let into the floor, giving efficient support to the roof, and these can be made useful in supporting the stand for flowers. They may also serve for training any one of the climbing plants, as the passion flower or canary creeper. As all the rafters will be equally deep, though not equally thick, this cross stay will support them all alike. When the roof is glazed, it will be necessary to have a strip of sheet lead closely attached to the wood plate against the wall, and wide enough to overlap the glass about 3in., to prevent the rain from making its way into the house. This lead must extend a little beyond the ends of the roof, and be laid down over them as closely as possible. In glazing the two ends of such a greenhouse the sheets of glass will lie in the rebates of the upright bars, and will abut against each other, but not lap; at least such is a common practice. If they are preferred to lap, which is the only way to keep out a *driving* rain, let a sprig be put in under each as it is put in place—before it is puttied, so that it shall not be able to slip downwards from its own weight. Another way to prevent this slipping from taking place, before the putty becomes dry and hard, is to put in the lowest sheet of glass first, and then bend over it a bit of window lead about a couple of inches long, turning up again the end which hangs outside so as to give the whole the form of an S. The second glass will rest in the outer loop of this, and as the lead is thin it can be readily unbent and drawn out after the putty has become hard. One reason against lapping the front and side glasses is that there soon accumulates in each lap a thick coat of green fungi, mosses, and dirt, which eventually looks untidy, and, in addition, keeps out not a little light. If the sheets, on the contrary, are cut clean and straight, and simply abut on each other, the joint will be close enough for all practical purposes, and have a much better appearance.

The front sashes are not very difficult to make, being simply of strips of clean deal, 2½in. wide, rebated like picture frames and mortised. The intermediate bars, also rebated to receive the glass, need not be above half or three-quarters of an inch thick at most, and 1¼in. wide. They need only be tenoned about half an inch at each end, as they cannot get loose. In old-fashioned greenhouses there were added cross bars at, perhaps, 9in. distance, or even less, so that a house of this kind might have almost as well borne the name of a wooden house as a glass one. It was the same in the residences of all classes, but was found to be a very bad way and to entail much useless expenditure of labour, to say nothing of most effectually shutting out an immense proportion of daylight—crossbars are now seldom, if ever, used, and if they should appear necessary to aid in stiffening a large sash, they are put as widely asunder as possible. Long narrow strips of glass are for all purposes the best to use, and the distance between the upright bars can be regulated accordingly. Wide and large panes become more costly because of breakages, which are sure to occur with unfortunate frequency. If the amateur should prefer such a course (and unless he is a pretty sure hand it may be a wiser plan), he can buy these front lights ready made and glazed almost as cheaply as he can make them. When living in the neighbourhood of Gloucester, in which town were then steam joinery works, we ourselves purchased a set for a house we had erected, at 5s. 6d. for each front light, and 7s. 6d. for the top ones. They were about 3ft. by 2ft. 6in., and 9ft. by 2ft. 6in., so far as we can remember. But no doubt, like all building material, the price would now be much higher — probably 7s. 6d. and 10s. at least. The

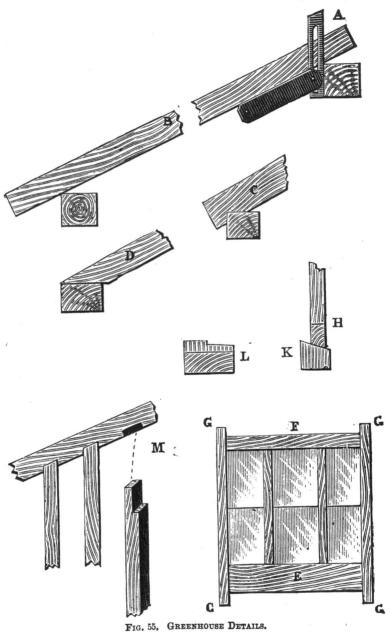

FIG. 55. GREENHOUSE DETAILS.

advantage, however, of having a hanging sash well made is great, for badly fitted mortices, needing perhaps corner clamps of iron within a few months, to prevent them from falling to pieces, are apt to put a young workman considerably out of conceit with the noble art of carpentry and joinery, to say nothing of damping, to some extent, his pleasure in horticultural affairs. At the same time such work as this is excellent practice, and should not if possible be "shied" at. Neither is it really very difficult work if such directions as we have already given, be closely attended to. Use the mortice gauge, compasses, and rule unsparingly with that *sine quâ non* the square. Let chisels be sharp as razors, and cut every mortice with care and deliberation, and you will succeed. The mortices should be one-third the width of the pieces used to make the lights, *i.e.*, if the stuff be an inch and a half thick by two and a half wide, the mortices, being cut in the thickness, will be just half-an-inch wide, leaving a similar width on each side. The bottom piece, however, of the light should be 3in. wide, and it will make the work stronger if these be the tenoned pieces. In the light given in the drawing, the top as well as the bottom is shown as made broader than the sides, to give better hold to the hinges—say 2½in. at the top, 3in. at bottom, and 2in. for the sides. The mortices are cut in the side pieces, and remember to leave these at least an inch too long until all are glued up, pinned, and dry. Then saw off level, and when planing up the lower piece E, chamfer it slightly like H, as also the wall plate seen in section at K; or, which will answer as well, let the wall plate remain as it is, and tack on, in each division a chamfered and rebated slip of wood like L, for the sash to shut and bed against. It will often be found that such details are omitted, or only very partially carried out, but a little extra trouble at the outset will be repaid by the snugness and neatness of the green-house.

It has, no doubt, been noticed in this description that there is no provision for ventilation—the usual sliding top sashes being wholly omitted. The reason for this is two-fold; first, it would add to the difficulty of building such house, and, secondly we have often found it a great drawback to make top-lights move at all. They require special apparatus in the way of ropes and pulleys to work them, are heavy and awkward to move, and very often, indeed, allow rain to penetrate. Hence it is a boon to get rid of them altogether. Two or three different modes have been devised, by which ventilation can be arranged. In the orchard houses, as they are called, patented by Sir Joseph Paxton, Rivers, and others, which are glasshouses on a large scale, and generally without front lights—the sashes reach in one slope from the ridge of the roof to the ground, or to a wall plate laid on a very low front wall, up to the level of which the soil outside is generally raised. These sashes are alternately broad and narrow, and the latter, being hinged like doors or French casements, may be opened singly or simultaneously by an arrangement of levers, giving thereby complete ventilation all over the house. Generally no artificial heat is used, the object being to protect fruit trees, and insure a crop without any great amount of actual forcing. All kinds of garden crops, however, are, of course, forwarded by being thus grown under shelter. This mode of ventilation we have not provided for in our present plan. But supposing the greenhouse to be, as designed, a lean-to, and the back wall not that of a dwelling house, it will suffice to put a few perforated bricks—or a perforated and a solid one alternately, just below the top wall plate, with a flap shutter to each—or a shutter that will take more than one, and which can be closed at pleasure; a single shutter the whole length will do almost as well, as it can be opened wholly or partially, according to the temperature. If always kept open it will hardly be found too much, for more plants are destroyed by damp and want of air than by the admission of the latter in undue quantity. When, however, the back wall is so situated as to render impossible the mode of ventilation we have described, panes of perforated zinc may be inserted in lieu of glass, in the upper part of the two ends of the house. Such zinc plates can be obtained finely perforated, and we have used them constantly, without any kind of shutter or flap to cover them. A very simple plan, however, which will give full power of increasing or diminishing the air space at pleasure, is to insert a cross bar between any two of the upright ones, so as to form a rebated frame, in which can be inserted either a pane of glass or a sheet of perforated zinc, either of which can be instantly secured by a button, and in very hot weather both can be laid aside, and the frame or frames left completely open. There are also to be obtained—but we cannot now recall the address of the maker—iron frames, fitted with Venetian shutters of glass. These shutters are slips of plate glass, about 2in. wide, set at each end into a metal socket, which is hinged at its centre, turning in fact upon a pin. By a simple arrangement, similar to that adopted in the larger Venetian blinds of wood, the slips can be made either slightly to overlap each other and fall down close, so as to form a single pane, or to open more or less widely asunder, so as to admit a current of air between them. We have had them in use in a dwelling house, made of the size of the ordinary panes in the windows of the room—one of these panes in fact has only to be removed, and the ventilator inserted in its place. This would answer our present purpose well. Like all patents there is in this case the drawback of expense, and the perforated zinc will answer quite as well.

The door of a greenhouse will be found as easy, or easier to make than a common panelled door. The styles and rails will only have to be rebated instead of being grooved in the upper part, the lower half being made, as usual, wholly of wood.

To set up such a house, first get the brick walls raised to the necessary height. Then lay on the front frame, wall plates, and all together, this being arranged in the workshop, and the mortices pegged, but the pegs not cut off, so that, if necessary, any part may be removed. Having set up the frame in its place, tack on a couple of temporary rafters as holdfasts, just a couple of planks or strips of quartering, not cut to length notched out, but held in place on the wall plate and top bars of the front frame by a couple of nails, so as to prevent the frame shifting. Then arrange the wall plate on one side, notching it into the front one and letting it into the wall after cutting a hole for that purpose. Now set up the uprights, which fit into mortices in this wall plate, and put on in a similar way the horizontal beam or bar which answers to the front plate—an upright rebated sash bar, remember, is needed close to the wall to take the last sheet of glass. This may be held by staples to the wall, if the horizontal bars be mortised into it, but if it be itself mortised into the upper and lower plate this will not be necessary, as it cannot shift its position. This side being thus raised, proceed with the opposite one, so as to erect the house to the general level of the front upper wall plate, pinning all the side tenons and mortices. Next proceed to cut the rafters to length and to the proper angle, as already described; but you cannot yet put up the two larger ones at the angle permanently, as you have to mark the places for the upright sash bars above the wall plate, to be mortised into them, using the bevel to insure their being correctly placed, i.e., perpendicularly. You can, if you like, however, in respect of these vertical sash bars at the ends of the house, mortise them into the top plate, and merely notch them into the sloping rafter like M, using the half lapped joint. They will be almost as firm as if mortised into both the plates and rafters, and some work will be also saved, for mortising is rather a tiresome operation if there is much to be fitted in this way. Having got up the corner rafters as directed, nothing is left but to put up the intermediate ones; first the heavy, then the lighter ones; each being now securely nailed to the wall plate at the back, and to the top bar of the front frame. Take great care to get them all level above, not caring so much about the under side. After all is in place, every bit of wood must have a coat of priming, and one of lead paint *before* putting the glass in its place; after which a second and third coat of colour, generally white, is laid on. Before this final painting, the front sashes are to be hinged on, if not previously done. Grease the screws by which the hinges are to be affixed, because it will prevent them from rusting, in case the sashes should need to be removed, which is very often the case with new ones, which frequently need replaning and refitting after the wood has been exposed to the action of the weather. For this reason, too, it is the best plan only to put two screws in each wing of the hinges at first, adding the third and fourth (if a large one with four holes) after you have had the greenhouse in use six months or so.

The irons, by which the windows are kept open to any desired degree, need no special description, as they can be inspected anywhere. The simplest are the best—a mere flat bar hinged to the bottom of the sash, and having holes about 3in. apart which fit over a pin in the window frame. This description of a greenhouse appears somewhat lengthy, but there were details into which we felt it absolutely necessary to enter, because ultimate success depends in this, as in other cases of the kind, on attention to what may appear minor particulars. We have had, in short, ample experience of a house in which the ambition of the amateur who built it exceeded very considerably his own powers of carpentry. The mortices are all strengthened, even at the corners of the hanging sashes, with angle plates of iron to prevent falling asunder—and wherever a leak was possible there it is—we hope our readers will do much better work.

CHAPTER VI.

ROUGH CURVED WORK—BENDING BY STEAM—VICE FOR CURVED WORK, &c.—CUTTING CURVES WITH SWEEP SAW—BUILT UP CURVED WORK—THE ELLIPSE—METHOD OF DESCRIBING AN ELLIPSE—THE TRAMMEL.

IT does not of course always happen that the work of the carpenter is bounded by straight lines. Not in wheels only, but in a number of other articles which fall under his hands in the ordinary way of business, he finds himself under the necessity of cutting out pieces of wood of varying curvature. If he combine the two trades of wheelwright and carpenter, and does an extensive business under the former head, it is probable that he will purchase his felloes roughly cut out at the steam saw mill, and confine himself to further finishing and fitting them together. If, however, his trade be more limited, he will rough out these at his own saw pit with the usual felloe saw already described, with which he will also cut out any articles of large size requiring curvature. The backs of chairs for instance, are cut with a similar saw, from a thick plank of suitable wood—beech, ash, birch or mahogany, in sets, and are subsequently finished to the required pattern. Besides this general plan, however, some of the larger work of this kind is produced by baking or by steaming the boards and bending them while still hot over cauls, or pattern blocks of cast iron. The chairs advertised as " Austrian bent wood " are thus steamed and worked, the advantage consisting in the fact that the grain of the wood follows the sweep of the curve, and the fibres are not cut across. This heating of the material gives it a pliancy far beyond what would be expected ; and where powerful apparatus is at hand to force the work into the required shape, tolerably thick pieces may be thus bent, and when cold will retain the form given to them. As a rule, however, a vast number of curved works are produced by the aid of the sweep or turn saw, such as the legs and claws of pillar tables, and those of chairs, trussed pianoforte legs, and smaller articles too numerous to describe in detail.

H

For cutting such curved pieces, especially if the curves vary much, we have found a vertical wooden vice of great service, and not only for such special purpose, but also for many operations in more general demand. It consists simply of an upright post A (Fig. 56) driven into the ground to a depth of 2ft., flat on one side, with a mortice cut near the bottom to receive the strip B, and a hole through the upper part for the screw, a nut being securely let into it. The post may be of ash, or beech, or elm; perhaps the first is, on the whole, preferable, as it is tough and durable. The vice is completed by the part C, which takes the screw through the upper end, and has the strip B pinned to it below, so as to form a joint. This strip allows the jaw to open to any desired width, like that of an iron parallel vice (a very useful article, by the way, but costly); a second pin is put through any one of the holes in this strip, and rests against the fixed post. The screw may be of iron or wood —preferably of iron, and of not too coarse a thread, and there must be a good-sized washer between the head of this screw and the upright post. A plate of iron may also with advantage be let into the loose jaw under the washer, and the nut of the screw should not be a small one, but consist of a square plate, bored and tapped, 3in. square, let in on the further side of the fixed post, so that the strain of the screw shall not tend to loosen it. The top of the vice should be about 2ft. 6in. from the floor, and we are sure that the experience of a few weeks will suffice to prove to the amateur that he has not a more serviceable tool or workshop appli-

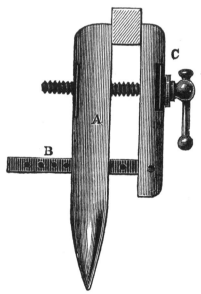

FIG. 56. WOODEN VICE.

ance anywhere. In the first place it is of firm construction, in the next it can be got at on all sides readily, then it will take very thick or very thin stuff, and will hold either in almost any position for sawing or for the action of the draw knife or spokeshave. We use it in sawing off firewood or pieces for the lathe, to grip pieces of varied curvature for our many jobs in carpentry and joinery, to hold the handles of rakes, hoes, and brooms while the iron parts are being fitted. If we add that we have used it to chain up a monkey and to secure a tame squirrel, it will be confessed that we find our wooden vice a veritable universal holdfast.

To commence a cut with the sweep saw or the fret saw, which is the same thing in miniature, it is only necessary, if the cut be not from the outside of the wood, to bore a hole with a centre-bit, large enough to allow the blade to enter, and, having loosed it from its frame, to insert it and set to work; generally, however, the cut extends to the outside of the piece, except in actual fretwork, and, therefore, can be begun at either end. Short quick strokes are to be made, and the saw kept at right angles to the cut, so that the wood is sawn equally on both sides. If the saw were held, as is usual in using the ordinary handsaw, on a slope, the curve might perhaps be followed correctly on one side or face of the work, while the other would not by any means be its counterpart. If the wood to be cut be two inches and upwards in thickness, and there be at hand, as recommended, a pattern template of thin wood, its outline should be marked on both sides of the piece, and sawn partly from one face and partly from the other. This course, moreover, should be pursued even in cutting along a straight line in every case where the wood is thick, or the saw will probably, in spite of all care, run out of cut on one side or the other.

It must not be imagined that all apparently curved work is in reality what it seems to be; a pillar, for instance, of wood, or a large wooden roller (not a field roller), will in all probability be built up of several flat boards, nailed to an internal frame or skeleton, and then it will be made cylindrical on the outside by means of the lathe, or by the use of planes; being, in fact, constructed something like a cask or barrel. There is a good deal of this framed work made and sold, for although it is not always very strongly put together, it is very light, easily movable, and, as the exterior alone is intended to be seen, it suffices for a great number of purposes, as well or better than solid work. A loo, or occasional table, intended to have a massive looking top, is made up in this way: A design being drawn to scale—elliptic or circular, or of varied curvature —the frame is first constructed by cutting out of a plank, two inches or more in thickness, several curved pieces, which when notched into each other will have the form required, and form not only the basis of the moulding round the edge of the top, but the outer frame to which the latter is to be attached. This is sometimes left independent of the rest of the ribs or framing, and sometimes the ends of the latter are mortised into it, so that the whole of the skeleton top is completed before the upper board is attached. The latter may thus be made of lighter substance than if it were not to be so supported, by which there is a saving of valuable material, to say nothing of a material diminution of weight. To mark out the curved pieces if the whole is to be circular, is a very easy matter. The material is laid upon the work bench or floor, and a lath or piece of string is used as the radius, a pencil being looped into one end, and an awl into the other, to form a pair of beam compasses. The awl is stuck into another board, and the pencil made to mark the curves on the piece to be cut.

We have already shown how to describe what is commonly called an oval by means of a loop of string with a nail at each end of it; and, on the whole, it is as useful and simple a method as can be devised for the purpose. There are, however, other methods which we will describe here, because the oval or ellipse answers for table tops, picture frames, and stands for clocks, statuettes, and many other articles of vertu.

In the first place let it be understood what an ellipse is. It is the figure formed by taking a slice off a cone in the direction A B (Fig. 57).

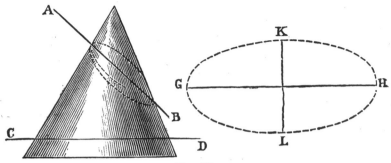

FIG. 57.

A similar slice in the direction C D would show a circle, and the nearer the cut is to the horizontal, or parallel to the base of the cone, the nearer will the resulting ellipse be to the form of a circle. If we draw the lines G H, K L, we have what are called the major and minor axes; and in the ellipse now to be described, we require the respective lengths of these to be first given. A circle is then to be described (Fig. 58), having the major axis for its diameter, as M N, and half its circumference is to be divided into as many equal parts as possible. Then draw lines from these perpendicular to the diameter already drawn, and, therefore, parallel to each other, until they meet the opposite side of the circle. Draw also a circle from the same centre as the first, but taking the minor axis of the proposed ellipse

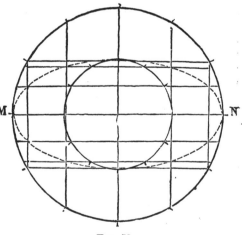

FIG. 58.

as the diameter; divide the circumference into as many parts as the first was divided into (or divide the half circumference and draw the parallels as before), but draw these last lines horizontally, i.e., parallel to the major axis or diameter of the larger circle. These lines will cut the first at certain points through which a curved line drawn by hand will describe the ellipse required. This is not at all difficult; if the description be carefully read and understood, although on first perusal it may seem a little complicated.

A third plan (Fig. 59), which, however, as well as that just described, will only approximate to a perfect ellipse, is to describe circles O P on the line

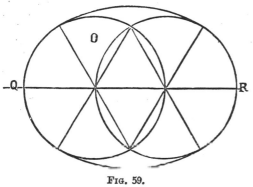

Q R, which is the major axis, then draw lines from the point where the circles cut, through their centres to the opposite part of the circumference. Place one point of the compasses on the point of intersection of the circles and take a radius to the other end of one of these lines last drawn, and complete the ellipse by striking the two small arcs which are

Fig. 59.

needed to unite the circles into one figure. This again is a rough and ready plan of general use, because the lath, bradawl, pencil, and carpenter's rule, suffice for the work, and it is seldom that a workman requires to be mathematically correct in drawing the shape of a table or of any other article of furniture.

The method first described, viz., with a string and two nails, is perhaps the easiest of all, but in this case, either trial must be made to find the distance between the pins, or a little more mathematics will be required for the purpose.

The following, however, is a practical demonstration of the mathematical part of the business, and will give the required distance at once. Let

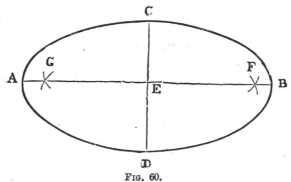

Fig. 60.

A B (Fig. 60) be the major axis, and C D the minor axis perpendicular to it. From centre C or D, with the distance equal to E A or E B describe arcs of circles, cutting each other in G and F on the major axis. These points

of intersection are the foci or points where the pins are to be inserted
Place the double string round these and knot it at the distance F B or A G.
It will be noticed that its total length when doubled and strained equals
the distance between the foci plus the distance between either focus and
the extremity of the major axis. In the drawings of these systems we
think the practical matter of striking ellipses will be clear to our readers.

Not forgetting, however, that we are giving instructions in carpentry,
and not upon the science of mathematics, on which carpentry is
based, we will now add one other method of striking elliptic curves, and
describe the mode of constructing the instrument by which it is done.
This is called a trammel (Fig. 61), and, for engineering drawings as well as

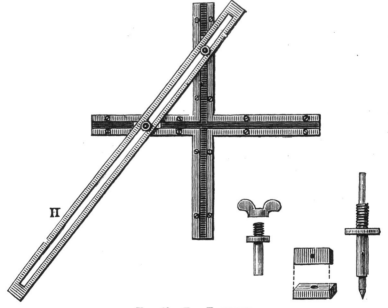

FIG. 61. THE TRAMMEL.

architectural, it is in constant use, being for that purpose beautifully made
in ebony or other hard wood, with ivory or metal edges and fittings. For
carpenter's work such costly material is unnecessary, and any bit of dry,
hard wood—mahogany by preference—will suffice. Cut out two strips,
1½in. wide and 18in. long and ¾in. thick, and with a sharp plough cut
a groove down the centre of them to a depth of ⅜in., the groove being
about ¼in. wide. Notch these into each other at their centres, exactly
at right angles, so that you may get a simple channelled cross, and if
you can get a piece of sheet brass about ¹⁄₁₆in. thick, and cut into the form
of a cross, you can strengthen the junction by letting this in underneath,
and attaching it by small screws, the channels being, remember, on the top
side, and the bottoms of these channels quite level one with the other. If

you can manage with $\frac{1}{2}$in. stuff, and work it up to a lighter section, so much the better, the thickness and general size depending on the powers of the workman and the use to which the instrument is to be put. Now cut out two small blocks of mahogany, or other hard and sound wood, to fit these grooves very exactly, so as to slide easily in them, but without shake. The blocks must be level with the upper edge of the grooves, or just a shade below, and may be 1$\frac{1}{4}$in. long. In the centre of each block drill a neat perpendicular hole, reaching almost through, and the size of a tolerably large knitting pin, $i.e.$ about $\frac{1}{10}$in. diameter. It only remains to add two strips of thin wood to prevent the blocks from falling out of their grooves, or, if you wish your work to look well, two strips of brass, each slightly overlapping the edge of the grooves, and attached by brass screws to the mahogany. These may overlap so as just to allow the pins, which will fit the holes in the blocks, to traverse freely up and down the slits thus formed. These strips must be eight in number, because they must not be continued across the centre of the trammel. This will be understood from the figure. Instead of proceeding in this way, the channels may be chamfered and also the blocks, in which case it will be easier to attach chamfered strips to a plain flat rule of mahogany ; but on the whole the method here given, if neatly finished in brass, will be the best to follow. There is now needed the actual beam compass, with which to draw the ellipse. It consists of a straight ruler of mahogany, marked H, in the figure of the trammel, having a narrow slit along its centre for the purpose of adjusting to any distance apart the two pins K L, which fit nicely the holes in the wooden blocks already described. These pins may be made of brass or iron, or better, steel wire of the form shown, $i.e.$, with a shoulder and washer, and a nut, the wire being screwed to receive it. Thus either pin can be fixed at any point in the ruler or beam, and clamped by the nut, and then the pins can be inserted in the holes of the little blocks, in which they will be free to turn as on a pivot. A third pin or rather socket to carry a pencil is similarly fitted into the groove in the ruler, and is also adjustable as to distance. It may be made of brass, like a hollow tube with a shoulder, and if a couple of saw cuts be made in it to allow a certain degree of elasticity, it will hold the pencil without any need of a clamp or tightening screw. Such is the trammel or ellipsograph for correct delineation of what is commonly called an oval. As to size, it may be made to pack in the pocket, or be as large as anyone chooses to make it. The distance between the pins will be the distance between the foci of the described ellipse, while the adjustibility of the pencil will give a good deal of range as regards the size, and also determine whether the figure shall approach a circular form, or be considerably elongated.

We strongly advise the reader to make one of these trammels, not only because it will assist him in any work of an elliptic form, but because it is a good plan to work at light as well as heavy articles. It prevents the hand from becoming too much accustomed to clumsy carpentry, and is in short work far more suitable for amateurs than building or "wheeling" as it is termed. Nevertheless, we know a clerical amateur in carpentry who builds his own carts for farm work, or for driving himself about, and who is as neat a hand at fine joiner's work as need be. The grand secret is to know how to carry out the elementary principles of mortising and framing; the rest depends upon practice, and upon a knowledge of the details of construction of the job in hand. Any amateur, for instance, who can cut a good tenon or mortice, can make a wheelbarrow, if he take the trouble to use his eyes and brains, and to notice the exact way in which such articles are usually framed up, and there is nothing like a barrow to test his power of putting work strongly together.

CHAPTER VII.

SIXTH LESSON.

CLAW AND PILLAR TABLE—CURVED SPOKESHAVE—CONSOLE TABLE—OAK READING DESK—PILLAR AND CLAW TELESCOPE READING DESK — DOUBLE PILLAR TELESCOPE READING TABLE—THE PERSPECTOGRAPH.

IN cutting out in the rough, for subsequent ornamentation, such an article as the leg of a pillar table, care should be taken to give the greatest possible amount of strength by allowing the grain of the wood to run, as nearly as possible, lengthwise as in Fig. 62, or it will probably not be long before it is broken across at the narrowest and most slender

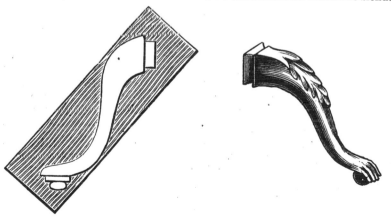

FIG. 62.   FIG. 63.

part. This is especially true of wood like deal, the grain of which is coarse and open. The harder woods, particularly those of tropical growth are almost equally strong in any direction of the grain, and do not so much need the above precaution to be observed. These small and useful tables are not by any means difficult to make, but require the aid of a lathe for turning the central pillar. The legs are three in number and are to be cut with a projecting tenon which is to be fitted into a mortice in the lower part of the pillar. This mortice is sometimes cut in a dove-tailed form, the tenon being made to slide in from below after being glued (Fig. 63) but it is more often made as a simple mortised and tenoned joint. Now this is the usual place in which fracture or separation occurs, and once divorced from its pedestal the leg will seldom consent to a perfect reunion, so that the table thus injured usually becomes a hopeless cripple whose ultimate abode is the lumber room. The reason is that the joint is difficult to fit together—is weak when fitted—and has to bear a strain, when the table is in use, tending to its disunion, and when this occurs a bit of the pillar is generally split off, especially if, to make a firmer junction, a dove-tailed tenon be used. To obviate this defect a plate of iron with three arms should always be fitted underneath, attached in the middle by a good screw to the pillar, and by other smaller screws to the under sides of the legs, where it will of course be out of sight. But we think it a better plan not to depend upon a single tenon, but to cut a shallow mortice only in the pillar, and attach the legs by dowels or strong wooden pegs glued into them and into the pillar, using a nose bit or centre bit to make the holes. Or it may be preferable to cut the leg with a projecting tenon as usual, but to cut away the central part so as to leave two tenons, which, being then rounded, serve as dowels, instead of making the latter as separate pegs. In either case the mortice has not to be cut with a chisel, but by the simpler and quicker action of a boring bit, and the further advantage is gained of a double tenon, which, in most cases will be found a great deal more secure than a single one of double the size. The iron plate ought still to be added as before. If the joint so made should at any time give way, there is nothing to cause the pedestal to splinter or split off, but the pins themselves will be the part broken, and may of course be very easily restored. Pillar and claw tables, however, are not very fit for knocking about in nurseries, or where they are likely to meet with rough usage. It must, however, be remembered that anything on three legs will stand firmly, though on an uneven floor, like the Isle of Man penny, *Stabit quocunque jeceris.*

For various surfaces, more or less curved, tools of special form are frequently needed. A curved shave, or double-handed draw knife, for example, like Fig. 64, is by no means a useless tool for hollowing the seat of a wooden chair and other parts of concave work not easily reached by the ordinary spokeshave. Children's wooden spades are so hollowed, and this sea-

Fig. 64.

side toy, so useful for digging all kinds of salt-water ponds, for the delectation of small fry, is cut out of wood steeped in water till quite soft, and of about the condition of cheese. Those who combine cabinet making with joinery—a by no means unusual combination—often make use of tools variously curved and intended for the work of the carver—gouges and chisels, for instance, with bent instead of straight shanks, curved files, called rifflers, and other queer-looking tools, called by queer-sounding names, are then in very general use, and, indeed, are absolutely essential to the proper and speedy performance of this class of work. Another tool still more generally used is a plane, the bottom of which forms a portion of a circle, being convex in regard to its length. This is for planing concave pieces, such as the inside of wheel felloes.

Among the more simple curved articles the legs of a console table or cabinet may be mentioned as easy to cut out and satisfactory in appearance when made. The usual form is shown in Fig. 65. The upper portion is part of a spiral or scroll, but is easily marked out by hand, and may be then cut out of a sheet of stiff brown paper and kept for future use. The leg will require a tenon to be left, as seen in the

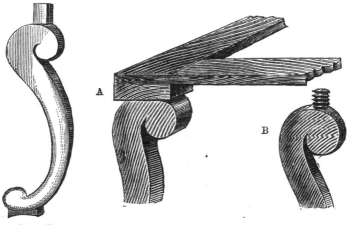

FIG. 65.   FIG. 66.

drawing, and may be framed up as if part of a straight table leg. With this form, however, it is not unusual to vary somewhat the mode of attachment to the frame, and to attach the legs by means of stout dowels. The frame will thus be independent of the legs, and the pins of the latter will be inserted and glued into blocks (A, Fig. 66), firmly screwed underneath to receive them. These tables are very generally made to stand against the wall of the room, and the two back legs are therefore made as in other tables, quite straight, and planed up; because turned ones would be out of character with these front legs. When a table is thus made care must be taken that the pins are of ample size. They can be made of beech if the table be of deal, and let into the scroll by means of a screw augur or American screw bit, and glued firmly. The rest of the pin can then be screwed (B) as already directed with a carpenter's screw box, and so attached to the block and upper frame of the table.

The top board of such a table must have a curved outline to look well. This plan of construction is not given as the best, but carpentry must be applicable to various sorts of framing, and sometimes a piece may be too short to allow a tenon to be cut, and may yet be sound and otherwise well suited for the intended purpose; and in these cases, as well as occasionally for mere practice, ordinary routine should give place to novel modes of work. A good carpenter, in short, ought to be able to use in a satisfactory way the stuff he may have in stock, and make it answer his purpose by dint of his ingenuity, if it be in any degree suitable. We have seen many a bit of wood chopped up for firing, and similarly wasted, that in good hands would have served not only for making some useful article, but even an ornamental one. Put an old oak or yew gate post in the hands of a clever carpenter or joiner, and he will show it to you subsequently in a new form, in which its value has been doubled and trebled by his ingenious mode of using it.

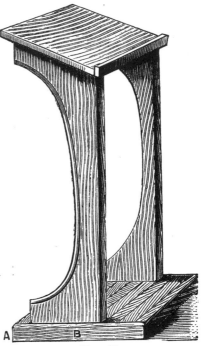

FIG. 67.

We introduce here a desk (Fig. 67) which can be made of a good dry bit of oak, and will be all the more handsome if the material be of gnarled and crooked grain, although such is far more difficult to work than the clean and straight grained stuff generally used in church architecture or for oak fittings in study or dining room. There is first of all the base, A, which, in the best work, consists of a platform with a solid moulded or chamfered oak frame running around it, seen at B in the perspective drawing. The oak frame may be of stuff 3in. by 2in., the narrow part upwards, and chamfered to 1in. If half this last be further rebated to take the boards of ½in. stuff, so that they lie flush with the edge, but on no account above it, it will make a good base of neat yet solid appearance. From this rise the two oak trusses which support the desk seen in profile in the figure, and which may be moulded at pleasure to any pattern preferred, or curved differently to the drawing. These will be of solid oak, 2in. thick, or 2in. to 3in. according to the width of the desk. If too thin in proportion the whole will look poor, if too thick it will be clumsy, but much will depend upon the moulding of the edges of these pieces. The desk itself, of oak or of deal lightly stained—for it is only old oak that is of very deep colour—will probably be 18in. to 24in. in length, and about 1ft. wide, with a rim at the bottom standing ¾in. above it. It is exceedingly difficult to give dimensions, so much depends upon the use to which a desk of this kind is likely to be put. For a church it would be made larger and more solid, for a study lighter, to be used as a reading desk, or for writing.

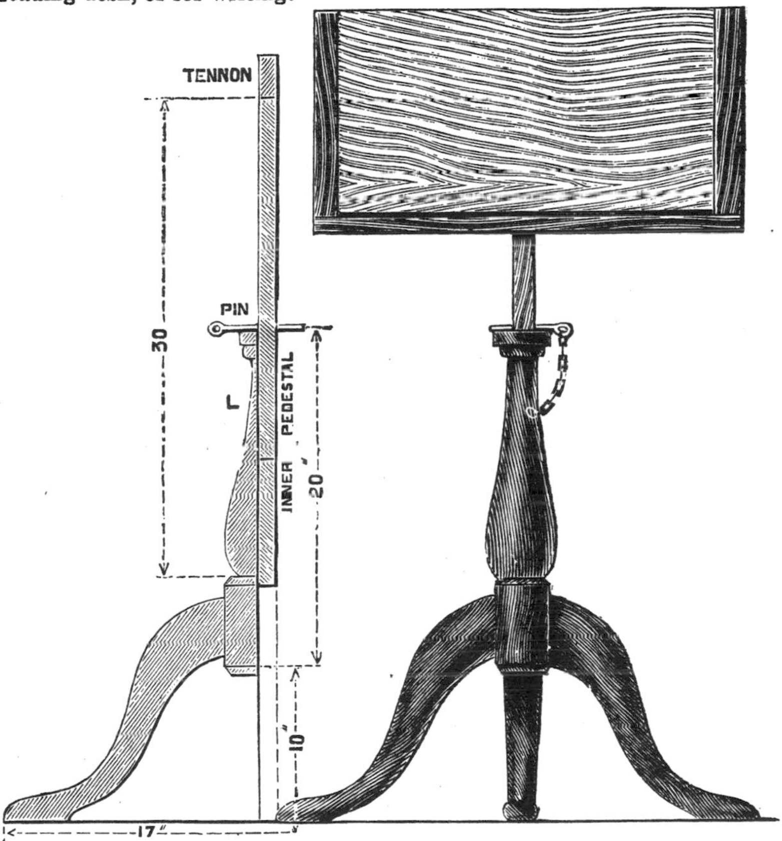

FIG. 68. ELEVATION AND HALF PROFILE OF PILLAR TELESCOPE READING DESK.

To make a reading table is not so very difficult a task to a tolerably practised hand; but although a step from one part of our description to the next is not great, it may and must premise a good deal of practice on the reader's part. These tables may be made with a central single pillar and three legs, or with two such pillars, each with its own pair of legs, which is generally the case if the table is of large size.

To begin with the first which is sketched complete in elevation in Fig. 68.

it must be understood that the pillar is hollow, and the desk is mounted on a square shaft, which slides up and down inside it. This can be checked and fixed at any desired height, either by a simple peg or by a spring catch. No one who has not tried it can conceive the relief of standing to read after a prolonged sitting at an ordinary table. It seems to renew one's powers of study in a wonderful manner. But to proceed. The single leg or claw of this table is to stand on the side opposite to that at which the reader will be placed when at work, so that the table, which is of light construction, will not be liable to tilt and fall over if he should chance to lean against it. This will also give him foot room between the other two legs. As regards height, the table when lowered upon the pedestal should enable anyone to sit at it comfortably to read and write—this will be about 2ft. 6in. or 2ft. 9in. from the floor, according to the height of the student. When drawn up the lowest part of the sloping desk should be 4ft. or so from the floor; the vertical height of the three claws to the bottom of the central pillar will be 10in., the pillar 20in., and then if the desk be drawn up to 4ft. as specified, there can be 18in. of the squared support above the pedestal, and 1ft. below within the pillar, which is the shortest length to be allowed, so that the whole length of this squared support will be 30in. The drawing has the above dimensions plainly marked upon it. When lowered to the utmost the bottom of the inner sliding pedestal will just touch the floor. With books at all heavy upon the desk when at its full height this table will be unsteady, unless the legs are made to spread considerably. They should reach 18in. from the central line of the main pillar. If, then, the desk itself be 24in. from side to side, or 12in. from the central line or axis, the legs will be 3in. beyond it, which will give a firm base, and make the table stand securely.

It will plainly be an impossible job to bore the main pillar through with a square hole, and not easy to do so with a round one. It is, therefore, to be built up of four sections, and these, when glued and dry, are to be put in the lathe and turned. They should have at each end an iron or brass hoop to keep them together, because when the desk is raised there is a good deal of strain upon them. The cross section of the pillar is shown in Fig. 69. These parts consist primarily of four strips of board, numbered 1, 2, 3, and 4, each 1in. thick, planed up truly and squarely on all sides. They will need to be 20in. long, and Nos. 1 and 4 must be 3½in. wide, while 2 and 3 must be 2in. These must be glued up together as shown by the shading, so as to make a long box. The circle drawn through this shows the cross section of the pillar when turned. Plane off now the angles AA, BB, CC, DD, and reduce the whole to an octagonal section ready for the lathe. Observe that by so doing the joints are necessarily weakened considerably by reducing their surfaces, but the parts cannot be nailed, because the turning tools would soon be ruined thereby. Hence take care to glue the work up well. Dowels or pins, HH, may with advantage be inserted before glueing the pieces, as they will materially add to the strength of the work. Several can be put in each piece, as the whole pedestal will be 20in. long. Put at least, however, three or four ¼in. or ⅜in. diameter, of mahogany, or beech, or ash. Now proceed to plug the two ends, using plugs like P of the figure. These are made of a round bit of ½in. wood, beech or ash, not deal, with a square block glued in the centre of it on one side about 1in. thick to fit the square hole in the pedestal—the fit is,to be exact, but not so tight as in the least to endanger separating the glued joints at the angles. The pillar may now be mounted as if a solid one between a prong chuck and back centre. Turn down, first of all, a recess at each end about ½in. wide and ¼in. deep, to take an iron or brass ring, already prepared. Brass will look best, as it can be turned up bright, but an iron one painted will answer. As soon as this has been done, put on the rings, one at each end. For this purpose mark the faces of the plugs, and notice which way the fork stands, so as to be able to replace all exactly as they were before. See that the fit is such that the rings will barely go on. Then warm them

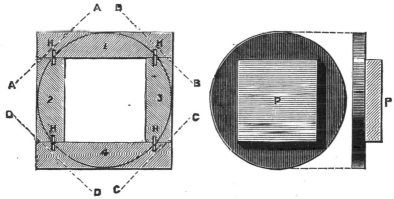

FIG. 68. CROSS SECTION OF PILLAR.

until so hot you cannot hold them, and they will go on easily, and when cold will grip the work very tightly, after which there will be no fear of the glued joints giving way. Now replace the pedestal and turn it something like profile L, Fig. 68.

You have now to consider the positions of the claws, because you should avoid mortising either into such a part of the pillar as will be upon or near one of the joints—although the rings of metal would prevent serious damage—for it would not be so secure an union as if placed elsewhere. To divide a circle into three equal parts you have only to remember that its circumference is about three times its diameter. You can, however, cut a strip of paper in this case, so as just to wrap round the lower part of the cylindrical pedestal, and then double it, or rather fold it, into three. See where these folds come, and move the paper about until you get each fold as far as you can from a joint, and mark these places as the centre of the mortices. You will not find it easy to get

clear of all the joints, but sufficiently so for the purpose. In turning the
pillar plenty of material can be left at those points; ½in. at least must be
left even at the parts immediately adjacent to the angles. For this
reason, too, cut the mortices for the legs about ½in. deep only, and be sure
to add the iron plate below as already directed—a couple of dowels, if they
can be added without going through to the inside of the hollow pedestal,
will give extra stability to the whole.

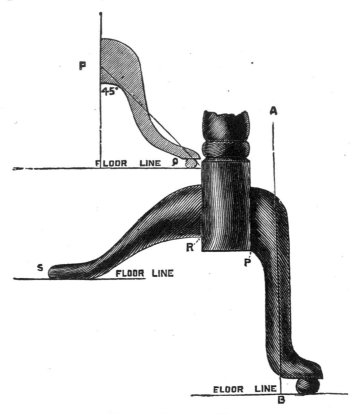

FIG. 70. POSITION OF LEGS.

In planning claw legs of this description it will be well to examine the
tendency that exists, to their being broken off or torn out of the socket by
the strain caused by the weight of the table top and its contents. A leg
like AB, Fig. 70, would sufficiently support any reasonable weight, because,
the pressure being directly downwards in the line AB, there is no strain
tending to disruption of the joint. If, in fact, the latter were hinged at P,
the weight would simply keep the joint quite close. But such a leg or three
so shaped would offer little resistance to upsetting the table, the base
formed by the feet being too small in proportion. On the other hand,

such a leg as R S would give a good broad base, preventing any chance of an upset, as the table would be more inclined to run along upon its castors or slide on the floor. But now the strain would be great, tending to open the joint at R, the point S being the fulcrum on which the leg would turn. The latter should be, therefore, so arranged as to divide the strain. Its central line P Q should make an angle of 45 deg. with the axis or central line of the pedestal. This will look well, and give an appearance of strength which is not deceptive. A comparison of this figure with the previous one will satisfy the mind at once as to which is the proper angle to be used in such a case. The tendency to tear out the leg by opening the joint is here not only small, but will be wholly counteracted by the iron

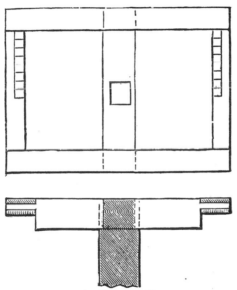

FIG. 71. PLAN OF FRAME.

plate underneath, and at the same time there will be little liability to upset the table by accident, especially if, as directed, the single leg be opposite to and farthest from the feet of the reader.

Pillar and claws being thus arranged, we have now to attend to the desk. First there is the 2in. square pedestal already described, and this is to be of hard wood; in short, the table should be of mahogany, as it is worth the additional expense, and will be much handsomer and fitter for the study. If not of this wood, nor of oak, which, unless of very straight grain, is difficult to manage, let the pedestal be of beech or ash, and the desk may be of deal, except the bar, which is fitted upon the pedestal. The plan is shown in Fig. 71 of the under framework, upon which is to be hinged the actual desk. This is 2ft. by 18in. The central bar is 3in. wide and 2in. thick; the side bars ½in. thick, and 2in. wide, the front and back the same or a little thicker, say ⅝in., as the front one has to take the hinges, and all three of the cross pieces may be mortised into the front and back ones. The lower figure shows the thick bar, and the frame must be so constructed as to be level on its upper side, underneath the central and front and back bars will be lower than the others. In mahogany these proportions will make a very stiff and strong frame, but a lighter one is not desirable. Into the central bar the pedestal is to be well mortised and it may be just cut away on two sides enough to make shallow shoulders. It will then be very firm when glued into its place. The weight of the desk, and strain, remember, will fall on this part, so that a badly fitted joint will be fatal to stability. Fig. 72 shows in profile the desk hinged to the front bar of the lower frame so that it can be raised or lowered. When raised it is kept up by a light frame B, the back or lower rail of which rests in any one of the notches cut upon half the width of the side bars of the lower frame, one of which is shown at C. The rail of B which rests in these notches at each end should extend a little beyond the sides. With this description of every detail of construction it ought not to prove to the reader a very difficult task to make such a table as this. The top board should have clamping pieces to prevent warping, as described in a former

FIG. 72. DESK AND SUPPORT.

chapter, and it should have a strip attached by screws to prevent the books falling off when the desk is raised. This strip, if preferred may be attached by two iron pins only, so as to be movable.

I will now describe a large elevating reading table. This, though similar to the last, is not constructed in precisely the same manner, as it has no central pedestal with claws, but a pedestal at each end, which are as often made square as round. The general plan of the framework has consequently to be somewhat modified. A desk of this kind may be of any size; 4ft. long by 2ft. 6in. wide would be a handy size for general use, without being so large as to be cumbersome. The desk of this table being heavy, all parts must be made strongly, and should be of mahogany. A table and also a section of one of the pillars is given in Fig. 73. A is a solid pedestal of beech or ash, 2in. square and 1ft. high, mortised into B with one tenon, and it may be further strengthened by a bed screw inserted from below the foot B. A plan of the latter is given at C. It consists of a piece of sound mahogany (or any wood selected instead), 1ft. 9in. in length, 4in. wide, and 2½in. thick. There will be of course a pair of these, as both pedestals are alike. This,

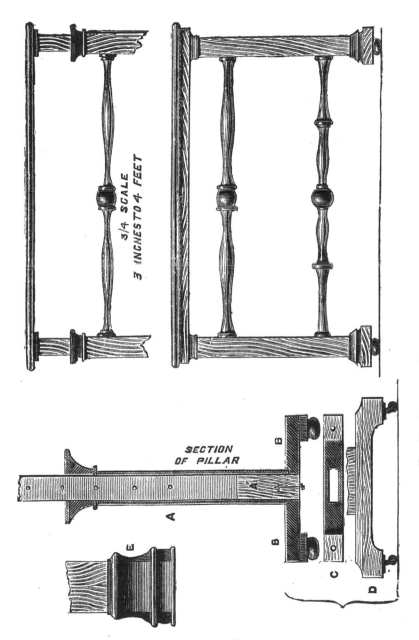

3/4 SCALE
3 INCHES TO 4 FEET

SECTION
OF PILLAR

FIG. 73. DETAILS OF LARGE ELEVATING READING TABLE.

12

remember, with the short piece mortised into it, forms the foundation of the table, and bad work here will prevent you from obtaining rigidity in other parts, as the desk will be unsteady and uncomfortable in use. The under side of this foot is made by adding knobs and castors to raise its centre from the floor, otherwise it must be of thicker stuff, cut out like D.

The hollow pillar has now to be built up of board, ½in. thick, which will in the present case be left as it is, except that a moulding run round it at the top and bottom will give it a handsome finish. The lathe will not be used in building up this hollow pedestal, therefore, do not let the edges of the boards get rounded or damaged, but keep them nice and even. Whenever work is to be square and sharp let it be really so, and the work will look as it ought to do. Edges like these should be shot with a trying plane and a shooting board, as being the easiest way to keep them true and square. Of course two of the boards will be narrower than the other two which have to overlap them; i.e., there will be two of them 3in. wide, and two 2in. wide, which will leave the hollow part 2in. square, the size of the fixed pedestal and of the rising one, by which the desk will be supported. These two pedestals are to be 2ft. 6in. high, measured from the floor, and after having been glued up and become dry, they are to be bound with an iron hoop at the top and bottom, which will be concealed by the mouldings at those places. These iron hoops—if we may call a square iron ferule by such a name—need not be more than ⅛in. thick, and ¼in. wide, and as the boards are of ½in. stuff, they can be let in flush by the help of a mitre saw and chisel. It will be also a very good plan to let the ends of the boards half an inch into the foot. This will even allow the lower hoop to be dispensed with, as their sole use is to prevent the pedestal from bursting open. If the solid part at the bottom be well planed up and glued, this will give a very firm hold to the boards, even if they were not also glued together at the edges. Of course, a few brads can be used to secure the joint until dry, and they are easily concealed, if it be preferred to leave them, by using a punch to drive them in below the surface of the wood and filling the hole with glue and dust from the saw.

It is usual to enlarge the base of the pedestal somewhat by a broad moulding, or rather a skirting like E (Fig. 73) which is a sectional drawing of such base. Some, however, enlarge the upper part instead, like H (Fig. 74); but to our eye this takes from it the appearance of its stability, and gives a topheavy look which we do not admire. In such matters Nature is the best guide to artistic taste, and we all know how she strengthens the forest giants by buttresses reared at their bases.

The inner pedestal on which the desk is raised is, as before, a piece of wood of the requisite length and 2in. square. This size need not be exceeded if the wood used be mahogany, because there are in this case two such supports; and a piece of mahogany of such sectional area will sustain with ease such a weight as is likely to be placed on a reading table. As the whole pedestal is 2ft. high exclusive of the foot, and the solid part mortised into the latter is 1ft., and is let into the foot 2½in., it will project 9½in. into the hollow part of the pedestal, leaving a clear space of 14½in. above it. As 2½in. must at least be left of the inner pedestal when drawn up to its full height, this will admit of a rise only of 1ft. above its ordinary level. If this be not likely to be sufficient, which will depend on the height of the reader, there are two ways in which the arrangement can be altered. First, by cutting the solid block A (Fig. 73) down to 6in. or 8in.; or, secondly, by making the original table stand 3ft. off the ground, and using a high chair or office stool instead of a low one.

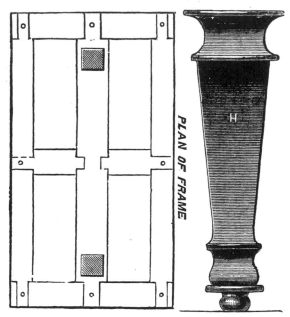

FIG. 74. FRAME AND PILLAR OF READING TABLE.

There is no reason, however, to be afraid of cutting down A thus much but if this be done, merely leaving it as a short block, it would be advisable to use ¾in. board for the inside boards of the standards of the hollow pillars instead of ½in., to allow a good solid bar from one pillar to the other. In any case, some such bar will be needed both here and lower down as stays and braces to the structure. Of course the lower one will be let well into the solid block just above the feet of the table, and this will, in all probability, act as a footstool to the reader. Both these stays are to be turned in the lathe, and should vary from 1½in. at the largest part, or 2in. if the moulding be of a bold character, to 1in. at each end where it is let into the pedestals.

We may now consider the framing of the upper part, which will be strong at all points. First run a flat bar from one upright to the other as the foundation of the whole; into this the two uprights have to be mortised securely, and therefore it will be as well to make it of stuff 1¼in. thick, and 3in. wide. Its length will be nearly that of the table, which may overlap it, however, an inch or so at each end. The frame may be completed as shown in plan, Fig. 74, but of stuff 2in. wide by 1in.thick, which will be substantial enough, as the frame is of no great size. Of course as the central bar is stouter than the other, there will be an overlap of its thickness. Keep, therefore, the upper side of the frame level, and allow this projection below where it will be of no importance.

Now, in constructing a table in this way, it is evidently quite impossible to tie together except by this one cross piece, the two pedestals which work up and down in the hollow pillars, and if they had to be drawn out to a considerable distance the whole plan would have to be modified by building the hollow pillars open on the sides opposite to each other, i.e., making them up of three boards instead of four, and securing them with an iron hoop as before at two points. It is then possible to run a bar or build up a light braced frame of an ornamental character between the two square pillar pistons, or whatever they may be named, so as to prevent any spreading of them apart or shakiness. In this case, the main or hollow pillars cannot be braced together by two single turned bars, but must have two flat ones attached to the outer boards of the pedestals. Practically, however, no tie is needed of the above character if the total rise of the inner supports be not more than 18in. In fact, after long practical use of these reading tables, we have never been annoyed by the defect hinted at.

With a heavy lot of books, however, it is not easy to raise these tables single handed, unless the hand be applied as nearly under the centre as possible, and the pistons move easily in their respective pedestals. These double-legged tables are very generally made with a rack to allow of their rising by the application of a lifting force, and which keeps them raised until the rack is released by a spring. The releasing gear ought, however, to be such as can be acted on by one hand, while the table top is supported and gently lowered by the other. Such a refinement, however, we have never yet seen practically applied. We shall, however, presently offer a suggestion for a method of raising such a table by the feet, leaving both hands free to move the detaining pins or catches. These complications, however, are merely questions intended to interest our mechanical readers; for our own part we should care but little for such gimcracks.

The top board of the table is to be clamped in a proper way by strips at each end to counteract the tendency to warp, or by cross pieces put on underneath by screws. Instead of a single book rest at the lower part of the desk, there may be a second movable bar about three parts distant from the front one. This is handy to retain any books of reference from slipping down upon those which are being read, or in which entries may be made in writing. The inkstand is also conveniently placed above this upper bar, unless a special place be made for it near the right hand lower down. Further description of this table will hardly be necessary with the plans, elevations, and details given herewith.

To recur, however, to the promised foot gear, there is one very simple mode of going to work, which will be found quite effective and very little trouble to rig up. A narrow slit is to be made in the inside boards of the pedestals from the level of the top of the solid block, about a foot in length, or, at any rate, almost up to the iron collar at the top of the pedestal. Just at the top of this slit, which is to be made in both pedestals, a pulley is to be fixed, over which a catgut cord, attached to the bottom of the rising pillar or piston, is to pass, so that by pulling down these cords the desk will be raised. The cross stays will not interfere if holes are made in each, just where the slit is made in the uprights, so as to allow the cords to pass freely. It is now only necessary to attach the loose ends of these cords to a roller, with a winch handle and check wheel near the right hand, or to a treadle bar to be depressed by the feet. The first is the best, because a treadle has hardly vertical motion to draw down the cord 1ft. or 18in. Both cords may, however, pass to one side, a second pulley being arranged for that purpose, and may pass down to a hand lever, to which greater play may be given. The rachet wheel and paul, with roller and winch handle, is the most complete plan, and will be perfectly effective, as the pins may be pulled out of both rising legs, and the table quietly lowered by one hand. In a large and heavy table some plan of this kind is not only serviceable but almost essential, unless one is content to call in a friend to assist at the operation. The holes into which the pins of the desk bars are inserted should be bushed with a short bit of brass tubing, or with a little plate of brass let into the surface of the table and drilled to fit the pins. If these pieces of brass be heated somewhat, and some glue be dropped into the places in which they are to be inserted, it will be found sufficient to retain them. If they be not first heated the glue will be chilled by touching them, and will not take hold of them at all.

The edges of the upper board which forms the desk may be either simply rounded off or moulded. The skirtings and moulding attached to the pedestals must be mitred at the angles, a work that should now by no means be fraught with difficulty.

Having lately been engaged upon a painting, it struck us that a description of an instrument not generally known, but requiring neatness of construction, would form another useful lesson in carpentry. The object of this instrument is to enable the sketcher to mark down upon his paper, direct from the scene, the various points of the latter: such as the corners of buildings, or position of a tree or other object. The result of connecting such points by lines will be an accurate perspective copy obtained with ease, and perfectly rendered. As a practical means of teaching perspective the perspectograph will be found a very handy instrument, well worth the attention of those who, like ourselves, practise the fine arts as well as carpentry. Fig. 75 shows, first of all, a flat board of ½in. deal or other material, which should have strips screwed on below, or should be clamped like a drawing board at each end to prevent it from warping. We can give no precise direction as to its width or length, because this will depend on the size of the

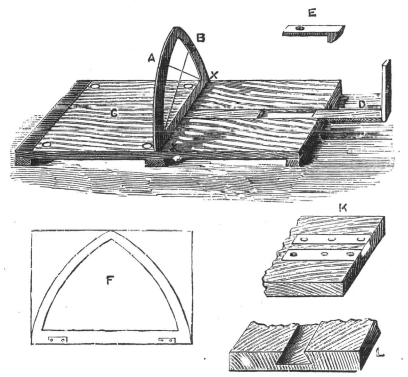

FIG. 75. THE PERSPECTOGRAPH.

largest sheet of drawing paper intended to be used with it, and which will be attached by drawing pins at C or by paste. If drawing pins are to be used, make the board of deal, as they will not penetrate hard wood. At D is seen a narrow strip of hard wood, made to slide in a chamfered groove, so that it can be drawn out, and at its extremity is fixed or hinged a short upright piece of thin brass, with a small hole drilled in it as an eye-hole, through which the scene is to be viewed. At a distance of half the length of the board from either end is hinged a frame, composed of two segments of a circle, the centres of which are at X, X, united at the point of intersection by a half lap glued joint, and at the base by a third straight piece of wood of the same thickness. This frame should be very light, about ⅛in. thick at most, and made of hard wood, not liable to split. Pear tree, of which drawing curves are made, will answer exceedingly well for the purpose, and is not liable to warp and twist under variations of temperature. This frame is hinged so that when not erected it will lie flat upon the sheet of drawing paper, and, when it is raised into a perpendicular position it is held up by a hinged hook of wood, like E of the figure. Slides of bent tin, or thin brass, fitting over the arcs A, B, so as to slide upon them easily, have each a piece of silk attached, which is fastened by its other end to the lower angles of the frame. These silks can thus be made to cross at any desired point.

Before describing a convenient modification of this frame, we shall describe the mode of using the instrument, which will also render clear the description already given of its construction. The complete instrument can be mounted like a camera for photographic purposes, upon a tripod stand, or it may rest on any table or level surface. The slide carrying the eye-piece is then drawn out and the frame erected. The sketcher now views the scene with one eye applied to the eye-hole in D, the other being closed, and, with the hand, the strings are made to cross upon any desired spot. The hook supporting the frame is then loosed, and the latter is allowed to fall upon the sheet of paper, when the point thus taken is transferred to the paper by a dot made with a sharp pointed pencil. Other points are subsequently taken, and similarly marked down to form the leading points of the picture. The result will be the same as if the frame (A B) were a sheet of glass, and each point marked upon it, which is practically what perspective, as a science, is founded upon.

An inspection of F, which represents the frame laid down upon the paper, shows that there are parts beyond it, upon which points cannot be marked by means of the crossed silks, hence we have designed a slight alteration in the mode of fixing the frame. Instead of attaching it at once by hinges to the base-board of the instrument, it is hinged to a narrow strip, which is fitted to slide in a groove running *across* the base-board so that the whole frame can be run to and fro sideways, by which movement its action becomes extended in either direction beyond the frame, and any point upon the drawing can be thus reached. In the construction of this instrument no difficulty will be experienced, unless perhaps in the fitting of the two sliding pieces, which must move easily, but with sufficient firmness not to shake or shift their position accidentally. The neatest way, as it gives a finish to the whole, is to plane first a rectangular groove, and then to let in two parallel plates of brass, as shown at K. The slide itself will then be simply rectangular in section, and the frame which rises from it will pass along the slit groove between the plates which overlap the channel but do not meet. Hard wood will answer as well as brass or metal if the latter be not at hand. A chamfered groove, L., may be substituted if desired, but is not so easily cut with the necessary smoothness and accuracy, nor does it afford as much support to the slide; we decidedly therefore recommend the method first described. A makeshift for a similar purpose can be constructed of thick cardboard to teach perspective in a room, but the above, neatly made of as light a material as possible, is far better and more accurate.

CHAPTER VIII.

SEVENTH LESSON.

VENEERING—SPECIAL TOOLS—VENEERING FLAT SURFACES—
VENEERING CURVED SURFACES—FRENCH POLISHING—CON-
CLUSION.

It has long been the custom where money is an object, which is unfortunately very generally the case, to make articles of furniture of deal, and
lay on outside it a thin coat of wood of a handsome kind, most generally
rosewood. This would be all very well, provided that the said outer coat were
not almost as frequently removable as one's own coat, and given to rise in
blisters, and scale off under the influence of a change of temperature. Like
French polish, which in effect has banished from the household the good
old housemaid, who used to keep the furniture bright by the copious use
of elbow grease, the veneered furniture has ousted the more solid, trustworthy articles, that in olden times descended from father to son through
many successive generations. But, somehow, our forefathers seem always
to have had cash to buy these better articles, or they used to be procurable
for less, or we have taken up too much of French polish ourselves, and
regard appearances more than solid work. Anyhow, we now unhesitatingly
purchase furniture warranted to fall to pieces in a year, if only it wear a
lustrous face, and has its weak points carefully hidden from our eyes.

After which snarl of bitter experience let us go on to speak of the way
in which the veneer is to be put on—it will come off of itself. In the
first place are required a few special tools : (1), a toothing plane ; (2),
a veneering hammer ; (3), a set of clamps and cauls, and a screw press
or some efficient substitute ; (4), glue pot, and some of the very best thin
transparent glue, with brush ; (5), a basin of boiling water, and a
sponge ; (6), a hot iron of some kind, a common flat iron will do for many
kinds of work, but its special use will be understood presently. The
veneers themselves must be bought. They are cut with a tremendously
big circular saw, built up, so to speak, on the edge of a large disc or wheel
of cast iron. The side next to the log is flat, the other is bevelled off so as
to cause the veneer to curl off side ways as it is cut. The thickness is
about 1-12th of an inch, but lately this has been reduced until the veneers

are cut as thin as paper, and indeed are used to cover walls in the same manner. The latter, however, are cut in a different way. The log is first turned on a lathe to a truly cylindrical form, and then placed between centres in a special machine, which gives it a slow rotation on its axis, while a knife or fine saw pares off a continuous coil much in the same way as you would pare a potato or reduce a cork. Ivory has been also similarly treated, by which a large and long sheet of that beautiful material has been cut and subsequently flattened by heat and pressure, so as to fit it for use as a veneer. Almost any of the foreign woods may be obtained in this form at a reasonable rate; and for any small job the amateur in town or country could readily suit his requirements at the nearest cabinet makers.

A piece must be cut with a knife, of the size and shape required to cover the object, the surface of which we will suppose to be flat in the first instance, as we will deal with curved surfaces presently. Have the glue boiling hot, which is best done by putting soda or salt in the water in the outer vessel. This, boiling at a higher temperature than pure water, will, if once boiled, retain the glue at boiling point. Veneering, however, should be always done in a workshop where a fire can be made, and the work should be within reach of the glue pot as it stands upon the hob. The basin of hot water being also at hand, score the surface upon which the veneer is to be placed with the toothing plane, and also that of the veneer, but to a very slight depth on account of its thinness. This is to give a better hold to the glue. Now damp the veneer on its upper side with the sponge and hot water, or when the glue is applied to the under side it will curl up. Warm the surface to which it is to be applied—if thin, on both sides —to prevent warping. Now quickly brush over with the glue—the consistency of cream—the surfaces of both the veneer and the article to which it is to be applied, and lay the former in its place. Then take the veneering hammer and use it as follows: it is called a hammer, and is, in fact, sometimes literally such, as the pane of a carpenter's hammer will answer for any small job. The real hammer, however, has a very broad pane or edge, and the handle is not inserted at right angles. It is held by the head, so as to rest the edge of its pane upon the work, and with this pressed down and moved in a wriggling way, the glue is pressed out, and the veneer laid flat. This is to be begun, therefore, in the centre of the work, and the pressure carried thence outwards so as to push before it both air bubbles and glue, which will ultimately escape at the edges. The heated iron is to be applied, and also the sponge and hot water if the glue chill and become hard too soon, or if any blister appear, caused by air underneath the veneer not being able to escape. A small flat piece of work may now be placed under a heavy weight, or screwed up in a press, and when dry will be found to be quite level and ready for the further operation of finishing and polishing. Any overhanging pieces must be cut off with a sharp knife or fine saw. The operation, so far, is extremely simple, and presents no apparent difficulty, but it nevertheless is one which frequently fails more or less from neglect of certain precautions, especially from not keeping the glue sufficiently hot, and from not working it out sufficiently at the edges. The more you squeeze out, remember, the better, because you are sure to leave quite enough to secure the union of the parts even after doing your best to squeeze out the whole. If one bit of veneer be not enough to cover the surface you may of course fit as many as you like and of all shapes, cutting them to line with a knife; but the more in number the pieces to be so arranged the more careful you must be to work quickly in arranging them side by side, and preventing them from slipping asunder when pressing out the glue. Do not, however, attempt too large a surface until after attaining a fair degree of skill. You may cover a part first, and when dry go on to a second section. But, if so, it is the better way at once to wipe off clean with a sponge and hot water the glue that oozes out upon the uncovered portion of the work, so that it shall not remain and harden upon it. If it should (and in any case it will form a thin glaze), it should be carefully scraped off and the toothing plane run over it again.

If the surface to be covered, instead of being plane, be of a curved or rounded form, it is evidently impossible to work in the above way; and the operation is not only more difficult but requires special screw clamps and cauls of wood or metal. The latter term is applied to pieces of wood or metal cut or bent to the exact shape of the surface to be veneered, forming thereto a kind of case, whereby the veneer is to be held in place until dry. Whenever, therefore, a cabinet maker designs a piece of furniture that is to be veneered, he also makes a special caul to fit the curved parts; and hence it is, among other causes, that we see so many repetitions of the same pattern issued from any particular shop, and such unwillingness to depart from it. There is far more freedom in this respect when veneer is not intended to be used, as in the best furniture.

Designing for cabinet makers is, as it deserves to be, a well-paid art, and a new pattern is not to be had without special outlay. Let us consider this *en passant*, as it is little understood by outsiders. First comes the rough sketch or original design—true artist's work of head and hand. If satisfactory, this has to be repeated to scale—one inch or half an inch of the drawing representing one foot of the work. This needs great care. Then come the details, the skeleton so to speak, each also to a given scale, with tenon and mortice, and curved and straight pieces of framework, in full detail, in plan, elevation, and, where necessary, in section; and when the drawing is complete it has to be repeated on tracing paper, perhaps several times, for the use of the workmen, and to send out to customers. Then come pattern pieces or templates of curved parts, made from the drawings, but of full size, in zinc, or wood, or paper, to be numbered or lettered for future use. Add to this the cauls and special clamps for veneered parts, and the trouble and risk of getting the workmen used to the new design, so as to understand it, and ample cause appears for making large numbers of articles of the same pattern before relinquishing it in favour of a new one. Hence, also, the immense advantage of the large shops, where capital is at hand to pay handsomely the most skilful and clever artists that can be engaged.

Metal cauls are not likely to be used by amateurs, as they are too costly, cumbrous, and otherwise ill-adapted to their use. In curved surfaces generally it is highly desirable to let the pressure begin on the centre, and gradually spread thence towards the edges of the work, as explained in treating of flat surfaces. Hence wooden cauls are made so as to be capable of bending *slightly* under pressure, and the middle of the curve is first clamped by their means, and other clamps added on each side working outwards. The glue is thus driven onward as before towards the edges. These cauls are always heated, so as to keep the glue under the veneers in a perfectly fluid state until the last clamp is screwed on. With iron clamps it is evident that this can be done to a far greater extent than with wood; and iron clamps and presses of great power and the heat of steam are largely used by pianoforte-case makers and others.

To amateurs, for whom we are specially writing, we may mention a makeshift often of great service in holding down veneers, viz., needle points, such as are used largely by upholsterers for fixing gilt mouldings and for other purposes. One of these driven here and there will hold the veneer firmly, and can be easily extracted after all is dry, leaving no appreciable mark, as the minute hole is at once filled up by the polish. They need only just penetrate the veneer enough to hold it securely, and the latter, being damp, will not be split by their use. No one knows how handy this plan will prove for little odd corners and places where no screw clamp will take hold. These clamps are of all shapes and sizes. The wooden ones of beech, with two wooden screws (cut by a screw box), as used by every carpenter, are of universal service; but in addition there can be had very convenient ones of metal, various patterns of which may be inspected at any tool shop.

On a *convex* surface, a very simple plan is to tie the work round at intervals with wire or string, putting little wedges of wood under it to prevent its cutting into the veneer, and to assist in tightening it to the requisite degree. The string should not be coiled, but passed round the work here and there, and each piece tied. Begin here also in the middle, so as to squeeze out the glue towards the edges of the work gradually. Always be careful to arrange the different slips of veneer so that the grain of the wood shall produce an artistic and beautiful effect, else the work will have a spotty appearance and general want of unity that will be displeasing to the eye. The various mouldings are of course not veneered, but cut out of the solid material, and should generally be of the same wood as the veneer.

As regards general effect it must not be forgotten that veneered work is a *sham,* and a sham is an attempt to deceive, and is of itself very detestable, under whatever aspect it may appear. Nevertheless your sham ought to look like reality, or it will be a *bad* sham, which is one degree worse. Take care, therefore, to make very close and accurate joints when any two slips of veneer meet together edgewise, and do not let the grain of one piece stand across that of the others, unless it be as part of a set design, apparent to the eye as a design, and not leaving in the mind any question as to whether it may not possibly be a mistake or want of skill on the part of the workman.

As a rule a strong and sharp knife, short in the blade and with a large handle, to give the hand a good grasp of the instrument, will be found preferable to a saw for cutting the various pieces. When, however, the wood is very hard or of very knotty and curled grain, a saw may be necessary to cut a straight line, and the finest tenon or mitring saw will then be the best tool to work with.

It now remains to polish the veneers, and as the same method is used as for solid work, we shall give full details. Knotted or cross-grained wood cannot be planed with the planes used for deal, but with a special tool, of which the iron is placed at a more obtuse angle. These planes can be had in wood or metal, and are in general use by cabinet makers. They are named according to the angle at which the iron is placed. For deal and soft wood this is 45 degs., or common pitch; for mahogany and hard wood 50 degs., or York pitch; while the iron set at 55 degs., middle pitch, or 60 degs., half pitch, is used for moulding planes for soft and hard wood. When the latter is, however, very knotty, it is worked over in all directions with a toothing plane, so as to cut across the fibres and reduce the surface to a general level. It is then finished by the scraper, often a piece of freshly broken glass, but more properly a thin plate of steel set in a piece of wood, and ground off quite square. The edge is then often rubbed with a burnisher, to turn up a slight wire edge. This will scrape down the surface of the wood until it is ready for " papering," i.e., being further smoothed by glass or sand paper. This is to be rubbed in all directions, until the work has an even surface, and the lines thus produced are further reduced by the finest sandpaper, marked 00. After this it is rubbed over with a bit of flannel, dipped in linseed oil, and allowed to dry. This oiling is then repeated, and the work again set aside for a day or more, until the oil is fairly absorbed.

If the wood is of a porous nature this process may be omitted, and, instead, the wood is to be rubbed over with a mixture of Russian tallow and plaster of Paris. After this is dry the same process is to be repeated until all the pores are well filled up and a good smooth surface obtained. When this is thoroughly dry the polishing may be commenced, and for the first coats plenty of the polish is to be taken on the rubber, so as to give a good body—but for the rest a very little is to be used, and thinner in quality. The polish—French polish—is made by dissolving shellac in spirits of wine or methylated spirit, or even naptha. This is facilitated by placing the jar or bottle in a warm place, on a stove or by the fire. Other gums are often added, but are not generally necessary. In short, no two polishers use precisely similar ingredients, but shellac is the base of all of them. We append a few recipes collected from various sources more or less reliable.

First, 4oz. shellac, 1 pint spirit of wine; *second*, 4oz. shellac, ½oz. sandarac, 1 pint spirit; *third*, finishing polish, best rectified spirit wine ¼ pint, shellac 2dr., gum benzoin 2dr. Put into a bottle, loosely corking it, and stand it near a fire, shaking it occasionally. When cold, add two teaspoonfuls of poppy oil, and shake well together. These, it must be remembered, are polishes to be applied by means of rubbers, and not by a brush. Those used in the latter way are varnishes such as are applied to cheap wares, and also to parts of furniture and such articles as are carved and cannot in consequence be finished by rubbing. Varnishes cannot be safely made by the amateur, as they require to be boiled—a dangerous process, for the ingredients include turpentine and linseed oil. Moreover, any of the varnishes can be readily procured in London, and many in our country towns.

It is necessary now to proceed with our directions for French polishing. In the first place, to insure absolute success the work should be done in a warm room, free from dust. Make a rubber of cotton wool, of a size suited to the work. For a small job it may be 2in. diameter, or less. For larger work it may be as big as a cricket ball. Roll it pretty tight, and cover with rag, tied securely. Sometimes list is rolled up and the rag tied over one end, which will make a very soft wad. In whatever way it is made, dip it into the polish, or pour a few drops upon it, and quickly cover it with another soft linen rag, wetted with a drop of raw linseed oil. This rag acts as a strainer, and the oil prevents it from sticking to the work, as it otherwise rather interferes with the process, and causes the polish to be full of smears and dull streaks. Rub lightly with circular sweeps, taking only a small part of the surface at one time, and continue until the rag begins to stick, or until it is dry enough to begin to scratch the surface; then take off the outer rag and repeat the process as before, with one drop only of oil each time. The work will gradually get a partial polish, still looking dull here and there and uneven. In taking off the rubber do not lift it straight up, or it will leave a mark—bring it with a sweep clean from the wood. Now set all aside for a day to dry thoroughly. Much of the polish will in a few hours sink into the face of the work, but this is of no consequence, and indeed it will improve matters if at this stage the whole surface is rubbed well with the finest sand or glass paper, which will leave it of a uniform dull grey colour. The pores, however, will now have been well filled up and a good foundation laid. Again, therefore, the polishing process is to be repeated, and this time the polish should not be too thick, and as little oil should be used as possible. When this is dry, if it look fairly well, it may not need another coat, but may be finished by putting on a clean rubber a few drops of spirits of wine, which will remove all the smears caused by the oil, and give a finished appearance to the whole. The above is the process of French polishing, but there is a great deal of knack and experience

K

necessary to secure perfection. It is by no means easy to polish equally all over any large surface. There is a good deal dependent on the touch, for after a time the workman is able to tell by the sense of feeling when the rubber is too dry, or whether it needs more or less oil or polish upon it. It must never stick in any case, if it does it needs oiling; but if this is overdone, the polish, however ·bright at the moment, will soon fade and leave the surface quite dull. The last few strokes with the spirits of wine only on the rubber should be in the direction of the grain, and not in a circle as before. There is in fact, no need now to rub the work, but it is finished by light sweeping strokes in one direction only. Even after this it will improve the appearance to let the surface get very dry and then give one more coat of thin polish, finishing again with the spirits of wine only.

For lathe work I have pursued a different course, and obtained a most brilliant polish. The polish itself I made thin, almost as liquid as milk. This I put in a bottle, and turning it upside down obtained a few drops on the cork, which was a nice soft one, out of a medicine bottle. Causing the work to revolve away from me, I held the cork against it, adding one drop of Rangoon oil. This is, I believe, sperm or olive oil, with a little paraffin added, at any rate the latter forms an excellent lubricant for all purposes. The polish gets absorbed, and, under pressure, exudes again from the pores of the cork. Alternating oil and polish, but chiefly the latter, I soon obtained a surface of exquisite brilliancy, far beyond that produced by an ordinary rubber, and I am inclined to think that a ball of cork shavings would prove superior to one of cotton wool, list, or other material. Of course, after polishing, the work must stand till the next day or longer, and then receive a finishing coat, because, however applied, the polish is quite sure to sink and render the work dull again; but any trouble is well repaid. The labour of French polishing in the lathe is nothing compared to similar work done by hand on a large surface, and so essential is practice to perfect success, that in many towns polishing is carried on as a separate trade.

Polishing must not be confounded with varnishing, and a good many articles are finished by the latter process, as it is quicker and less laborious. But the surface obtained in this way bears no comparison to that produced by the rubber. The cheapest of the varnishes used chiefly for toys is made of rosin dissolved by the aid of heat in turpentine. Sandarac is used instead for the white hard varnish, and this gum finds a place also in French polish with many workmen. The following are from Holtzapffel's work on The Lathe: 1lb. hard wood lacquer, 2lb. shellac, 1 gall. of spirits of wine, or 1lb. seed lac, 1lb. white rosin, 1 gall. spirits of wine. To be used as French polish in the lathe. The varnishes are laid on with a brush made for the purpose. If the wood be of a very porous nature, like deal, it is usual to save polish by first filling the pores with size made either of very thin glue or parchment shavings boiled in water. When dry the surface is well rubbed down with very fine sand paper, and the process repeated. When again dry it is rubbed very smooth, and the French polishing or varnishing proceeded with.

In many books are recipes for staining wood or ivory of various colours, but now it is hardly worth while to make stains, because Stephen's wood stains, which answer far better than home-made ones, and Judson's dyes, supply every need, and are procurable in nearly every town of note in England. Cabinet makers will also generally spare the amateur small quantities either of varnish or polish, as will also painters and paper-hangers, who use several kinds of excellent varnishes.

We must now bid adieu once more to our readers, hoping that our endeavours to instruct them in the useful art of carpentry will not be wholly thrown away. Our book upon the subject is by no means of a pretentious character, nor do we pretend to lay before the reader the whole details of a joiner's business, which embraces hand railing for staircases, window sashes, and shop fronts, with other interior fittings of the house, be it cottage or palace. With these the amateur is never likely to deal, and the complications of hand railing for balusters are so numerous that many country carpenters are incompetent to undertake them. No amount of reading will, be it remembered, render anyone a proficient in carpentry or any other art. Nothing but constant practice with tools will teach their use, but directions clearly given will suggest the proper way of setting to work, and prevent the tyro from falling into any great errors. A blind man may eventually find his way to the desired spot, but he will do so more quickly and certainly by the aid of a kindly leader, though such leader may be no more than his little faithful doggie. We trust our friendly guidance of the amateur along the path of carpentry and joinery may prove as faithful and efficient.

INDEX.

A.

Adzes 8
Augers 31
Awls 30
Axes 6

B.

Bassoolah 9
Bedstead 84
Bench fittings 35
Bending by steam 113
Bevels 43
Blind dovetail 69
Boring tools 30
Box, tool 59
Brace and bits 31
Built-up curved work 115

C.

Cabinet door 48
Carpenter's bench 35
Chest of drawers 76
Chisels 11
Classification of tools 5
Claw and pillar table . . . 121
Console table 123
Curved spokeshave 122
   Surface veneering . . . 142
   Work, built-up 115
   Work, rough 113
   Work, vice for 114

Curves, cutting with sweep
   saw 114
Cutting curves with sweep saw 114

D.

Desk, double pillar telescope
   reading 130
   Oak reading 124
   Pillar and claw telescope
     reading 125
   Writing 66
Doors for cabinet 48
   Panelled 50
Double pillar telescope read-
   ing table 130
Dovetails 56
   Blind 69
Dowelling 56
Drawers, chest of 76
   Nest of 62
Draw knife 13
   Curved 122

E.

Ellipse 116

F.

Flat surfaces, veneering . . 141
Frame, light mortised . . . 52
French polishing 144

G.

Gauges	45
Gimlets	30
Gluing	59
Gouges	12
Greenhouses	101
Grindstones	32
Groving	49

H.

Hammers	10
Holdfast	39
Hones	33
Hot water plant case	90

I.

Indian wardrobe	82
Introduction	3

L.

Lamp heated plant cases	95
Light mortised frames	52

M.

Mallet	10
Method of describing an ellipse	115
Mitred and dovetailed joint	71
Mitre keys	66
Mitres	65
Mitring	65
And shooting block	66
Box	39
Mortice, open	56
Mortised frame, light	52
Mortising	45

N.

Nest of drawers	62

O.

Oak reading desk	124
Oil stones	33
Open mortice	56
Ovals	115

P.

Panelled doors	50
Panelling	50
Perspectograph	136
Pillar and claw telescope reading desk	125
Pitch of planes	144
Planes	23
Pitch of	144
Plant case, hot water	90
Lamp heated	95
Polishes	145
Polishing, French	144
Preparation of material	43

R.

Reading desk, oak	124
Rebating	48
Rough curved work	113

S.

Saws	14
Screw block and taps	81
Secret dovetails	69
Sharpening tools	32
Shooting board	40
Special tools for veneering	140
Spokeshaves	13
Curved	122
Squares	43
Squaring up	43
Surfaces, curved, veneering	142
Flat, veneering	141
Staining	147
Steam, bending by	113

T.

Tables, double pillar telescope reading	130
Console	123
Pillar and claw	121
Pillar and claw telescopes reading	125
Tenons	47
Wedging	55
Tongue and groove	49
Tool box	59
Tools, adze	8
Auger	31

Tools, awl and gimlets . . . 30
    Axe 6
    Bench 35
    Bevels 43
    Boring 30
    Brace and bits 31
    Chisels 11
    Classification of 5
    Draw knife 13
    Draw knife, curved . . . 122
    Gauges 45
    Gimlet 30
    Gouges 12
    Grindstones 32
    Hammers 10
    Holdfast 39
    Hones 33
    Mallet 10
    Mitring and shooting block 66
    Mitring box 39
    Oil stones 33
    Planes 23
    Saws 14
    Screw block and taps . . 81

Tools, sharpening 32
    Shooting board 40
    Spokeshave 13
    Spokeshave, curved . . 122
    Squares 43
    Trammel 118
    Veneering 140
    Vices 35
    Vices, wooden universal . 114
Trammel 118

V.

Varnishing 146
Veneering 140
    Curved surfaces 142
    Flat surfaces 141
    Tools 140
Vice for curved work, &c. . . 114

W.

Wardrobe, Indian 82
Washstand 72
Wedging tenons 55

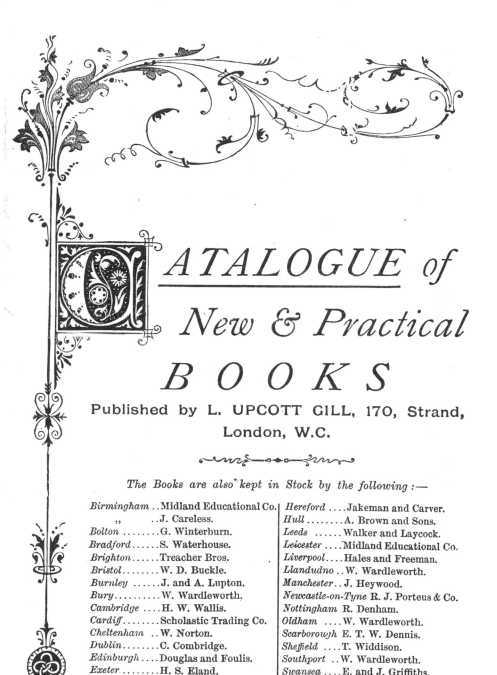

ATALOGUE of
New & Practical
BOOKS

Published by L. UPCOTT GILL, 170, Strand, London, W.C.

The Books are also kept in Stock by the following :—

Birmingham ..Midland Educational Co.	*Hereford* ....Jakeman and Carver.
,, ..J. Careless.	*Hull* ....A. Brown and Sons.
Bolton ....G. Winterburn.	*Leeds* ......Walker and Laycock.
Bradford......S. Waterhouse.	*Leicester* ....Midland Educational Co.
Brighton......Treacher Bros.	*Liverpool*....Hales and Freeman.
Bristol........W. D. Buckle.	*Llandudno* ..W. Wardleworth.
Burnley ......J. and A. Lupton.	*Manchester*..J. Heywood.
Bury..........W. Wardleworth.	*Newcastle-on-Tyne* R. J. Porteus & Co.
Cambridge ....H. W. Wallis.	*Nottingham* R. Denham.
Cardiff........Scholastic Trading Co.	*Oldham* ....W. Wardleworth.
Cheltenham ..W. Norton.	*Scarborough* E. T. W. Dennis.
Dublin........C. Combridge.	*Sheffield* ....T. Widdison.
Edinburgh ....Douglas and Foulis.	*Southport* ..W. Wardleworth.
Exeter ....H. S. Eland.	*Swansea* ....E. and J. Griffiths.
Glasgow ......W. and R. Holmes.	*Taunton* ....Barnicott and Son.
Gt.Yarmouth..A. and W. Huke.	*Torquay* ....A. Iredale.
Halifax ......J. Crossley.	

No. 2.— 1886.

❮ CATALOGUE ❯

OF

PRACTICAL HANDBOOKS.

₊ *All Books sent Carriage Free on Receipt of Remittance.*

ANIMALS.

BREAKING AND TRAINING DOGS.
Being Concise Directions for the proper
Education of Dogs, both for the Field and
for Companions. Second Edition. By
"Pathfinder." With Chapters by HUGH

DALZIEL, on
Work of Spe-
cial Breeds;
Trail or Drag
H o u n d s;
T r a i n i n g
B l o o d -
hounds; Defenders and Watch-dogs;
Sheepdogs—Stock Tenders; Life Savers—
Water Dogs; Vermin Destroyers; House
Manners; Behaviour Out of Doors. Illus-
trated. In cloth gilt, **price 6s. 6d.**

PRACTICAL DAIRY FARMING. A
short Treatise on the Profitable Management of a Dairy Farm.
Illustrated. By G. SEA-
WARD WITCOMBE. In
paper, **price 1s. 6d.**
"A mass of interesting
material."—*The Field.*

BOOK OF THE GOAT. Containing full
particulars of the various Breeds of Goats,
and their Profitable Management. With
many plates. By H.
STEPHEN HOLMES
PEGLER. Third Edi-
tion, revised, enlarged,
and with additional
illustrations and
coloured frontispiece.
In cloth gilt, **price
4s. 6d.** "The best
book we know on the
subject."—*Chambers's Journal.*

GOAT-KEEPING FOR AMATEURS
Being the Practical Manage-
ment of Goats for Milking
Purposes. Abridged from
"The Book of the Goat,"
by H. S. HOLMES PEGLER.
Illustrated. Now ready.
In paper, **price 1s.**

DISEASES OF DOGS: Their Pathology,
Diagnosis, and Treatment; to which is
added a complete Dictionary of Canine
Materia Medica; Modes of Administering
Medicines; Treatment in cases of Poison-
ing, and the
Value of Dis-
infectants.
For the of
Amateurs.
By H U G H
D A L Z I E L,
Author of "British Dogs," &c. New,
Revised, and Greatly Enlarged Edition.
In paper, **price 1s.**; in cloth gilt, **2s.**
"Will enable anybody who keeps a dog to
deal with cases of ordinary indisposition or
injury."—*The Scotsman.*

OF ENGLISHE DOGGES. The Diversi-
ties, the Names, the Natures, and the Pro-
perties. Date 1576. Re-
printed verbatim.
[Note. — This is the
earliest book in the
English language on
the subject, and should
be in the hands of all
who take an interest in
Dogs.] In boards, **price
2s. 6d.** "It cannot fail
to commend itself to all." — *Live Stock
Journal.*

☞ *All Books sent Carriage Free.*

L. UPCOTT GILL, Publisher, 170, Strand, London, W.C.

DISEASES OF HORSES : Their Pathology, Diagnosis, and Treatment ; to which is added a complete Dictionary of Equine Materia Medica. For the Use of Amateurs. By HUGH DALZIEL. In paper, **price 1s. 6d.** "Should be in the hands of every horse owner."—*Sporting Chronicle.*

EXHIBITION ACCOUNT BOOKS. For use at all Dog, Poultry, Pigeon, Rabbit, and Cage Bird Shows. In Four Books, comprising : I. Minute Book ; II. Cash Book ; III. Entries Book ; IV. Ledger. With Full Directions and Illustrative Examples for Working them. N.B.—The Set of Four Books is kept in Three Series : No. 1, for Show of 500 Entries, **5s.** the set ; No. 2, for 1000 Entries, **7s. 6d.** the set ; and No. 3, for 1500 Entries, **12s. 6d.** the set. Larger sizes in proportion. The books can be had separate. MINUTE BOOK, No. 1, **1s.** ; No. 2, **1s. 3d.** : No. 3, **2s.** ; CASH BOOK, No. 1, **2s.** ; No. 2, **2s. 6d.** ; No. 3, **4s.** ENTRIES BOOK, No. 1, **2s.** ; No. 2, **2s. 6d.** ; No. 3, **4s.** LEDGER, No. 1, **2s.** ; No. 2, **2s. 6d.** ; No. 3, **4s.** "Just what are wanted, for a set of these books will save a vast amount of labour and trouble."—*The Stock-keeper.*

BOOK OF THE PIG. Containing the Selection, Breeding, Feeding, and Management of the Pig ; the Treatment of its Diseases ; the Curing and Preserving of Hams, Bacon, and other Pork Foods ; and

other information appertaining to Pork Farming. By Professor JAMES LONG. Fully Illustrated with Portraits of Prize Pigs, by HARRISON WEIR and other Artists, Plans of Model Piggeries, &c. In cloth gilt, **price 15s.** "This is assuredly a publication to be proud of. It goes a good deal further than any book on the subject which has been issued before, and, without being infallible, is well informed, well illustrated, and well written."—*The Field.*

PIG KEEPING FOR AMATEURS. A Practical Guide to the Profitable Management of Pigs. By G. GILBERT ("Gurth"). In paper, **price 1s.** "Not merely a good deal of useful and practical information, but many bits of homely folk-lore."—*Spectator.*

RABBITS FOR PRIZES AND PROFIT. Containing Full Directions for the proper Management of Fancy Rabbits in Health and Disease, for Pets or the Market ; and Descriptions of every known Variety, with Instructions for Breeding good specimens. Illustrated. By the late CHARLES RAYSON. Revised by the Editor of "The Book of the Rabbit." In cloth gilt, **price 2s. 6d.** "We have often had occasion to recommend this work."—*The Field.* [May also be had in two parts, as follow :]

GENERAL MANAGEMENT OF RABBITS. Including Hutches, Breeding, Feeding, Diseases and their Treatment, Rabbit Coverts, &c. Fully illustrated. (*Forming Part I. of "Rabbits for Prizes and Profit."*) In paper, **price 1s.**

EXHIBITION RABBITS. Being Descriptions of all Varieties of Fancy Rabbits, their Points of Excellence, and how to obtain them. Illustrated. (*Forming Part II. of "Rabbits for Prizes and Profit."*) In paper, **price 1s.**

FERRETS AND FERRETING. Containing Instructions for the Breeding, Management, and Working of Ferrets. In paper, **price 6d.** "Well worthy of perusal . . . . Contains valuable information."—*Sportsman.*

FANCY MICE—Their Varieties, Management, and Breeding. Re-issue, with Criticisms, &c., by Dr. CARTER BLAKE. Illustrated. In paper, **price 6d.** "Goes thoroughly into the subject."—*Cambridge Chronicle.*

KENNEL DIARY. A Register for Owners, Breeders, and Exhibitors of Dogs, wherein they can keep full particulars of their Studs in a convenient and comprehensive manner. Contains : 1. Index Diary ; 2. Owner's Diary ; 3. Breeder's Diary ; 4. Diary of Pups ; 5. Stud Diary ; 6. Exhibition Diary ; 7. General Diary ; 8. Pedigree Diary ; 9. Receipts ; 10. Expenditure ; 11. General Balance Sheet. In cloth, with pockets for certificates, **3s. 6d.** "The Editor has left little room for improvement."—*Live Stock Journal.*

☞ *All Books sent Carriage Free.*

L. UPCOTT GILL, Publisher, **170, Strand, London, W.C.**

THE GUINEA PIG, for Food, Fur, and Fancy. Illustrated with Coloured  Frontispiece and Engravings. An exhaustive book on the Varieties of the Guinea Pig, or Cavy, and their Management for Pleasure or Profit. By C. CUMBERLAND, F.Z.S. In cloth gilt, **price 2s. 6d.**

ART AND VIRTU.

PRACTICAL VIOLIN SCHOOL for Home Students. A Practical Book of Instructions and Exercises in Violin Playing, for the use  of Amateurs, Self-learners, Teachers, and others. By J. M. FLEMING, Author of "Old Violins and their Makers." Now ready, 1 vol., demy 4to, cloth gilt, **price 7s. 6d.** In Parts, **7d.** Monthly.

MIRROR PAINTING in the Italian Style. A Practical Manual of Instruc- tion for Amateurs. This highly decorative art has be- come very popular, but the execution is not always worthy of the design, in con- sequence of want of know- ledge on the part of the Artist. This book will supply the deficiency. By Mrs. SHARP-AYRES. **Price 1s.**

ARTISTIC AMUSEMENTS. Being In- structions in Colouring Photographs, Imitation Stained Glass, Decalcomanie, Queen Shell Work, Painting on China, Japanese Lacquer Work, Stencilling, Painting Magic Lan- tern Slides, Menu and Guest Cards,  Spatter Work, Pic- ture and Scrap Screens, Frosted Sil- ver Work, Picture Cleaning and Restoring, Illuminating and Symbolical Colouring. Illustrated. In cloth gilt, **price 2s. 6d.** "Practical, satis- factory in its treatment, and very interest- ing."—*The Queen.*

CHINA PAINTING. Its Principles and Practice. A Guide to Amateurs and others commencing the Art  of Painting on China. By WALTER HARVEY. Illustrated. In paper, **price 1s.** "Just what is wanted."— *Ladies' Journal.*

ALL ABOUT PAINTING ON CHINA. With Twelve Descriptive Lessons. The object of this little book is to teach, by easy progressive Lessons, all that a beginner requires to know about China Painting. By Mrs. CONYERS MORRELL. Second Edition. In paper, **price 9d.**

DECORATIVE PAINTING. A Prac- tical Handbook on Painting and Etching upon Textiles, Pottery, Porcelain, Paper, Vellum, Leather, Glass, Wood, Stone, Metals, and Plaster, for the Decoration of our Homes. By B. C. SAWARD. In the new "Renaissance" bind- ing, **price 7s. 6d.** "Spared no pains to give useful information as to the various processes of Decorative Painting."—*Aca- demy.*

A GUIDE TO THE COINS of Great Britain and Ireland, in Gold, Silver, and Copper, from the Earliest Period to the Present Time, with their Value. By Major W. STEWART THORBURN.' Of immense value to collec- tors and dealers. Plates in Gold, Silver, and Cop- per. In gold cloth, with Silver Fac-similes of Coins, **price 6s. 6d.** "Such a book as this has never before been placed within the reach of the ordinary collector . . . . A model of careful and accurate work."— *The Queen.*

ENGLISH POTTERY AND PORCE- lain. A Manual for Collectors. Being a Concise Account of the Development of the Potter's Art in England. Profusely Illustrated with Marks, Monograms, and En- gravings of Characteristic Speci- mens. New Edition. In cloth gilt, **price 3s. 6d.** "The collector will find the work invaluable."—*Broad Arrow.*

BEES AND BIRDS.

BEES AND BEE-KEEPING—Scientific and Practical. VOL. I., SCIENTIFIC. A com- plete Treatise on the Ana- tomy and Physiology of the Hive Bee. By F. R. CHES- HIRE, F.L.S., F.R.M.S., Lec- turer on Apiculture at South Kensington. In cloth gilt, **price 7s. 6d.**; also in Monthly Parts, **price 7d.** VOL. II., PRACTICAL, will deal exhaustively with the Profitable Manage- ment of Bees.

☞ *All Books sent Carriage Free.*

L. UPCOTT GILL, Publisher, 170, Strand, London, W.C.

POULTRY for PRIZES and PROFIT.
Contains : Breeding Poultry for Prizes, Exhibition Poultry, and Management of the Poultry Yard. Handsomely Illustrated. New Edition, Revised and Enlarged. By Professor JAMES LONG. In cloth gilt, **price 3s. 6d.**

DUCKS AND GEESE. Their Characteristics, Points, and Management. The only Book on the subject of Domestic Waterfowl and their Proper Treatment. By Various Breeders. Splendidly Illustrated. In paper, **price 1s. 6d.** "A very desirable little work."—*The Queen.*

POULTRY AILMENTS and their Treatment. A Book for the Use of all Poultry Keepers, describing the Causes, Symptoms, and Cure of Diseases affecting Domestic Fowl. By D. J. THOMPSON GRAY. In paper boards, **price 1s.**

EXHIBITION ACCOUNT BOOKS. For use at all Dog, Poultry, Pigeon, Rabbit, and Cage Bird Shows. In Four Books, comprising : I. Minute Book; II. Cash Book; III. Entries Book; IV. Ledger. With Full Directions and Illustrative Examples for Working them. N.B.—The set of Four Books is kept in Three Series ; No. 1, for Show of 500 Entries, **5s.** the set ; No. 2, for 1000 Entries, **7s. 6d.** the set ; and No. 3, for 1500 Entries, **12s. 6d.** the set. Larger sizes in proportion. The books can be had separate. MINUTE

BOOK, No. 1, **1s.** ; No. 2, **1s. 3d.** ; No. 3, **2s.** CASH BOOK, No. 1, **2s.** ; No. 2, **2s. 6d.** ; No. 3, **4s.** ENTRIES BOOK, No. 1, **2s.** ; No. 2, **2s. 6d.** ; No. 3, **4s.** LEDGER, No. 1, **2s.** ; No. 2, **2s. 6d.** ; No. 3, **4s.** "We can recommend the books as admirably adapted for the purposes for which they are intended."—*The Field.*

THE SITTING HEN RECORD. Forming a convenient Record of all Eggs Set, and supplying in a handy and concise form Labels which can be readily attached to or above the Nest-boxes, showing at a glance the number of Eggs under the Hen, the Variety, and when they should be brought off. Price—50 Forms, **6d.** ; 100 Forms, **1s.**

DISEASES OF CAGE BIRDS. Their Cause, Symptoms, and Treatment. A Handbook which should be in the hands of everyone who keeps a Bird, as successful cure of ailments depends on knowing what to do, and *doing it promptly.* By Dr. W. T. GREENE, F.Z.S. In paper, **price 1s.**

FOREIGN CAGE BIRDS. Containing Full Directions for Successfully Breeding, Rearing, and Managing the various Beautiful Cage Birds imported into this Country. Beautifully Illustrated. By C. W. GEDNEY. In cloth gilt, in two vols., **price 8s. 6d.** ; in extra cloth gilt, gilt edges, in one vol., **price 9s. 6d.** "Full of information on every point." — *Public Opinion.*

PARROTS, PARRAKEETS, Cockatoos, Lories, and Macaws : Their Varieties, Breeding, and Management. Illustrated. (*Forming Vol. I. of "Foreign Cage Birds."*) In cloth gilt, **price 3s. 6d.**

WAXBILLS, FINCHES, Weavers, Orioles, and Other Small Foreign Aviary Birds : Their Varieties, Breeding, and Management. Beautifully Illustrated. (*Forming Vol. II. of " Foreign Cage Birds."*) In cloth gilt, **price 5s.**

FANCY PIGEONS. Containing Full Directions for the Breeding and Management of Fancy Pigeons, and Descriptions of every known variety, together with all other information of interest or use to Pigeon Fanciers. Third Edition, bringing the subject down to the present. COLOURED PLATES and other Illustrations. By J. C. LYELL. In Monthly parts, **price 7d.** "One of the best of the kind."—*Bell's Life.*

BRITISH CAGE BIRDS. Containing Full Directions for Successfully Breeding, Rearing, and Managing the various British Birds that can be kept in confinement. Illustrated with COLOURED PLATES and numerous finely-cut Wood Engravings. By R. L. WALLACE. In monthly parts, **price 7d.** To be complete in about Thirteen Parts.

☞ *All Books sent Carriage Free.*

L. UPCOTT GILL, Publisher, 170, Strand, London, W.C.

CANARY BOOK. Containing Full Directions for the Breeding, Rearing, and Management of all Varieties of Canaries and Canary Mules, the Promotion and Management of Canary Societies and Exhibitions, and all other matters connected with this Fancy. By ROBERT L. WALLACE. Second Edition, Enlarged and Revised. With many new Illustrations of Prize Birds, Cages, &c. In cloth gilt, **price 5s.** "This very comprehensive work . . . . which is one of a most practical character . . . may be safely consulted by all canary fanciers." —*The Field.* [May also be had in two Sections, as follows :]

GENERAL MANAGEMENT OF CANARIES: Including Cages and Cage Making, Breeding Managing, Mule Breeding, Diseases and their Treatment, Moulting, Rats and Mice, &c. Illustrated. Second Edition. Revised and Greatly Enlarged. (*Forming Section I. of the "Canary Book."*) In cloth, **price 2s. 6d.**

EXHIBITION CANARIES : Containing Full Particulars of all the different Varieties, their Points of Excellence, Preparing Birds for Exhibition, Formation and Management of Canary Societies and Exhibitions. Illustrated. (*Forming Section II. of the "Canary Book."*) Second Edition, Revised and Enlarged. In cloth, **price 2s. 6d.**

AMATEUR'S AVIARY OF FOREIGN Birds ; or, how to Keep and Breed Foreign Birds with Pleasure and Profit in England. Illustrated. By W. T. GREENE, M.D., M.A., F.Z.S., F.S.S., &c., Author of "Parrots in Captivity," &c. In cloth gilt, **price 3s. 6d.** "Is worthy of a hearty welcome from all breeders and keepers of foreign birds."—*Live Stock Journal.*

THE SPEAKING PARROTS. A Scientific Manual on the Art of Keeping and Breeding the principal Talking Parrots in confinement, by Dr. KARL RUSS, Author of "The Foreign Aviary Birds," "Manual for Bird Fanciers," &c. Illustrated with COLOURED PLATES. In Monthly Parts, **price 7d.**, or complete in cloth gilt **price 6s. 6d.** "Here is all that can be desired ; the directions how to feed and how to keep foreign birds in health are given by the greatest authority living."—*Public Opinion.*

BIRDS I HAVE KEPT IN YEARS Gone By. With Original Anecdotes, and Full Directions for Keeping them Successfully. By W. T. GREENE, M.A., M.D., F.Z.S., &c., Author of "Parrots in Captivity," "The Amateur's Aviary"; Editor of "Notes on Cage Birds," &c., &c. With COLOURED PLATES. In cloth gilt, **price 5s.** "A prettier present for anyone who is fond of these household pets it would be difficult to find."—*Stock-keeper.*

GARDENING.

DICTIONARY OF GARDENING. A Practical Encyclopædia of Horticulture for Amateurs and Professionals. Illustrated with upwards of 2000 Engravings. Edited by G. NICHOLSON, of Royal Botanic Gardens, Kew, assisted by Prof. Trail, M.D., Rev. P. W. Myles, M.A., B. W. Hemsley, A.L.S., W. Watson, J. Garrett, and other specialists. Vol. I., A to E, 552pp., 743 Illustrations, and Vol. II., F to O, 544pp., and 811 Illustrations, now ready, **price 15s.** each. Also in Monthly Parts, **price 1s.** "No work of the kind could be of more use to the professional and amateur gardener." — *Public Opinion.* "The fullest information is given, and the illustrations, which are exceedingly numerous, are first rate."—*The World.*

LILY OF THE VALLEY. All About It, and How to Grow It. Forced indoors, and out of doors in various ways. By WILLIAM ROBERTS. In paper covers, **price 6d.** "Lovers of these beautiful flowers will welcome this edition." —*Paper and Printing Trades Journal.*

HARDY PERENNIALS and Old-fashioned Garden Flowers. Descriptions, alphabetically arranged, of the most desirable Plants for Borders, Rockeries, and Shrubberies, including Foliage as well as Flowering Plants. Profusely Illustrated. By J. WOOD. In cloth, **price 5s.** "Seems particularly useful."—*Athenæum.*

☞ *All Books sent Carriage Free.*

L. UPCOTT GILL, Publisher, 170, Strand, London, W.C.

GREENHOUSE MANAGEMENT FOR Amateurs.

Descriptions of the best Greenhouses and Frames, with Instructions for Building them, particulars of the various methods of Heating, Illustrated Descriptions of the most suitable Plants, with general and special Cultural Directions, and all necessary information for the Guidance of the Amateur.  Second Edition, revised and enlarged. Magnificently Illustrated. By W. J. MAY. In cloth gilt, **price 5s.** "Ought to be in the hands of everybody."—*The Queen.*

VINE CULTURE FOR AMATEURS.

Being Plain Directions for the successful Growing of Grapes with the Means and Appliances usually at the command of Amateurs. Illustrated. Grapes are so generally grown in villa greenhouses, that this book cannot fail to be of great service to many persons. By W. J. MAY. In paper, **price 1s.** "Plain and practical."—*The Queen.*

PRUNING, GRAFTING, AND BUDding Fruit Trees.

 Illustrated with Ninety-three Diagrams. A book which can be followed with advantage by amateur fruit growers. By D. T. FISH. In paper, **price 1s.** "One of the few gardening books that will suit everybody."— *Gardener's Magazine.*

GARDEN PESTS AND THEIR Eradication.

Containing Practical Instructions for the Amateur to Overcome the Enemies of the Garden. With numerous Illustrations.  In paper, **price 1s.** "It is just the sort of book one would refer to in emergency."—*The Florist and Pomologist.*

ORCHIDS FOR AMATEURS.

Containing Descriptions of Orchids suited to  the requirements of the Amateur, with full Instructions for their successful Cultivation. With numerous beautiful Illustrations. By JAMES BRITTEN, F.L.S., and W. H. GOWER. In cloth gilt, **price 7s. 6d.** "The joint work of a competent botanist . . . and a successful cultivator with the experience of a quarter of a century."— *Gardener's Chronicle.*

BULBS AND BULB CULTURE.

Being descriptions, both Historical and Botanical, of the principal Bulbs and Bulbous Plants grown in this Country, and their Chief Varieties; with Full and Practical Instructions for their Successful Cultivation, both in and out of doors. Illustrated. By D. T. FISH. In cloth gilt, in one vol., 465pp., **price 5s.** "One of the best and most trustworthy books on bulb culture that have been put before the public." —*Gardener's Chronicle.*

ROSE BUDDING.

Containing full Instructions for the successful performance  of this interesting operation. Illustrated. Amateurs will find the information here given of great assistance. By D. T. FISH. In paper, **price 6d.** "Full, practical, ... and contains many valuable hints."—*Garden.*

CHRYSANTHEMUM.

Its History, Varieties, Cultivation, and Diseases. A small work which gives a large amount of useful information and instruction in growing to perfection one of the most popular autumn plants. By D. T. FISH. In paper, **price 6d.** "Replete with valuable hints and sound information."—*The Stationer.*

CUCUMBER CULTURE FOR AMAteurs.

Including also Melons, Vegetable Marrows, and Gourds. Illustrated. By W. J. MAY. In paper, **price 1s.** "Evidently the work of a thoroughly practical writer."—*Brief.*

ARBORICULTURE FOR AMAteurs.

Being Instructions for the Planting and Cultivation of Trees for Ornament or Use, and Selections and Descriptions of those suited to special requirements as to Soil, Situation, &c. By WILLIAM H. ABLETT, Author of "English Trees and Tree Planting," &c. In cloth gilt, **price 2s. 6d.** "Full of practical remarks, tending to make it a reliable and useful guide to amateur gardeners."—*The Farmer.*

☞ *All Books sent Carriage Free.*

L. UPCOTT GILL, Publisher, **170, Strand, London, W.C.**

VEGETABLE CULTURE FOR AMA-teurs. Concise Directions for the Culti-vation of Vege-tables, so as to insure good crops in small Gardens, with Lists of the best Varieties of each sort. By W. J. MAY. In paper, **price 1s.** "None more simple and prac-tically useful."—*The British Mail.*

PROFITABLE MARKET GARDEN-ing. Adapted for the use of all Growers and Gardeners. By WILLIAM EARLEY, Au-thor of "High Class Kitchen Gardening," &c. In cloth, **price 2s.** "La-bour greatly assisted by a perusal of this work."—*North British Agriculturist.*

MUSHROOM CULTURE FOR AMA-teurs. With full Directions for Success-ful Growth in Houses, Sheds, Cellars, and Pots, on Shelves, and Out of Doors. Illustrated. By W. J. MAY, Author of "Vine Culture for Ama-teurs," "Vegetable Culture for Amateurs," "Cucumber Culture for Amateurs." In paper, **price 1s.** "This excellent little book gives every direction necessary."—*Daily Bristol Times and Mirror.*

GENERAL LITERATURE.

A GUIDE TO THE LEGAL PRO-fession. A Practical Treatise on the various Methods of Entering either Branch of the Legal Profession ; also a Course of Study for each of the Examinations, and selected Papers of Questions ; forming a Complete Guide to every Department Legal Preparation. By J. H. SLATER, Barrister-at-Law, of the Middle Temple. **Price 7s. 6d.** "Any-one who, before en-tering on either branch of the profession desires information to determine which branch it shall be, will find a great deal here that will assist him." — *The Law Student's Journal.*

A GUIDE TO DEGREES in Arts, Science, Literature, Law, Music, and Divinity, in the United Kingdom, the Colonies, the Continent, and the United States. By E. WOOTON, Author of "A Guide to the Medical Profession," &c. In cloth, **price 15s.** "Is a complete store-house of educational information."—*The Graphic.*

THE LIBRARY MANUAL. A Guide to the Formation of a Library, and the Valuation of Rare and Standard Books. By J. H. SLA-TER, Barrister-at-Law, Au-thor of "A Guide to the Legal Profes-sion." Second Edition. In cloth, 112pp., **price 2s. 6d.** "A most ex-cellent and useful handbook." — *Public Opinion.*

CHARACTER INDICATED BY Handwriting. With Illustrations in support of the Theories advanced, tak-en from Auto-graph Letters of Statesmen, Lawyers, Sol-diers, Ecclesi-astics, Authors Poets, Musicians, Actors, and other persons. Second Edition, revised and enlarged. By R. BAUGHAN. In cloth gilt, **price 2s. 6d.**

PRACTICAL JOURNALISM. How to Enter Thereon and Succeed. A Manual for Beginners and Amateurs. A book for all who think of "writing for the press." By JOHN DAWSON. In cloth gilt, **price 2s. 6d.** "A very practical and sen-sible little book."—*Spectator.*

SHORTHAND SYSTEMS: Which is the Best? Being a Discussion by various English Authors and Experts on the Merits and Demerits of Taylor's, Gur-ney's, Pitman's, Everett's, Janes', Pock-nell's, Peachey's, Guest's, Williams', Odell's, and Red-fern's Systems, with Illustrative Examples. Edited by THOMAS ANDERSON, Author of "History of Shorthand," &c. In paper, **price 1s.** This is a book which ought to be carefully read by every person who is about to take up the study of Shorthand. "Is certain to be very much appreciated." —*The Derby Mercury.*

☞ *All Books sent Carriage Free.*

L. UPCOTT GILL, Publisher, 170, Strand, London, W.C.

LESSONS IN SHORTHAND, on Gurney's System (Improved). Being Instruction in the Art of Shorthand Writing, as used in the Service of the Two Houses of Parliament. By R. E. MILLER (of Dublin University; formerly Parliamentary Reporter; Fellow of the Shorthand Society). In paper, **price 1s.** "A very entertaining and able little book."— *Literary World.*

CHURCH FESTIVAL DECORATIONS. Comprising Directions and Designs for the Suitable Decoration of Churches for Christmas, Easter, Whitsuntide, and Harvest. Illustrated. A useful book for the Clergy and their Lay Assistants. In paper, **price 1s.** "Much valuable and practical information."— *Sylvia's Home Journal.*

GUIDES TO PLACES.

THE UPPER THAMES. From Richmond to Oxford. A Guide for Boating Men, Anglers, Picnic Parties, and all Pleasure Seekers on the River. Arranged on an entirely new plan. Illustrated. In paper, **price 1s.**; in cloth, with elastic band and pocket, **2s.** "One of the most useful handbooks to the river yet published."— *The Graphic.*

LAND OF THE BROADS. A Practical Guide for Yachtsmen, Anglers, Tourists, and other pleasure seekers on the Broads and Rivers of Norfolk and Suffolk. With map, **price 1s. 6d.** "A capital guide to the angler, the yachtsman, or the artist."— *Scotsman.*

WINTER HAVENS IN THE SUNNY South. A complete Handbook to the Riviera, with a notice of the new station, Alassio. Splendidly Illustrated. By ROSA BAUGHAN, Author of "The Northern Watering Places of France." In cloth gilt, **price 2s. 6d.** "It is a model 'guide,' and supplies a want."— *The Field.*

DICTIONARY OF FOREIGN Watering Places, Seaside and Inland. Contains Routes, Climate, and Season, Waters recommended for, Scenery, Objects of Interest, Amusements, Churches, Doctors, Boarding Establishments, Hotels, House Agents, Newspapers, &c. In cloth, **price 2s.** "We know of no other work in which all this information is to be obtained."— *The Broad Arrow.*

SEASIDE WATERING PLACES. A description of Holiday Resorts on the Coasts of England and Wales, the Channel Islands, and the Isle of Man, including the gayest and most quiet places, giving full particulars of them and their attractions, and all other information likely to assist persons in selecting places in which to spend their Holidays according to their individual tastes, with Business Directory of Tradesmen, arranged in order of the Town. Fifth Edition, with Maps and Illustrations. In cloth, **price 2s. 6d.** "One of the most complete guides to our English holiday resorts that paterfamilias could desire."— *Bell's Life.*

TOUR IN THE STATES AND Canada. Out and Home in Six Weeks. By THOMAS GREENWOOD. Illustrated. In cloth gilt, **price 2s. 6d.** "We can confidently recommend this book."— *The Literary World.*

NORTHERN WATERING PLACES of France. A Guide for English People to the Holiday Resorts on the Coasts of the French Netherlands, Picardy, Normandy, and Brittany. By ROSA BAUGHAN, Author of "Winter Havens in the Sunny South," &c. In paper, **price 2s.** "We have pleasure in recommending this work." — *Cook's Excursionist.*

THE TOURIST'S ROUTE MAP OF ENGLAND AND WALES. Shows clearly all the Main and most of the Cross Roads, and the Distances between the Chief Towns marked in small figures, as well as the Mileage from London. In addition to this, Routes of *Thirty* of the *most interesting Tours* are specially indicated, and marked in red. The Map in mounted on linen, so as not to tear, and is inclosed

☞ All Books sent Carriage Free.

L. UPCOTT GILL, Publisher, 170, Strand, London, W.C.

in a strong cloth case. It is thus in a convenient form for the pocket, and will not suffer from ordinary fair wear and tear, as is the case with most maps. **Price 1s. 2d.**, post free.

HOUSEHOLD.

PRACTICAL DRESSMAKING. Being Plain Directions for Taking Patterns, Fitting on, Cutting out, Making up, and Trimming Ladies' and Children's Dresses. By R. MUNROE. In paper, **price 1s.** "It is just the sort of book that anyone should have at hand to take counsel with."—*The Queen.*

THE DICTIONARY OF NEEDLE-work. An Encyclopædia of Artistic, Plain, and Fancy Needlework; Plain, practical, complete, and magnificiently Illustrated. By S. F. A. CAULFEILD and B. C. SAWARD. Accepted by H.M. the Queen, H.R.H. the Princess of Wales, H.R.H. the Duchess of Edinburgh, H.R.H. the Duchess of Connaught, and H.R.H. the Duchess of Albany. Dedicated by special permission to H.R.H. Princess Louise, Marchioness of Lorne. In demy 4to, 528pp.,

829 illustrations, extra cloth gilt, plain edges, cushioned bevelled boards, **price 21s.**; with COLOURED PLATES, elegant fancy binding, and coloured edges (for presentation), **31s. 6d.** Also in Monthly Parts, **price 1s.** "This very complete and rather luxurious volume is a thorough encyclopædia of artistic, plain, and fancy needlework. . . . After being submitted to the severe test of feminine criticism, the Dictionary emerges triumphant. . . . The volume, as a whole, deserves no small commendation." — *The Standard.* "This volume, one of the handsomest of its kind, is illustrated in the best sense of the term. . . . It is useful and concise—in fact, it is exactly what it professes to be. . . . This book has endured the severest test at our command with rare success."—*The Athenæum.*

HONITON LACE BOOK. Containing Full and Practical Instructions for Making Honiton Lace. With numerous Illustrations. In cloth gilt, **price 3s. 6d.** "We have seldom seen a book of this class better got up."—*Bell's Weekly Messenger.*

ARTISTIC FANCY WORK SERIES. A series of Illustrated Manuals on Artistic and Popular Fancy Work of various kinds. Each number is complete in itself, and issued at the uniform **price** of **6d.**

Now ready—
(1) MACRAMÉ LACE,
(2) PATCHWORK
(3) TATTING,
(4) CREWEL WORK,
(5) APPLIQUE.
"Will prove a valuable acquisition to the student of art needlework." — *The Englishwoman's Review.*

CHURCH EMBROIDERY: Its Early History and Manner of Working, Materials Used and Stitches Employed ; Raised and Flat Couching, Appliqué, &c., &c., including Church Work over Cardboard. Illustrated. **Price 1s.**

SICK NURSING AT HOME. Being Plain Directions and Hints for the Proper Nursing of Sick Persons, and the Home Treatment of Diseases and Accidents in case of sudden emergencies. By S F. A. CAULFEILD. In paper, **price 1s.**; in cloth, **price 1s. 6d.** "A copy ought to be in every nursery."—*Society.*

PRACTICAL HINTS ON COFFEE Stall Management, and other Temperance Work for the Laity. In paper, **price 1s.**

☞ *All Books sent Carriage Free.*

L. UPCOTT GILL, Publisher, 170, Strand, London, W.C.

COOKERY FOR AMATEURS: or, **French Dishes for English Homes of all Classes.** Includes Simple Cookery, Middle-class Cookery, Superior Cookery, Cookery for Invalids, and Breakfast and Luncheon Cookery. By MADAME VALÉRIE. Second Edition. In paper, **price 1s.** "Is admirably suited to its purpose."—*The Broad Arrow.*

INDIAN OUTFITS AND ESTAB-lishments. A Practical Guide for Persons about to reside in India; detailing the articles which should be taken out, and the requirements of home life and management there. By an ANGLO-INDIAN. In cloth, **price 2s. 6d.** "Is thoroughly healthy in tone, and practical."—*Saturday Review.*

MECHANICS.

REPOUSSÉ WORK FOR AMA-TEURS: Being the Art of Ornamenting Thin Metal with Raised Figures. By L. L. HASLOPE. Illustrated. Cloth, **price 2s. 6d.**

BOOKBINDING FOR AMATEURS. Being Descriptions of the various Tools and Appliances required, and Minute Instructions for their Effective Use. By W. J. E. CRANE. Illustrated with 156 Engravings. In cloth gilt, **price 2s. 6d.** "A handy manual for the study of an interesting and important art."—*The Graphic.*

PRACTICAL ARCHITECTURE. As applied to Farm Buildings of every description (Cow, Cattle and Calf Houses, Stables, Piggeries, Sheep Shelter Sheds, Root and other Stores, Poultry Houses), Dairies, and Country Houses and Cottages. Profusely Illustrated with Diagrams and Plans. By ROBERT SCOTT BURN. In cloth gilt, **price 5s.** "A valuable handbook for ready reference."—*Journal of Forestry.*

PRACTICAL BOAT BUILDING FOR Amateurs. Containing full Instructions for Designing and Building Punts, Skiffs, Canoes, Sailing Boats, &c. Fully illustrated with working Diagrams. By ADRIAN NEISON C.E. New Edition, revised and enlarged, by DIXON KEMP, Author of "Yacht Designing," "A Manual of Yacht and Boat Sailing," &c.. In cloth gilt, **price 2s. 6d.** "Possesses the great merit of being thoroughly practical."—*Bell's Life.*

PICTURE FRAME MAKING FOR Amateurs. Being Practical Instructions in the Making of various kinds of Frames for Paintings, Drawings, Photographs, and Engravings. Illustrated. By the Author of "Carpentry and Joinery," &c. In cloth gilt, **price 2s.** "The book is thoroughly exhaustive."—*The Building World.*

WORKING IN SHEET METAL. Being Practical Instructions for Making and Mending small Articles in Tin, Copper, Iron, Zinc, and Brass. Illustrated. Third Edition. By the Author of "Turning for Amateurs," &c. In paper, **price 6d.** "Every possible information is given."—*The Reliquary.*

ART OF PYROTECHNY. Being Comprehensive and Practical Instructions for the Manufacture of Fireworks, specially designed for the use of Amateurs. Profusely illustrated. By W. H. BROWNE, Ph.D., M.A., L.R.C.P., &c. Second Edition. In cloth gilt, **price 2s. 6d.** "A most complete little handbook."—*The Field.*

CARPENTRY AND JOINERY FOR Amateurs. Contains full Descriptions of the various Tools required in the above Arts, together with Practical Instructions for their use. By the Author of "Turning for Amateurs," &c. In cloth gilt, **price 2s. 6d.** "The best of the book consists of practical instructions."—*Iron.*

☞ *All Books sent Carriage Free.*

L. UPCOTT GILL, Publisher, 170, Strand, London, W.C.

TURNING FOR AMATEURS. Being Descriptions of the Lathe and its Attachments and Tools, with Minute Instructions for their Effective Use on Wood, Metal,

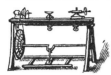

Ivory, and other Materials. New Edition, Revised and Enlarged. By JAMES LUKIN, B.A., Author of "The Lathe and its Uses," &c. Illustrated with 144 Engravings. In cloth gilt, **price 2s. 6d.** "Gives the amateur copious descriptions of tools and methods of working."—*The Builder.*

PRINTING FOR AMATEURS. A Practical Guide to the Art of Printing; containing Descriptions of Presses and Materials, together with Details of the Processes employed, to which is added a Glossary of

Technical Terms. Illustrated. By P. E. RAYNOR. In paper, **price 1s.** "Concise and comprehensive."—*The Figaro.*

WOOD CARVING FOR AMATEURS. Containing Descriptions of all the requisite

Tools, and full instructions for their use in producing different varieties of Carvings. Illustrated. A book of very complete instructions for the Amateur Wood Carver. In paper, **price 1s.** "Will be found of great interest."—*Illustrated Carpenter and Builder.*

TUNING AND REPAIRING PIANO-Fortes. The Amateur's Guide to the Practical Management of a Piano without the intervention of a Professional. By CHARLES BABBINGTON. In paper **price 6d.** "A very useful little book."—*Sylvia's Home Journal.*

MODEL YACHTS AND BOATS—Their Designing, Making, and Sailing. Illustrated with

118 Designs and Working Diagrams. By J. DU V. GROSVENOR. In leatherette, **price 5s.** "We can safely commend the volume."—*The Graphic.*

TOYMAKING FOR AMATEURS. Containing Instructions for the Home Construction of Simple Wooden Toys, and of

others that are moved or driven by Weights, Clockwork, Steam, Electricity, &c. Illustrated. By JAMES LUKIN, B.A., Author of "Turning for Amateurs," &c. In cloth gilt, **price 4s.** "A capital book for boys."—*Dispatch.*

NATURAL HISTORY.

PRACTICAL TAXIDERMY. A Manual of Instruction to the Amateur in Collecting, Preserving, and Setting-up Natural History Specimens of all kinds. Fully Illustrated, with Engravings of Tools, Examples, and Working Diagrams. By MONTAGU BROWNE, F.Z.S., Curator of Leicester Museum. New and Enlarged Edition. In cloth gilt, **price 7s. 6d.** "Throughout the volume is essentially practical."—*Daily Telegraph.*

ZOOLOGICAL NOTES on the Structure, Affinities, Habits, and Faculties of Snakes, Marsupials, and Birds; with Adventures among, and Anecdotes of, them. By ARTHUR NICOLS, F.G.S., F.R.G.S., Author of "Natural History Sketches." In walnut or sycamore, 8vo, **price 7s. 6d.** From PROFESSOR RUSKIN.— "I have just opened your proofs, and am entirely delighted by the glance at them.... The engraving of the cobra—Mr. Babbage's — is the only true drawing of it I ever saw."

NATURAL HISTORY SKETCHES among the Carnivora — Wild and Domesticated. With observations on their Habits and Mental Faculties. By ARTHUR NICOLS, F.G.S., F.R.G.S., Author of "Zoological Notes," "The Puzzle of Life." Illustrated by J. T. Nettleship, C. E. Brittan, and T. W. Wood. In cloth gilt, **price 5s.**

"This little volume is full of interest."—*Nature.*

All Books sent Carriage Free.

L. UPCOTT GILL, Publisher, 170, Strand, London, W.C.

BRITISH MARINE ALGÆ. Being a Popular Account of the Seaweeds of Great  Britain, their Collection and Preservation. Magnificently illustrated with 205 Engravings. A work of great interest to all residents at, or visitors to, the seaside, and one that will give an additional charm to their stay. By W. H. GRATTAN. In cloth gilt, **price 5s. 6d.** "A really useful handbook."—*Public Opinion.*

COLLECTING BUTTERFLIES AND Moths. Being Directions for Capturing Killing, and Preserving Lepidoptera and their Larvæ. Illustrated. Reprinted, with additions, from "Practical Taxidermy." By MONTAGU BROWNE, Author of "Practical Taxidermy." In paper, **price 1s.** "One of the handiest little helps yet published."—*Excelsior.*

SPORTS AND PASTIMES.

PRACTICAL FISHERMAN. Dealing with the Natural History, the Legendary Lore, the Capture of British Freshwater Fish, and Tackle and Tackle Making. Beautifully Illustrated. By J. H. KEENE. In cloth gilt, gilt edges,

price 10s. 6d. "It is by a thoroughly practical angler ... Will form a valuable addition to the angler's library."—*Fishing Gazette.*

SKATING CARDS. A Series of Cards of convenient size *for use on the Ice*, containing Clear Instructions and Diagrams, for Learning the whole art of Figure Skating. One of the Cards, containing the figure to be learnt, is held in the hand whilst Skating, so that the directions are read and acted on simultaneously.

Tinted cards, gilt edges, round corners, inclosed in strong leather pocket book, **price 3s. 6d.**; or in extra calf, satin lined (for presentation), **price 5s. 6d.** "An ingenious method ... and the instructions are brief and clear."—*The Queen.*

SLEIGHT OF HAND. A Practical Manual of Legerdemain for Amateurs and Others. New Edition, Revised and Enlarged. Profusely Illustrated. By EDWIN SACHS. In cloth gilt, **price 6s. 6d.**

"No one interested in conjuring should be without this work."—*Saturday Review.*

PRACTICAL BOAT BUILDING AND Sailing. Containing Full Instructions for Designing and Building Punts, Skiffs, Canoes, Sailing Boats, &c. Particulars of the most suitable Sailing Boats and Yachts for Amateurs, and Instructions for their proper handling. Fully Illustrated with Designs and Working Diagrams. By ADRIAN NEISON, C.E., DIXON KEMP, A.I.N.A., and G. CHRISTOPHER DAVIES. In One Volume, cloth gilt, **price 7s. 6d.** "A capital manual. ... All is clearly and concisely explained."—*The Graphic.*

PRACTICAL GAME PRESERVING. Containing the fullest Directions for Rearing and Preserving both Winged and Ground Game, and Destroying Vermin; with other information of Value to the Game Preserver. Illustrated. By WILLIAM CARNEGIE. In cloth gilt, demy 8vo, **price 21s.**

"Mr. Carnegie gives a great variety of useful information as to game and game preserving. ... We are glad to repeat that the volume contains much useful information, with many valuable suggestions. ... The instructions as to pheasant rearing are sound, and nearly exhaustive."—*The Times.* "It is practical, straightforward, and always lucid. The chapters on poaching and poachers, both human and animal, are particularly to the point, and amusing withal."—*The World.*

NOTES ON GAME AND GAME Shooting. Miscellaneous Observations on Birds and Animals, and on the Sport they Afford for the Gun in Great Britain, including Grouse, Partridges, Pheasants, Hares, Rabbits, Quails, Woodcocks, Snipe, and Rooks. By J. J. MANLEY, M.A., Author of "Notes on Fish and Fishing."

Illustrated. In cloth gilt, 400 pp., **price 7s. 6d.** "A thoroughly practical, as well as a very interesting book."—*The Graphic.*

☞ *All Books sent Carriage Free.*

L. UPCOTT GILL, Publisher, 170, Strand, London, W.C.

BOAT SAILING FOR AMATEURS. Containing Particulars of the most Suitable Sailing Boats and Yachts for Amateurs, and Instructions for their Proper Handling, &c. Illustrated with numerous Diagrams. By G. CHRISTOPHER DAVIES. Second Edition, Revised and Enlarged, and with several New Plans of Yachts. In cloth gilt, **price 5s.** "We know of no better companion for the young Yachtsman."—*Sporting Chronicle.*

BICYCLES AND TRICYCLES OF THE YEAR. Descriptions of the New Inventions and Improvements for the present Season. Designed to assist intending purchasers in the choice of a machine. Illustrated. By HARRY HEWITT GRIFFIN. (Published Annually.) In paper, **price 1s.** "It is as comprehensive as could be desired . . . We can readily testify to the strict impartiality of the Author."—*The Field.*

PRACTICAL PHOTOGRAPHY. Being the Science and Art of Photography, both Wet Collodion and the various Dry Plate Processes. Developed for Amateurs and Beginners. Illustrated. By O. E. WHEELER. In cloth gilt, **price 1s.** "Alike valuable to the beginner and the practised photographer."—*Photographic News.*

THEATRICALS AND TABLEAUX Vivants for Amateurs. Giving full Directions as to Stage Arrangements, "Making up," Costumes and Acting, with numerous Illustrations. By CHAS. HARRISON. In cloth gilt, **price 2s. 6d.** "Will be found invaluable."—*Court Journal.*

BAZAARS AND FANCY FAIRS, A Guide To. Their Organization and Management, with Details of Various Devices for Extracting Money from the Visitors. In paper, **price 1s.** "Most amusing. . . A better book cannot be purchased."—*Ladies' Journal.*

CARDS AND CARD TRICKS. Containing a brief History of Playing Cards, Full Instructions, with Illustrated Hands, for playing nearly all known games of chance or skill, from Whist to Napoleon and Patience, and directions for performing a number of amusing Tricks. Illustrated. By H. E. HEATHER. In cloth gilt, **price 5s.** "Deserves a large share of popularity."—*The Figaro.*

SIX PLAYS FOR CHILDREN. Written specially for Representation by Children, and Designed to Interest both Actors and Audience. With Instructions for Impromptu Scenery, Costumes, and Effects, and the Airs of the various Songs. By CHAS. HARRISON, Author of "Amateur Theatricals and Tableaux Vivants." **Price 1s.** "We can heartily commend these six plays."—*Ladies' Journal.*

PRACTICAL TRAPPING. Being some Papers on Traps and Trapping for Vermin, with a chapter on General Bird Trapping and Snaring. By W. CARNEGIE. In paper, **price 1s.** "Cleverly written and illustrated."—*Sportsman.*

IN THE PRESS.

BRITISH DOGS. Their Varieties, History, Characteristics, Breeding, Management, and Exhibition. By HUGH DALZIEL, Author of "The Diseases of Dogs," "The Diseases of Horses," &c., assisted by Eminent Fanciers. Illustrated with COLOURED PLATES and Special Engravings. This will be the fullest and most recent work on the various breeds of dogs kept in England, and, as its author is one of the first living authorities on the subject, its accuracy can be relied upon. In Monthly Parts, **price 7d.**

☞ *All Books sent Carriage Free.*

L. UPCOTT GILL, Publisher, 170, Strand, London, W.C.

NOTICE.

NEW BOOKS on Useful Subjects especially adapted to the requirements of Amateurs are constantly added to the List, and if a book on any subject not on the present List be wanted, the Publisher will be pleased to report whether he has one in the Press.

THE KENNEL CHRONICLE.

PUBLISHED MONTHLY, 1d.   Yearly Subscription is 1s. 6d., Post Free.

THE "KENNEL CHRONICLE" is the most complete and compact Chronicle of Dog Shows, a List of the Prize Winners at every Exhibition held in the United Kingdom, and at the most important Shows abroad, being given in its pages, and these fully indexed, so that ready reference can be made to facts, giving invaluable aid to Purchasers, Breeders, and others, in PROVING OR DISPROVING STATEMENTS MADE RESPECTING DOGS OFFERED FOR SALE OR AT STUD, &c.

In addition to the above features, the "KENNEL CHRONICLE" contains Registers of Births of Pups, Dogs at Stud, Change of Ownership, Stud Visits, List of Champions, &c., and Notes on all occurrences of permanent interest in canine circles.

Entry Fees.—PEDIGREE REGISTER: Winners of a Prize at any Public Show, FREE; Non-winners, 1s. each. PRODUCE, NAME, and SALE REGISTERS, 6d. each. STUD REGISTER, 1d. for Two Words.

The Yearly Vols. of the "KENNEL CHRONICLE," neatly Bound in Cloth, 2s. 6d. each; or, with Forms and Memorandum Pages for the entry of Kennel matters, making a valuable Diary and Register for Dog Owners, price 5s., by post 5s. 4d.

OFFICE: 170, STRAND, LONDON, W.C.

A CLEAR COMPLEXION.

PIMPLES, Black Specks, Sunburn, Freckles, and unsightly Blotches on the Face, Neck, Arms, and Hands, can be instantly removed by using Mrs. JAMES'S HERBAL OINTMENT, made from herbs only, and warranted harmless. It imparts such a lovely clearness to the skin that astonishes everyone. Of all chemists, 1s. 1½d. A box (with directions) sent free from observation, post free, on receipt of 15 stamps to—

Mrs. A. JAMES, 268, Caledonian Road, London, N.

LUXURIANT HAIR.

LONG, FLOWING EYELASHES, EYEBROWS, &c., are QUICKLY PRODUCED by using JAMES'S HERBAL POMADE. It is invaluable for the production of Whiskers, Beards, and Moustachios; it causes the hair to grow on bald places and scanty partings. Of most chemists, 1s.; or a box of it sent free from observation, post free, for 15 stamps.—

Mrs. A. JAMES, 268, Caledonian Road, London, N.

HAIR DESTROYER.

JAMES'S DEPILATORY Instantly Removes Superfluous Hairs from the Face, Neck, or Arms, without Injury to the Skin. Of most chemists, 1s.; or sent, wi   directions for use, free from observation, post free, for 15 stamps.—

Mrs. A. JAMES, 268, Caledonian Road, London, N.

BOOKS ✦ ON ✦ ANGLING.

ROWLANDS' MACASSAR OIL,

Known for more than 80 years as the best and safest preserver of the hair; it contains no Lead, Mineral, Poisonous, or Spirituous ingredients, and is especially adapted for the hair of children. It can now also be had in a golden colour, which is specially suited for fair and golden-haired persons and children.

Sizes, 3s. 6d., 7s., 10s. 6d., and 21s.

ROWLANDS' KALYDOR

Beautifies the complexion and removes all cutaneous defects; it is a most cooling wash for the face and hands during hot weather, and eradicates all Freckles, Tan, Sunburn, Stings of Insects, &c.

The bottle has on it a 6d. Government Stamp.

ROWLANDS' ODONTO

Is the purest and most fragrant dentifrice ever made; all dentists will allow that neither washes nor pastes can possibly be as efficacious for polishing the teeth and keeping them sound and white as a pure and non-gritty tooth powder. Such ROWLANDS' ODONTO has always proved itself to be.

The box has on it a 3d. Government Stamp.

ROWLANDS' EUKONIA

Is a beautifully pure, delicate, and fragrant Toilet Powder, and has lately been much improved. Each box has inside the lid a certificate of purity from Dr. Redwood, Ph.D., F.C.S., &c. Sold in three tints, white, rose, and cream, 2s. 6d. per box; double that size, with puff, 4s.

Ask any Chemist or Hairdresser for Rowlands' Articles, of 20, Hatton Garden, and avoid spurious worthless imitations under the same or similar names.

Any of these can be sent by post on receipt of 3d. above these prices.

Why many Persons Permanently Submit

to the

vexatious

and

unsightly

appear-

ance

of

" For every defect of Nature   *Art offers a remedy."*

GREY HAIR

Rather than attempt to Restore it.

1st.—Because the old fashioned and objectionable Hair Dyes dry up and spoil the Hair.

2nd.—Because the majority of "Hair Restorers" bring the users into ridicule by producing only a sickly yellow tint or dirty greenish stain, instead of a proper colour.

The following Testimonials (of many hundreds received) declare the value of

LATREILLE'S HYPERION HAIR RESTORER

As positively restoring grey or white hair to the REALLY NATURAL colour, gloss, softness, luxuriance, and beauty of youth; it so perfectly accomplishes its work and fulfils its promise, that in brilliant sunshine, or under glaring gaslight, the user can alike defy detection in ever having been grey, or used a remedy, while as a nourisher and strengthener of weak hair it has no equal.

Price 3s. 6d., sent in return for Postal Order or Stamps, by the Proprietors, **LATREILLE & CO., Walworth, London,** or may be had of Chemists;

But it is strongly advised that anything else, offered from interested motives, be resolutely refused, as Latreille's Hyperion NEVER DISAPPOINTS. All Chemists can readily procure through wholesale houses, if they have it not themselves in stock.

SPECIMEN TESTIMONIALS.

⁎⁎⁎ Be careful to ask for Latreille's Hyperion Hair Restorer, as the manufacturer is also proprietor of Latreille's Excelsior Lotion, which is a separate preparation, of universal repute for 25 years past, as a Producer of Hair.